The Complete
Job-Search Handbook

HOWARD FIGLER

THE COMPLETE *JOB-SEARCH* HANDBOOK

► *All the Skills You Need* ◄ *to Get Any Job and Have a Good Time Doing It*

REVISED AND EXPANDED EDITION

An Owl Book

HENRY HOLT AND COMPANY   NEW YORK

Copyright © 1979, 1988 by Howard Figler
All rights reserved, including the right to reproduce this
book or portions thereof in any form.
Published by Henry Holt and Company, Inc.,
115 West 18th Street, New York, New York 10011.
Published in Canada by Fitzhenry & Whiteside Limited,
195 Allstate Parkway, Markham, Ontario L3R 4T8.

Library of Congress Cataloging-in-Publication Data
Figler, Howard.
The complete job-search handbook : all the skills you need to get
any job and have a good time doing it / Howard Figler. — 1st ed.
p.   cm.
"An Owl book."
New, expanded ed. of the 1979 title.
Bibliography: p.
Includes index.
ISBN 0-8050-0537-4
1. Job hunting.   I. Title.
HF5382.7.F54   1988
650.1'4—dc19   87-26610
                                                                            CIP

Designed by Kate Nichols
Printed in the United States of America
1 3 5 7 9 10 8 6 4 2

The author is grateful to the following publisher for
permission to reprint previously copyrighted material:
From *PATH: A Career Workbook for Liberal Arts Students*
by Howard E. Figler: copyright © 1979 by Howard E. Figler.
Reprinted by permission of the Carroll Press.
Cranston, Rhode Island.

ISBN 0-8050-0537-4

*To Mom
who encouraged my career
when I needed it the most*

Contents

PART III
Communication Skills

PART IV
Skills for Selling Yourself

PART V
Special Problems and Special Solutions

PART VI
Other Perspectives

Acknowledgments

The revisions in this book were inspired by many friends and colleagues in career counseling who taught me how job-search principles are played out when real people try to apply them. Gutsy counselors make this book possible, because they test our ideas in the hard light of job-search counseling.

My coworkers at the University of Texas at Austin have helped me greatly to understand and refine my ideas about effective job hunting. Kathy Strawser, Sande Schrier, Dick Pyle, Lynne Milburn, Linda Johnson, and Suzy Ticer enabled me to separate workable concepts from impractical ones.

I would like to thank my publisher for supporting the original edition of this book so fully and consistently with strong distribution and promotion. Their confidence in the book helped to establish its place in the market.

My editor, Tracy Bernstein, helped me with this revision as only a first-class editor can—with honest assessments, key reorganizations, and a superb talent for finding every unnecessary, careless, or overblown paragraph I tried to sneak past her gaze.

Finally, I want to acknowledge the ongoing march of job hunters who endure hard work, anxiety, and the indignities of job searching in exchange for uncertain and intermittent rewards. Job hunting may not be as much fun as I say it is, but your day is coming. I appreciate your bearing with us authors who think it's all supposed to happen just the way we write about it.

The Complete
Job-Search Handbook

Introduction

Some people in this world can advance their careers simply by declaring
they are available. Like blaring trumpets, their credentials speak for themselves, announcing the presence of persons who are obviously suited to
perform particular jobs. Such people are renowned for certain public
achievements, or possess advanced degrees that automatically qualify
them for certain work, or have rare or outstanding talents, or can measure
their previous accomplishments on dollar scales that preclude the need
for further certification. These individuals have career opportunities dropped
into their laps.

Let's suppose you are seeking better work but have no single outstanding credential you can use in marketing yourself. You have done
very competent and dedicated work for many years and have been appreciated by your peers and superiors. The trouble is, you have no highly
visible way to call attention to the work you have done. You know you
are good at what you do, but cannot translate this into words, numbers,
or other marketable symbols. Every time you proceed to look for an
improvement in your career, it's as though you're starting all over again.
No one outside your present colleagues knows what you are capable of
doing. Applying for a new job becomes a trial of persuading yourself and
others that you are not faking, stepping out of your league, or otherwise
misrepresenting yourself. This predicament describes 98 percent of us
at one time or another. We are struggling to be noticed, searching for
the key phrases that will tell a prospective employer everything we are
capable of doing, without seeming pretentious.

If you have not won awards for your past work performance, are not famous, cannot announce your potency in terms of dollar sales, you are a mere mortal in the career-search process. There is no magic available for you. The success of your search will depend upon how well you understand the process of finding better work.

Many readers have been tantalized by reports of the hidden job market. Philosophers of the career search have encouraged people to seek new opportunities by using take-charge methods to uncover unadvertised jobs. Once having tried these methods, many are frustrated by their apparent inability to acquire these unseen career opportunities. They are unsuccessful because they lack the skills to put a take-charge attitude into action.

You-can-do-it philosophies invest you with courage, but courage is not enough. You must have the tools to accompany your firm resolve—the skills of self-assessment, detective work, communication, and selling yourself.

Advocates of the self-directed career search have done an admirable job of outlining successful job-hunting strategies, but they have not been clear enough about the specific skills that are prerequisite to these strategies. They have implied what these skills are but have not defined them and have not made it clear that people must learn these skills and practice them in their daily routine while they are tackling the target employers.

Career skills are like wilderness skills. When you are lost deep in the woods of unknown territory, you have no clues on how to get out of the predicament, but you know you will manage to survive and prosper because you understand the land and how to use its resources. Similarly, you want to be able to survive in new career landscapes without resorting to magical assistance from other sources.

► Everyone Needs ◄ Career Skills

Perhaps at times you have felt you have certain advantages that allow you to be casual, even lazy, about looking for better work. Consider yourself among the 2 percent in the privileged class of job seekers if you are in the top 10 percent of your college class, your IQ is above 135, you are a former athlete or other visible public figure, you are extraordinarily beautiful or six feet three and handsome, you are a graduate of an Ivy League or other prestigious university, or you are naturally gifted as a salesperson for yourself. If any of these is true of you, you may not be sure whether you need this book. Be assured, however, that relying on a single great talent or personal characteristic can be dangerous over the long haul. Beauty fades, talent wanes, and circumstances change unexpectedly. In the long run, nothing can substitute for a knowledge of how to develop and use career skills.

For most ordinary folk, comfort, peace of mind, and self-assurance in the career search derive not from knowing that you possess one great talent to depend on, but from knowing you possess the appropriate skills to find other work if this talent should dissipate or lose its natural market.

Those 98 percent who are plain looking, possess average college grades, have no great accomplishments, graduated from nonprestigious universities, receive little recognition on the job, have checkered career patterns, or are otherwise inheritors of ordinariness actually can, and do, turn the tables on the privileged by learning to acquire career skills from the very start. By having to survive, they learn to be superior survivors. The ordinary folk become stronger; the inheritors of great career wealth lose their potency when they can no longer receive automatic appointments based on their appearance, credentials, or birthright.

Fear not the burden of being ordinary. I know the hordes of job competitors you imagine make you highly anxious, but you can turn this anxiety to your advantage. So many talented and untalented people depend on luck, magic formulas, handouts from family or friends, or whims of the marketplace that a little initiative and focused effort can yield a greater gain. While they are wasting their energies looking for handouts, your knowledge of the secrets of the career-search process will pay off.

► You Have Been Told ◄ to Work Too Hard

Despite the value of career skills, many in the vast middle class of job hunting are discouraged by well-intentioned friends or counselors who say: "Job hunting is hard work, so push yourself, make an all-out effort"; or "Know *exactly* what you want before making an application"; or "Get out there and take control of the process, take charge!" (as though you were a football quarterback being exhorted by the fiery coach).

These are empty messages. They serve more to frustrate you than stir you to action. Admonished to work hard, work harder, know thyself, drive, drive, drive, you wonder what you are supposed to do first.

Most of all, you do not want to work hard. You do not want to embrace a philosophy of career seeking that sounds as if it were written for Superman. You want a career search strategy that will not rip your life apart or double your anxiety level in one swift stroke.

In all likelihood, you have already devised a homemade strategy for your career search and have built it into your daily routine. You are making some progress on your wits and common sense, without having to quit your present work, spend a fortune on career consultants, or have your palm read for further clues. In short, you are doing a decent job of job hunting on your own. However, you need a few hints about what you are doing wrong. These clues should suggest where you can make adjustments in your search while not disturbing the life routine to which you have become accustomed.

It has been said that getting a job is harder than any job you will ever do. Don't let that scare you. Landing a job is easier than you may believe. You can use the model of twenty career skills in this book to decide which skills you have been neglecting. You will see that you are already using many career skills very effectively and will be encouraged to perfect your own methods.

► The Blessings of the ◄ Career Search

While you are pleased to know there is hope for ordinary folk who seek better work, there is another part of you that says the career search is the curse of the employment misfit, or your penalty for being so untalented that no one notices you, or simply a bigger pain than anything else imaginable. It is a mistake to believe that a career search is a punishment for past failures. What may appear to be the curses of an extended exploration for better work are truly blessings in disguise:

- The curse of having to make the rounds of many employers, endure many interviews, and read numerous career materials before you decide becomes the blessing of reaching a large number of professional people who are acquainted with you and your work and can thus serve as your present and future contacts.
- The curse of struggling to identify your hidden talents—your subtle, not easily labeled abilities—becomes the blessing of discovering that you have many qualifications and skills that are marketable in a wide variety of employment contexts.
- The curse of not knowing exactly what your future will be, of living with unknown options and uncertain timetables, becomes the blessing of being secure enough so you don't jump at the first job opportunity; you enjoy playing with the many creative possibilities on your career landscape and trust that the mysterious plot in your career story will be resolved in your favor.
- The curse of having to ask many people a lot of questions, probe their psyches, and intrude upon their valuable time becomes the blessing of learning interview skills so you can elicit information and attitudes from anyone with ease in a way that makes the

interview even more pleasing to the other people than to yourself.
- The curse of having to explain yourself to everyone, justify your reasons for even wanting to talk about career matters, becomes the blessing of having the skills to portray yourself clearly, creatively, and in terms that are marketable without being pretentious or self-conscious.
- And the curse of taking on a task that seems to be a job in itself becomes the blessing of learning that most elements of the career search are already entwined in your daily routine of work and play and need only be improved or emphasized by a more conscious and focused effort on your part.

Perhaps the greatest blessing of career skills is that they can be used long before you are interviewed for your next job. You begin your search for your next position the very day you are hired in your present one.

There is a prevailing myth that all judgments of you as a job candidate are held in suspense until you arrive for the formal interview. That is why so many interviewees practice trying on new clothes and muttering magic phrases they hope will capture the interviewer's attention. This sort of preparation is self-defeating; if you believe that key words, manner of dress, or significant glances during a job interview will make the difference, you will find it extremely difficult to be your natural self. You will be one more victim of interview psychosis.

But if you take advantage of career skills long before the formal interviews, you will already know a lot about your target employer, who will also know a lot about you. As you will see in the forthcoming chapters, you can assess yourself, detect the available jobs, become expert about prospective employers, practice your communication skills, establish a network of helpers, and spend many hours with the people for whom you would like to work long before you decide to announce your intentions. The courtship is what counts; the wedding ceremony is a mere formality.

► Who and What This ◄
Book Is For

This book is for college graduates, career changers, returning workers, midlife-crisis and second-career people, and any others who feel they deserve better careers than they currently have. I assume you have opened this book not for casual reasons, but because you need some immediate help with your special career predicament. Career decisions probably are not new to you; I suspect you believe you already know a lot about the subject. You may already have tried several systems that disappointed you and may be curious to see if anything new can be said.

You are open to a new approach, anything that will dislodge you from your present rut.

If you are like most people, you prefer not to read a whole book to extract the information you need. To accommodate your desire to get information quickly, I have organized this volume so you can see at a glance what topics are covered. Like a patient who prefers a quick diagnosis to having the entire body examined, you prefer the shortest of shortcuts possible to obtain relief. You can skip around in this book, read the parts you like best or need most. I wrote it to be used that way because you are probably already doing many things right in the career search. You are also doing a few things wrong and want to know what they are and how to correct yourself quickly.

How is this book different from other books on career guidance? First of all, it does its best to illuminate the entire *process* that occurs when a person seeks better work. This process consists of using skills career advisors have heretofore taken for granted or ignored. The book spells out every skill you need to conduct a successful career search. I propose that these career skills will come more naturally to you than job-hunting techniques and that you will not need to depend on placement help once you become familiar with these skills.

I call these essential processes *career skills;* I maintain that you can enhance and improve every one of them with ordinary effort, simply by using them routinely in your career search.

Second, I propose that most of your career-search activity can and ought to be initiated long before the formalities of résumé preparation and job interviews. If you wait until you *must* have a new job or career next month, you will have allowed most of your opportunities to pass you by. You can and should do career exploration every day of your life.

Third, most career processes or skills have not been clarified before because they are connected to certain generic life skills that you already use to solve other life problems. You have been using career skills every day, probably unconsciously. The purpose here is to make sure you use and refine your career skills more deliberately and with greater proficiency.

Thus, this is a book that focuses on the twenty generic life skills that come into play whenever an individual acts to seek a new career. Past volumes have paid scant attention to specific skills. Instead, they exhort the individual to "know thyself," "take the initiative," and "be persistent," without ever explaining the processes involved. Many career seekers find it difficult to make progress following this standard advice, but cannot determine why they are failing. A highly structured program may tell them what to do on Day 1, Day 2, and so forth, but they cannot put the advice to use. Why? Because people lack the skills to carry out well-meant advice. A person told to prepare for a job interview must guess what that means when he or she has no research skills. A person cautioned to speak more clearly needs help with communication skills. An individual told to look harder needs detective skills to translate the advice into action. Advice givers who criticize clients without teaching the necessary skills are only creating frustration.

While I encourage you to diagnose and treat your career-search problems through use of several skills that seem appropriate, I caution you not to expect a cookbook solution to your difficulty. I cannot tell you what to do in ten easy steps. Precious few successful career searches are conducted in so mechanical a fashion. You must decide the best sequence of events for yourself.

A small but important proportion of readers will be systematic and patient enough to digest the book from beginning to end. Those who do will discover that the twenty career skills are presented in an orderly sequence, as outlined in Chart 1. Though many individuals will practice these skills in a sequence different from the one I have presented, I believe this sequence best represents the order of events in a career search.

You must begin with an understanding of your uniqueness (self-assessment skills) in order to determine which employers are most likely to be interested in you. Specific methods of exploration and information gathering (detective skills) then enable you to accumulate a list of prospective organizations and become knowledgeable about the employers at the top of your list. The skills of interpersonal exchange (communication skills) are vitally necessary for the many occasions when you talk with or write to an individual who has career possibilities for you. Skills for selling yourself are then used as you seek to fit your talents and motivations to the needs of the employer.

Chart 1. The Twenty Skills of the Career Search

Self-Assessment Skills	Detective Skills	Communication Skills	Skills for Selling Yourself
Values	Prospect List	Listening	Self-Marketing
Money	Personal Referral Network	Questioning	Getting Experience
Skills		Assertiveness	Interim Jobs
Creativity	Information Interviewing	Self-Disclosure	Selling Yourself Long-Distance
Decision Making	Library Research	Writing	
Reality Testing			Interviewing

The chart allows you to see the entire career search process as an organic unity, reminding you that the several parts of career exploration are interconnected and that proficiency in one career skill undoubtedly aids progress in all the others.

► The Twenty Skills ◄ of the Career Search

The twenty skills discussed in this book fall into four categories: self-assessment, detective, communication, and selling yourself. Each skill is briefly discussed below.

Self-Assessment Skills

1. *Values* Identifying and clarifying the highest-priority rewards and satisfactions you hope to obtain in your career, discriminating sharply among competing alternatives.
2. *Money* Evaluating the importance of financial security and high earnings in your career equation. Deciding how money will rate compared to other sources of satisfaction.
3. *Skills* Identifying and labeling your most prominent strengths or abilities and choosing the ones you most enjoy using in work situations.
4. *Creativity* Learning to envision new and previously unimagined career possibilities by using creative thought processes such as adapting, reversing, combining, and magnifying.
5. *Decision Making* Comparing the desirability of several career alternatives, in terms of the factors you consider most significant. Using structured and unstructured methods for making these comparisons.
6. *Reality Testing* Acquiring experiences that enable you to compare your expectations about a career and your relevant skills with firsthand exposure to the actual field of work. Participating in a career setting without having to make a commitment to it.

Detective Skills

7. *Prospect List* Building a comprehensive list of people, organizations, and situations that seem most likely to offer the kinds of work you desire.
8. *Personal Referral Network* Learning how to create contacts for yourself by establishing relationships with people who can refer you to other people who can help you.

9. *Information Interviewing* Obtaining information and insight directly from people in careers you may desire to enter; learning what questions to ask and how to conduct the entire exchange.
10. *Library Research* Using readily available published materials to quickly obtain data about a target employer, an industry, or a given individual you hope to meet.

Communication Skills

11. *Listening* Attending fully to another person's words, feelings, hidden messages, and subtle meanings; learning how to detect when you are not listening effectively.
12. *Questioning* Using questions in ways that encourage the other person to talk freely and offer more information that will aid your exploration; learning effective and noneffective methods of questioning.
13. *Assertiveness* Taking initiatives in the career-search process; learning nonaggressive methods to interest people in talking with you and providing you with assistance.
14. *Self-Disclosure* Expressing yourself freely and comfortably when asked to talk about your accomplishments, aspirations, and past experiences; practicing self-disclosure.
15. *Writing* Using written forms of communication in a personal way; writing letters to prospective employers that convey your inner motivations and spark a personal response.

Skills for Selling Yourself

16. *Self-Marketing* Sensitizing yourself to elements of your background that are most likely to be marketable; collecting evidence of your abilities so it can be presented to an employer.
17. *Getting Experience* Numerous ways you can acquire experience that will enhance your presentation to an employer; translating indirect experience into skills and knowledge that are directly relevant to the job you want.
18. *Interim Jobs* Accepting stopgap employment that allows you to survive financially but also makes it possible for you to continue exploration toward your career goals.
19. *Selling Yourself Long-Distance* Practicing your career skills when you are far away from your target geographical area; deciding what skills to use before the move and when to move to the target area.

20. *Interviewing*   Acquiring the skills necessary to deal with the nine-item hidden agenda in any job interview; learning to understand what interviewers look for and how to follow up.

► Diagnose Your Own ◄ Career Ailment

Perhaps you already understand many of the career skills and have used them successfully. Or perhaps you have precious little time and must be selective in deciding where to devote your energies. Or maybe many of the skills simply do not apply to your situation. Even if you can eliminate some career skills from your agenda, you may still be confused about where to start. You don't care to do everything, but would like some definite instructions to follow. To help you use your time most judiciously, I have distilled several typical career search problems and proposed that each problem can be attacked best by concentrating on a small number of skills. Your special predicament requires that you look at certain career skills before you look at others. In other words, I am giving specific directions for the shortcut that best applies to you.

Find yourself in the six problem situations described below. You may be out of work and desperate for anything that pays money, or you may be solidly entrenched in a job but bored enough to contemplate a new career. Go directly to the problem that correlates best with yours, and put those skills listed into practice without delay. As your career search proceeds, you will use other skills, but I have advised you to use these skills first because they will produce results most quickly.

All these shortcut strategies are designed to reduce your task to a manageable size so that you do not feel overwhelmed. There is nothing sacred about the skills chosen for each problem. You may choose skills other than those I have proposed. You may see yourself in more than one problem area and thus have to concoct your own strategy. My main concern is that you use a strategy simple and brief enough so you don't wear yourself out, but specific enough so you are enthusiastic about getting started.

► Problem One: I'm Panicked, Desperate, at My Wits' End

I need to find work in a hurry. My income is fast shrinking toward zero. I have little time to spare, must get a job the fastest way possible.

Interim Job (Skill 18)   In your impoverished state, you must first get a job that provides enough income for survival. But make sure this is also a job that allows you sufficient freedom to keep looking for your real vocational goal.

Prospect List (Skill 7) Most panic results from not knowing where the jobs are. This skill teaches you how to uncover potential employers with a minimum of effort, so you can conduct your search in an organized manner.

Personal Referral Network (Skill 8) Once having developed a list of prospects, you need to establish personal contact with them. This skill tells you how to attract personal attention from people who offer career possibilities that interest you.

Selling Yourself Long-Distance (Skill 19) Your panic may result from being far away from your target geographical area. A special strategy is necessary for searching at a distance, knowing when to move and how to manage the transition between long-distance searching and in-person exploration.

Getting Experience (Skill 17) Drop back and get a slice of experience in the field where you are trying so hard to find work. Volunteer your services, work part-time, or get a field experience in a college course. Sometimes a little firsthand exposure will give you just the confidence you may need.

► **Problem Two: I'm Bored, I Need a New Challenge**

I am secure in my present job situation, but cannot stand this place anymore. I have fulfilled my usefulness here, solved the big problems, and now need a new challenge to get the juices flowing again.

Information Interviewing (Skill 9) You probably have been in your present job a long while; hence, you must reactivate the skill of getting information from others. Information interviewing is the key link between you and a new career. This skill gives you specific guidelines for gathering data from other people.

Questioning (Skill 12) The success of your information interviews will depend heavily on your ability to question tactfully and with clarity. Certain questioning methods have a high likelihood of yielding positive results; others are almost certain to discourage your respondent.

Reality Testing (Skill 6) If you are determined to leap into a difficult field, you should participate in it directly before deciding you want to embrace it. This skill reveals how you can sample a work environment before committing yourself to an irreversible change.

Self-Marketing (Skill 16)   When changing occupational fields, you must be aware of the marketable talents you can transfer from one field to the other. This skill tells you how to assess your marketability and how to present yourself to a new employer.

▶ **Problem Three: I Have
Been in School and Have Little
Work Experience**

I don't know where to start. I have never been in the real world before. My only experience is in the classroom.

Skills (Skill 3)   Make a thorough review of your prominent strengths. Persuade yourself that you do have a lot to offer, even if you are young and inexperienced. By knowing your own assets, you can judge which jobs need you more than others.

Values (Skill 1)   Obstacles move aside for people who know what they want. Take a close look at the activities you find most satisfying and the reasons these activities stimulate you. You need not have work experience to discover career-related values. These values appear in your informal, out-of-classroom experiences.

Self-Disclosure (Skill 14)   As soon as you have a firm grip on what your strengths are, you should learn to talk about yourself and practice with others until it becomes second nature; this skill tells you how to describe yourself without appearing to be overly self-important.

Prospect List (Skill 7)   While you have access to a career resource library (in your school's guidance office or career planning center) and other libraries, this skill is easy to develop. You can put together a list of prospective places of employment by using these handy reference materials. Use these resources to convince yourself there are jobs out there when you're ready to find them.

Library Research (Skill 10)   Once again, your access to libraries gives you the advantage of gathering research data about employers long before they interview you. Let the research competencies you developed through your academic work prepare you for future career exploration.

► **Problem Four: I Don't Want to
Change My Job, Just My Assignment**

I don't want to move from my present employer at all, but I do need a different kind of work, a different project, assignment.

Values (Skill 1) Review the sources of your disenchantment by clarifying the values you feel are not satisfied in your present job responsibilities. Try to define or identify positions in the organization that would rekindle your enthusiasm.

Self-Marketing (Skill 16) When leaving a comfortable position for a new assignment, you should review what is most marketable in your work background so you can readily interest another department in your services.

Assertiveness (Skill 13) In order to change assignments or job titles, you'll probably have to initiate the request, follow it up, and perhaps persuade someone else to be uprooted. All this requires assertive skill, the ability to present ideas openly to those in power.

Information Interviewing (Skill 9) Because you are already on site, you have abundant opportunity to interview people about their work in other departments. Even though you may believe you already know what they do, a few interviews will convince you otherwise.

Decision Making (Skill 5) Your values and skills have changed since you first took this job. Determine which of your attributes are most important to you now, and check to see which new job assignments would satisfy most of these. Don't change assignments until you find one that meets a lot of your present needs.

► **Problem Five: I'm a Late Entry,
Returning to the Work Force**

I've been away from organized employment for many years. I've been a homemaker, odd jobber, traveler, or self-employed person.

Skills (Skill 3) You will feel out of place and somewhat immobilized until you use skills-identification methods to generate some self-esteem. You'll discover that you have cultivated numerous job skills even though you weren't paid for them.

Personal Referral Network (Skill 8) To acquaint yourself with job markets you've hitherto ignored, you should tap a pool of personal contacts who can lead you to sources of employment. This skill details how anyone can build a personal referral network, especially those who have not been employed by someone else recently.

Assertiveness (Skill 13)   Anyone has the right to initiate contact with a target employer, but many people don't know how to practice the skill. Assertiveness is always painless and usually pleasurable when done correctly; the skill can be practiced in many everyday settings.

Prospect List (Skill 7)   In addition to your personal referral network, you should use readily available employer directories to build a list of possible places of work. Using these directories gets you started quickly; with these and other prospecting materials, you can generate a list long enough to keep you occupied indefinitely.

Creativity (Skill 4)   As a person new to the career search, you will probably overlook many career fields that might interest you. You should stimulate your thinking by applying a few creative processes to your own background, and be willing to try the results.

Interviewing (Skill 20)   Get as many job interviews as you can, so that you can practice these skills and become comfortable with the process of talking about yourself. Learn the art of selling yourself by talking about your past experiences, skills, and motivations.

▶ **Problem Six: I'm Trapped**

I know I must make a change, but family and financial priorities prevent me from considering it. I am sad to admit that this will probably be my position for many years to come.

Selling Yourself Long-Distance (Skill 19)   Just for your own mental health, take a fantasy trip to places and career settings where you'd like to be if you could free yourself. Draw as clearly as possible the pictures you imagine and then use long-distance skills to identify organizations and people who might satisfy your career wishes.

Values (Skill 1)   Isolate the factors that make your present work unhappy; this is the most demanding of career search skills, but worth the effort. What sources of reward would make a difference to you? Don't be vague; pin down the activities, resources, and specific tasks that would be most likely to change your attitude.

Library Research (Skill 10)   This skill allows you to explore your new interests with a minimal time investment. Use the nearest library for newspapers and journals that focus on your target interests, and write away to organizations for their free literature. Stimulate your imagination with these materials; perhaps these materials will prepare you for the day when you are no longer so "trapped."

Writing (Skill 15)   This skill encourages you to take an additional step toward creating a fantasy job while you are stuck in your present one. If you establish correspondence with just one or two people in a fantasy field, you have made contacts and probably the beginnings of friendships as well. Letters need not be scholarly or pushy, just personal, enthusiastic, and genuine.

Reality Testing (Skill 6)   You are never trapped as long as you can get exposure to other alternatives and learn that many people have changed their jobs and careers. Ask people who made career shifts how they managed the financial difficulties and what inspired them to overcome the obstacles.

► Five Key Assumptions ◄

Several assumptions pervade the recommendations given in this book; collectively they make up an attitude about the career search that is different from the view that job hunting is dreadfully hard work, highly competitive, and pressure laden. I believe it is important to bring these central assumptions into the open so that you can understand a little better the attitudes and emotional tone of this volume.

The Career Search Is Fun   As long as you regard looking for work as drudgery or as punishment for leaving your last job, you will try to terminate it as quickly as possible and will accept the first thing that comes your way. I assume throughout this volume that the career search is an activity you can look forward to and become enthusiastic about. I believe it will become enjoyable for you about the moment you realize that you do have many options, that you can turn down an offer, safe in the assurance that you will find a better one. You can look forward to a job interview, instead of dreading it, because you will regard it as a chance to be curious and explore, rather than as an all-or-nothing situation.

The Career Search Involves Exploring, Not Hunting   Job seekers lose their patience and will because they are too single-minded about the task at hand. They easily become anxious and frustrated because they are trapped by the mentality that says: "If I don't get what I want the next time around, I will stop trying." Anything short of a job offer is interpreted as a failure.

People make the mistake of *hunting*, rather than *exploring*, for their work. Hunting implies the direct pursuit of quarry, zeroing in on a known adversary, and moving in for the kill. Exploration, by contrast, is a process you conduct in a carefree, information-seeking manner designed to satisfy your curiosity. Hunting is deadly; exploration is for fun.

Job hunting is an all-or-nothing game that has many unpleasant conditions about it—long trips across town, detailed arrangements in advance, talking to strangers who ask you questions you may not understand, getting dressed up, acting sophisticated, and, worst of all, trying to convey your personal capabilities within a brief time.

I don't believe you will last long in the work search unless you treat it as an exploration process rather than a deadly hunt. Therefore, I recommend that your initial career search activity follow certain rules designed to maximize your positive experiences and minimize your negative ones.

Multiple Skills Are More Important   One of the complaints most frequently heard from job seekers is the no-talent refrain: "I don't do anything especially well, so why hire me?" Many people believe that a single prominent talent is necessary to attract employers; if you are not a financial wizard, an exceptional speaker, a skilled artist, or a persuasive writer, you may fear you are destined for mediocrity.

The power of a highly visible talent is somewhat overrated. Very few jobs exist that permit a person to depend solely upon one talent for success. It is far more commonly true that *multiple competencies* are necessary in any job for highest-level performance. For example, an effective insurance salesperson must possess persuasiveness, competency with numbers, and long-range planning ability when discussing estate matters with clients.

In most cases, the combination of competencies is more powerful than any single talent could be. I assume this is true because I want you to recognize that all your strengths can be put to use.

The Career Search Is Largely Detective Work   I assume throughout this volume that the most effective career search is fundamentally an exercise of detective skills, that the largest part of one's effort should be devoted to *finding* the right work situations. For every promising job you have found, another two remain undiscovered. The wise individual understands this and looks further. About 80 percent of your time should be devoted to detective work, because the seek-and-ye-shall-find motif

incorporates all four of the skills categories; the detective attitude is at work in self-assessment, identifying job leads, communication skills, and selling yourself.

Detective work is a state of mind. Once you adopt this attitude, you will regard your career as a complicated mystery story and become absorbed in following the clues and looking for new evidence; you will enjoy being the Perry Mason of your own career.

You Need Time on Your Side, Not Against You   Time works against you if you force yourself to make an instant career decision. Your strategy requires time, and you can buy time by either staying in your present situation or acquiring an interim job (see skill 18). Time allows you to maintain the search at a comfortable level and to let informal contacts begin working in your favor. The harder you look for work, the more it may elude you. It is an axiom among employers that the applicant who too clearly wants to be hired has a tough time convincing the employer that she or he is competent. Instead of mounting a campaign worthy of Sherman's army, let your search take a more leisurely course. The lower your desperation quotient, the easier it is for you to exchange views with a potential employer on a level of parity. Therefore, I assume in this volume that the career search is best conducted many months before you must actually make a change; if you practice these skills before your situation becomes urgent, they will work doubly well for you when you embark on an actual job search.

▶ The Career Search Is an ◀ Everyday Thing

Looking for better work is rather like learning to tie your shoes by yourself. You have to do it several times before you get it right, but once you have it, you wonder how you ever allowed anyone else to do it for you.

We have tried desperately to make a science of career decision making, and have succeeded in making a mystique of it. In fact, choosing a career is the most obvious of functions, relying on the natural rhythms of self-reflection and human interaction. An army of career-choice "experts" has mobilized because of people's inability to recognize their own opportunities for career exploration. The less we do for ourselves, the more we assume that expert advice, outside consultation, and placement assistance are necessary. It is time to restore the natural order of things. Job seeking is as natural as any other kind of social interchange. By turning matters over to the pseudoscientists, we have assumed that (1) we know nothing or little about ourselves, (2) no one in our own circle of acquaintances can possibly be helpful, and (3) job getting requires a sophisticated set of techniques known only to the select few. The ultimate extension of this absurdity is to designate personnel officials as the soothsayers of the employment world, presumably capable of reading our palms, feeling our foreheads, or otherwise determining our capabilities from arcane criteria.

The more you believe that your ideal job is hidden away in a cave that can be discovered only by an experienced guide, the more helpless you will feel. Helplessness will lead you to desperation and a willingness to accept any employment as good fortune. By contrast, if you recognize that the skills of the work search are ordinary life skills and that they are available to anyone who cares to practice them, you can attend to the task yourself.

Looking for better work is fun. You can do it by yourself. It is relatively easy. Often it is about the least expensive thing to do with your time. Why is it necessary to state that the career search is pleasurable, self-propelling, and not complicated? Because of the way you've interpreted your previous job-seeking experiences. When you have obtained a job, you've assumed that your success was largely a matter of luck, fortuitous circumstances, or being in the right place at the right time. When you were not successful, you blamed bad luck, waited to see if your luck would change, and when it didn't, set about the chore of job hunting. And what a chore you made it! You laboriously typed application letters, sent out hundreds of résumés, spent hours scanning classified ads in the newspapers, and underwent interviews with potential employers to demonstrate your dedication to the Great American Work Ethic.

Let's take a closer look at the first part, the "I was lucky" statement, often used to interpret a previous job-seeking experience.

EXAMPLE ▶ After Eileen's children completed their schooling, she decided to reenter the work force. Because she had not been in a paid job for twenty years, she didn't know where to begin looking. While at the beauty salon, she sought the advice of her hairdresser and asked if she knew of anyone looking for part-time help. "It just so happened" that the director of placement at a local college had confided to the hairdresser that she was "terribly busy—her assistant had just left." The hairdresser made a personal reference to the director. Eileen followed this up with a telephone call and her résumé and got the job. Later, the job was made into a full-time assistant director's position. Eileen feels she was lucky in getting the job.

Was it just "lucky" that Eileen stepped into her new career as a function of her visit to the hairdresser? Or was she smart enough to take advantage of a natural referral network that exists simply because people are curious about each other and enjoy passing information around? What would have happened to Eileen if she had followed only formal channels in her efforts to find work? Only her hairdresser knows for sure.

EXAMPLE ► Bob wanted a job with a youth recreation group, so he hung around and helped out the local YMCA with its basketball games, its field trips, and anything else. He got to know Jane, one of the leaders, pretty well and showed her how the program could be expanded to include kids in his neighborhood. One day Jane invited him to a staff meeting; after the meeting there was a picnic. One thing led to another; a man was there from out of town who needed an assistant leader in his recreation center. Jane mentioned Bob's name, and he was hired a few weeks later. "All in all," Bob said, "I was pretty lucky."

Lucky, my foot. The young man in this example practiced naturally many of the skills outlined and detailed in this book. He found the target employer, asserted himself to become involved in its activities, used a personal referral to learn about a job opportunity, did information interviews with staff people, observed the activities of the center. No doubt he also used many self-assessment skills to decide that the YMCA was a good target employer and many communication skills in talking with the staff there.

People meet their lovers and employers in the strangest places. Exactly what implications does this have for you? It means simply that all your life activity can contribute to your work search. It means that your typical ways of getting together with people can be turned to your advantage. It means you can have your fun and profit by it too.

► Stop Making Excuses ◄ for Yourself

Like the child who can think of a thousand reasons for going outside, or ten thousand reasons for not doing his homework, many people have bottomless wells of excuses for their fear of getting involved in the business of searching for better work. It probably requires only one of the following to arrest any work-seeking behavior, and chances are you can lay claim to several.

I'm Too Old A person my age doesn't do all that running around looking for a different job. It takes too much foolish energy that I must be careful to conserve. Furthermore, I think it's a little undignified to admit I made a mistake in the past and go around confessing it to everyone.

Answer: Older folks look for new challenges because they have already licked several tough problems and want new ones. Changing work is not the confession of a sinner, but the spirit of a missionary who has something good to offer and wants to pass the wealth around.

I Can't Do Anything Else I must admit, if you press me, that I am afraid there's nothing else I can do as well as what I am currently doing.

I'm afraid of getting caught in the middle, losing my present work, and being unable to make the grade elsewhere. I was lucky to get my present work and am not so sure I'd be that lucky again.

Answer: The major currency in your work experience is transferable skills, which are abilities that can be marketed in numerous contexts. For example, if you have been an effective organizer in your present office, church, or community, chances are you can carry these abilities to a different work setting and put them to use without starting all over again.

I'd Better Hang on to What I've Got   There is no sense in building a record of good work and then throwing it away by looking for something new. Maybe my work isn't the greatest, but I should capitalize on the progress I have made, and not dismiss it for some uncertain future. I can't afford to surrender the experience I've accumulated.

Answer: No one is asking you to start over at the bottom. When you find a setting where your skills are transferable, you can reasonably request an appropriate level. If you are bored with your current situation, you cannot afford *not* to look for something more stimulating.

My Job Takes All My Time   My work doesn't give me time to think about doing anything else. I would have to take three weeks off just to explore this subject and would undermine my present responsibilities in the process. It's too large a price to pay for just shopping around in the dark.

Answer: Take a close look at the people you encounter routinely in your work and ask yourself how they might lead you to others. Whom do they know in other fields of work? Don't be so busy painting yourself into a corner that you fail to look for a way out.

I Don't Like Rejection   I would rather not push myself in situations where I am probably going to be turned away. No one likes that kind of treatment, and I am no exception. Why walk into a buzz saw when you know it's there? That sort of experience will only tend to reduce my confidence.

Answer: When you set about the work search, it is *you* who are doing the choosing, not the other way around. There is no risk of failure when you are the customer rather than the salesperson. Perambulate through the work search as a data gatherer and let the job offers take care of themselves.

Let Fate Take Over   I would prefer to trust that the unseen hand, the mysterious flow of events that has been my life so far, will continue to shape the story of my career. I like surprises and have faith that good things will happen, that whatever comes my way, I can handle it and adjust to it. Going out to make my own changes is too much like tampering with a higher-order process. To my vocation I will be called. I believe opportunities will cross my path and I will be wise enough to know which ones are marked for me.

Answer: If you are so closely in touch with divine powers that you prefer not to develop an organizer strategy, then play it your way. However, allow me to suggest it is not fate that guides you, but your sensitivity to yourself and your willingness to trust your instincts.

I Am Just a Complainer I am really a chronic malcontent. It's just a life-style with me. I really don't want to change, but would simply rather complain, moan, attract sympathy, and just stay put where I am.

Answer: There are better ways to entertain yourself than crying wolf. I believe people who grouse about their work are in need of help, but don't know how to ask for it. If you are sinking in vocational quicksand, please call for a rope and pull yourself out.

The Alternative Might Be Worse What I like about the miserable work I've got is that at least I know what sort of misery to expect each day. Whatever job I might get in exchange could be worse, even more debilitating. I am comfortable in a perverse sort of way with my present situation.

Answer: Risk is the tariff for leaving the Land of Predictable Misery. Secure a temporary visa—give yourself permission to roam the countryside and look at what other people are doing. If the alternatives demand too high a price in uncertainty, you can still come home again if you insist on it.

It Doesn't Hurt Enough Yet I really cannot change because my present work is tolerable. I have nothing much to look forward to, but I can keep the pain to a minimum by dodging around, doing a little something different, and fantasizing that it will get better. I'm sure other people have it much worse, so why shouldn't I put up with my share of discomfort?

Answer: Is the pain really tolerable or is your head just numb from repeated encounters with the wall? When *will* it hurt enough—when your children talk about what a kind, calm, and likable person you *used* to be?

I Don't Want to Shake Things Up Life is comfortable and predictable, even if it is not exciting and filled with challenges. If I look around for a change now, I will have to unsettle myself, my entire family, and everything that is orderly in my life. That's an awful price to pay in search of a rainbow that might not be there. I will not take chances with my family's security.

Answer: The emotional health of you and your family may be more important than a certain amount of financial sacrifice. Ask your family members first before you make assumptions about how they would regard a shakeup. Perhaps they have been waiting for you to give the word.

Nothing May Turn Up   Then what? Suppose I pour myself into a search for something better and then discover, after all that turmoil, that nothing is available, that I must stay where I am after all? Wouldn't that be a terrible waste of effort? Why even expose myself to that possibility? At least when I go to a store, I know I will usually find merchandise. Job hunting is shaky business. I don't like the odds.

Answer: Sure, and there may be no trout in the stream, no friends at the golf course, but you still go there hoping something lucky will occur. Charles Kettering's well-known saying about luck is especially apt here: "No one ever stumbled across anything sitting down."

No One Encourages Me   I am not being cheered on by those around me. My family and friends really don't know how I feel about my present work, so they see no great urgency for me to change. Besides, it is more comfortable for those close to me if I stay put. They won't have to adjust to my new ways or ideas.

Answer: You probably have not allowed them into your secret chambers. Any person with whom you share your struggle will cheer you on, because he or she wants the same attention when getting up the courage to move in a new direction. Don't suffer in silence; you will become your own worst critic.

► Conclusion ◄

Of course, you have looked for work before. You probably did so, however, as an adolescent might seek to break into a strange social group. Job hunting has much the flavor of a ritual dance in which the initiate must perform in certain prescribed ways. The dance is a passionless affair because the individual does as told—send your forms here, sit there, talk now, go have this or that examined, cross your fingers, breathe deeply, wait . . . and wait some more. Ritual dances, with employers calling the tunes and job seekers dancing to them, will remain the dominant rites until work seekers learn to orchestrate their own methods.

You cannot depend entirely on college degrees, reference letters, other people, good fortune, or paper qualifications to get the job that is best for you. You must exert more active control over the process and take initiatives as often as possible.

Your success will depend heavily on your ability to use many skills of the career-search process. Without these skills, you are at the mercy of other people's arbitrary judgments and whims.

No doubt you already apply many of the career skills naturally in your normal life routine. Other skills probably represent areas of serious deficiency for you. The following chapters will show you how to acquire the skills you need most.

Career skills are lifetime skills. They can be used repeatedly in a person's life and work history. By possessing these skills you can reduce your fear of the career search because you can take better control of the search process.

You are most likely to regard the career search as enjoyable and effective if you put the skills to use many months before you have an urgent need to change your employment or your career direction.

PART

I

*Self-Assessment
Skills*

1
Values

He who has a why to live can bear with almost any how.
—Friedrich Nietzsche

What we call "creative work" ought not to be called work at all, because it isn't. . . . I imagine that Thomas Edison never did a day's work in his last fifty years.
—Stephen Leacock

Values are the emotional salary of work, and some folks are drawing no wages at all. "I can't quite put my finger on it, but I feel empty all the time on my job." "I can't figure out why I am doing this; it all seems to add up to so much nothing." "It's just a job. Why should I expect anything more? So what if there are no fireworks; it's a living. . . . But I'm not living very much." And so we defend ourselves against criticism or regret about job choices we have made that defy the laws of emotional gravity, jobs we took because they were there, jobs devoid of purpose and redeeming virtue. The choice seemed reasonable at the time: "I had to do something, and this seemed as good as anything else."

Many people literally hate their work because they can find little or no value in it. As used in this chapter, the word *value* has a personal meaning: it reflects how you feel about the work itself and the contribution it makes to others. Value has other meanings (How much value will this product have in the marketplace? How valuable is this employee to our profit picture?) that are separate from the values that must dictate your individual choice.

Your selection of one particular kind of work from among the thousands available must reflect what you regard as important, worth doing, inherently valuable. If you do not value the work you do, then no other incentive can possibly compensate for your lost sense of being significant, important, part of something you value. On the other hand, if you value the work you have chosen, then neither small office, nor lack of recognition, nor poor working conditions can stay you from your appointed rounds or dissuade you from your objectives.

Most folks dance the Safety, Security, Seniority, Longevity Polka. Security is the usual trade-off for work a person regards as dull, routine, and meaningless. "I would have quit long ago, but the paychecks keep coming in." "I just can't afford to surrender the terrific security this place gives you." "I put up with this place because they don't make you fight for your job every week." "I'll hold on to this job if it kills me." How many unhappy people do you know who buttress their positions with arguments of that kind? How much mediocrity, ennui, and routine acceptance of things as they are masquerade as job security?

▶ Why Work? ◀

When everything else about a job is stripped away, the Values remain. "Why do this job? Why work in the first place?" To earn a living? To have a good time? To have something to do each day? To do something interesting? To have something to write home about? To be a part of whatever action is going on in your town? To offer something that other people will value? To keep from sliding into the pit of uselessness? To not get shown up by your friends? To pull your oar in the great ship of life? Yes, all of these reasons and more.

Values are at the center of every career decision. This is not just a matter for social-service types to think about, but bankers, government workers, accountants, real estate salespeople, urban planners, oceanographers, retail clerks—everyone. Why *this* job and not any other? Is it just a matter of what is available at the time? I hope not. Will your choice be the best reflection of what you think makes work worthwhile (your values), or the lowest common denominator—you work just because everybody else does?

What Everyone Wants from a Job

No matter who you are, what you do, or how much ambition you have, you want the same things from your work that I do and everyone else does: (a) work that is interesting for its own sake; (b) work that we can be respected for, because we do it well; (c) work that has some value for others. If your work does not fulfill any deeper need than survival, it will grate on you and make the rest of your day unrewarding too.

Values can be assessed by every job seeker along four dimensions:

Material How much will I gain from this job? Will I earn a lot? Will I make a comfortable living? Will the pay and benefits help me get the things I want in life? Will those I live with be comfortable? The chapter on money (pages 45–54) discusses how you can incorporate financial questions into your overall career decision.

Social Are these people I work with the ones I want to be part of? Do I like their company enough to be around them every day? Will I develop friendships here that will carry over to my personal life? Will I enjoy the companionship as much as the work?

Emotional Will I enjoy the work itself, the experience of doing it? Will I look forward to being involved with the problems of the job, and feel challenged by trying to solve these problems? Will this enjoyment be strong enough to counter the frustrations that will inevitably appear on the job?

Spiritual Will this work contribute to the greater good? This question is not just for people in the helping professions; it applies to every kind of work. "Does the bank provide services I feel are worthwhile?" "How do I feel about these singing telegrams that I do?" "Do my customers appreciate the work I am doing?" "How much would my work be missed, if I were not here to do it?"

Few people will embrace these four Values dimensions equally, but all four are part of every job or career choice. Why is it important to highlight them? Any dimension that is ignored completely will come back to haunt a person. For example, if you're satisfied on the Material, Emotional, and Spiritual dimensions, but the Social is lacking, the job will eventually become a problem. You'll only be able to stand the people in it for so long, before you want out.

The process of job hunting is often so complex and chaotic, and the task of just finding job opportunities so time consuming, that you may simply choose a job because it is available. Then, when you discover weeks or months later that it does not fit you, you'll suffer personal loss trying to find another, and meanwhile the employer will suffer from your lack of productivity, which won't help your market value either.

People think that getting a job is the hard part: not so. Staying interested enough in the job to do it well and with enthusiasm is the real challenge. That's probably why you are reading this book—you've been through a few Doggy Jobs already and don't care to find any more.

It's one thing to have a job, get paid, come home, go to work again, and join the car pool parade with little sense of anticipation. Ho hum. It's quite another to be doing something you value, affecting the world around you, and feeling involved in a worthwhile goal.

No job will have all four ideal conditions. But if you look for them, you're more likely to find them. Because your values are at stake, don't settle for a humdrum job.

Regardless of the job you have, there are three things you can do to change it, if it does not satisfy you:

1. *Change the job from within.* Ask for responsibilities that fit your abilities better. Volunteer for tasks that you find interesting. Get involved in things you think are worth doing. Seek out the coworkers you'd like to know better. If your job is boring, create a challenge for yourself.
2. *Define a new job, and seek it.* So you've done what you could to change the job, and it wasn't enough. Before you hit the streets to find a new one, shape a concept in your mind's eye of what you want that next job to look like. What will you be doing—can you see it? When it comes into focus, start looking for people who do this kind of work. Do *not* apply for such a job until you meet at least five people who are in that line of work. See the chapter on Information Interviewing (pages 132–141) to figure out how to get the best information from them.
3. *Seek unpaid work experience.* In some cases neither the old job nor the new job will satisfy you. Don't set out looking for another job too quickly. Instead, ask yourself: "What am I not getting from this job that I could seek outside of paid employment?" Is it use of a certain skill? Or involvement with certain kinds of people? Or a sense of challenge that is missing? Or is there certain subject matter that you want? Whatever it is, look for an opportunity to pursue it on a voluntary basis. This is a necessary safety valve, because few jobs will offer all the things you want. So what? Do them anyway.

Who would want to work and not get paid for it? You do it all the time—in the community work you do, the sports teams you play on, the organizations you belong to, the gardens you cultivate, or the projects you have around the house. Unpaid work serves three major purposes:

1. Unpaid work satisfies needs not met by your paid employment. Jobs may be dull or frustrating no matter what we do to spice them up, so we need other work to keep us fired up.
2. Unpaid work may provide a foundation for future paid work. Unpaid activities can grow into careers, either second careers or replacements for your primary work. Part-time involvement allows you to accumulate knowledge without risking the family fortune. One day you may want to market what you know, if you get fed up with your present job.
3. Unpaid work enhances your paid employment. Writing books and articles in a professional field . . . serving on community boards . . . giving free service to friends (tax accounting, car repair, etc.) . . . research projects . . . conducting free clinics (sports, health, etc.). These are examples of work which pays

little or nothing but, in terms of the skills we develop, the knowledge we acquire, and the experience we accumulate, helps us do our primary jobs better.

Most dream careers start with unpaid work. If there is a career you've dreamed of having, you've probably already been doing it, and thinking about it, and reading about it, long before you ever get paid for it, whether it's being a rock guitarist, a writer, a counselor, or an entrepreneur with an idea for a new business.

As you take steps toward starting your dream career, you are going to experience risk—risk of failure, risk that you will be disappointed in yourself, and the risk of unforeseen factors and events. Risk is the price of admission. Be a risk taker. It's the only way you will find out what you have to offer and how much value your work has for others. People who sit around wondering where to find the forty-year no-cut contract will probably immobilize themselves, because they are afraid of making a mistake. Those who look for the sure thing do not make good workers.

► Spotting Your Key Value ◄

Many readers will recognize that the four Values dimensions mentioned earlier are often clustered together when they find a job that really fits them. Often this is because the job captures an underlying value that is of special appeal.

Many of us have one Key Value, a theme that is so appealing, a subject matter that is so interesting to us, or a work environment we find so irresistible that we are naturally attracted to it. Examples of key values include:

- Working with disabled people
- Being around big money deals
- Being in the center of activity for a town or city
- Competing with others verbally
- Being around athletic events
- Teaching
- Being involved with dancing
- Helping children to grow up
- Getting to talk with as many different people as possible
- Working with plants and flowers
- Involving myself in social change
- Making decisions with numbers
- Selling ideas

EXAMPLE ► Joan is a person whom no four walls can contain. She feels imprisoned when she is sitting down for more than an hour. She works as a counselor in a community college. The job is all right, and most of the people are too, but Joan's one key value involves being outside, being physically active, and experiencing a love of nature. What can she do about it?

Solution: Joan tried backpacking on weekends for a while, but that was not enough. She kept the counselor job for security reasons, but eventually found her way to long-distance running, which gave her an excuse to be outside almost every day of the year. Today she is an ultra-distance runner, and probably spends as much time per week "working" outdoors as she does in the counseling office. Joan is in touch with her one key value and is doing pretty well in acting on it. Her next step may be to become a mountain guide . . . or perhaps buy a cabin in the foothills . . . or maybe design programs for the college that involve outdoor activity . . . or find some combination of these that fits her life situation best.

By searching for your one key value, you can kill four birds with one stone; that is, the one key value will usually point you toward a kind of work that will satisfy all four Values dimensions—Material, Social, Emotional, and Spiritual. You probably have had a few clues but are not sure whether to act on them. Or perhaps you know the one key value, but you believe there is no market for it. It's enough at this point to identify what the one key value is. Let's leave later chapters to tell you how to act on it.

► I Just Wanna Earn a Living ◄

There are those who will say: "Never mind Values. I just want to work so that I can produce an income, feed a family, and live comfortably. I entered the restaurant supply business because it is a good way to make money—that's it. There is nothing interesting about it." The one key value for these folks is to stay close to the market and do what is necessary to earn a comfortable and predictable income. However, I would bet that these people still have the four Values dimensions taken care of. Obviously the Material draws their attention. But also, they manage to work around people they like pretty well (Social). They find it reasonably enjoyable and a challenge to keep producing income (Emotional), and they believe their work gives others a decent product or service (Spiritual). If they were not getting some satisfaction in these four areas, I believe they would have gotten out a long time ago and looked for a different place to "just earn a living." Some people are not conscious of Values when they make their career choices; nonetheless these Values are present and accounted for.

A Word on Behalf of Social Consciousness

For some, career choice is focused on helping others or making a contribution to society. Counselors, ministers, social workers, probation officers, artists, etc., come to mind. Most others think that Social consciousness is for do-gooders, not for them. They would claim it is not a part of their career choice. But every career choice affects other people in some way. The dental hygienist can affect my attitude toward dental care; the person who answers the phone can make me not want to do business with a particular store; my tax accountant can affect my life in a hundred ways.

Work has no meaning at all unless it creates value. The work that you do will not be honored or respected, nor will it earn the money you want, unless it has value for others. We pay to hear songs sung, to have walls painted, to have parklands protected, to buy vehicles to carry us around, and for anything else we value. We pay you to provide us something we want and cannot provide for ourselves. Without us, your career does not exist.

I say this because "values" in career choice are often interpreted to mean, What can *I* get out of my career? Yes, your enjoyment, challenge, and life-style are important, but they are possible only if you consistently create something of value for others. Career choices that focus on just you and your needs eventually become empty and unsatisfying. People who reach levels of success and ask: "Why am I doing this?" or "Is this all there is?" have lost their core reasons for working.

The fear of losing ground in the race for economic comforts is sometimes overpowering. People often make career choices based upon whatever will give them their fair share of the pie, and then some. Such choices come back to bite you. If you find a niche where you are not accountable to anyone, you will lose sight of what doing a good job means, and will lose the capacity to evaluate yourself. People in such circumstances become bored and dissatisfied and do not understand why.

Social consciousness can be considered by everyone in contemplating various careers:

- Will I be helping people with these bank loans?
- Do I believe the services that this company offers are valuable?
- How do my graphics make these publications more readable, and thus educate people better?

The best jobs and careers are those in which the individuals *believe* in the value of what they are doing. They believe the product is a good one. As a result, they sell it better, invest more money in it, persist with it, and attract others to work with them.

Every successful career has a theme of social consciousness about it. A new tool won't sell unless it does someone some good. Government programs work best when they answer a need; teachers work best when students learn; and new businesses don't get very far unless people want what they are offering. So, don't think that social consciousness went out with the sixties. It is and always will be a factor in career choice.

Cynics may say that people act only in their own self-interest: Does a pawnbroker care? Does a marketing executive give a hoot as long as the product sells? Does a lawyer care as long as he/she wins the case? Self-interest exists and is powerful, but when self-interest and social good coincide, everyone walks away happy: "I like doing physical therapy and so do my clients." "I make money as a consultant because my clients profit by my recommendations."

A Sense of Purpose

Have you ever wondered what keeps people going in difficult jobs: years on a research project . . . struggling through the thickets of politics . . . running a restaurant for ninety hours a week . . . building a house . . . coaching a team of deaf athletes . . . writing a book for which the audience is uncertain . . . supervising a much-maligned police department . . . starting a program in the face of community opposition?

It's not the money. It's not the glory either. It's not even the promise of successful outcomes. It is the hope that something good might happen, and underneath that is a sense of purpose, a belief that the work is worth doing, a goal that lies outside the needs of the person working toward it.

In her long-range study of people and their careers, Gail Sheehy writes:

> What first emerged from the surveys and interviews was an outline of that enviable creature, the person who enjoys optimum well-being. . . . The person of optimum well-being is best characterized by the ten statements of self-description that follow. . . . 1. "My life has meaning and direction." This is the characteristic that correlates most closely with optimum life satisfaction. People of high well-being find meaning in an involvement with something beyond themselves; a work, an idea, other people, a social objective.[1]

I would suspect that this could be confirmed in any sample of people who are happy in their work, professional or otherwise. "Purpose" gets us involved in the big, ambitious projects, the goals not yet reached, the search for new discoveries, the quests that are exciting; it keeps us going in the face of repeated setbacks. "Purpose" can be more enticing than money, security, and status, because it deals with living problems. If your work does not affect anyone, then why do it? If your work does touch someone, then what more reason do you need?

► Defining Your Values ◄

Raths, Harmin, and Simon, in their book *Values and Teaching,* define values as "those elements which show how a person has decided to use his/her life."[2] Work values are those enduring dimensions or aspects of our work that we regard as important sources of satisfaction.

Here is a representative list of work values:

Help Society: Do something to contribute to the betterment of the world I live in.

Help Others: Be involved in helping other people in a direct way, either individually or in small groups.

Public Contact: Have a lot of day-to-day contact with people.

Work with Others: Have close working relationships with a group; work as a team toward common goals.

Affiliation: Be recognized as a member of a particular organization.

Friendships: Develop close personal relationships with people as a result of my work activities.

Competition: Engage in activities which pit my abilities against others where there are clear win-and-lose outcomes.

Make Decisions: Have the power to decide courses of action, policies, etc.

Work Under Pressure: Work in situations where time pressure is prevalent and/or the quality of my work is judged critically by supervisors, customers, or others.

Power and Authority: Control the work activities or (partially) the destinies of other people.

Influence People: Be in a position to change attitudes or opinions of other people.

Work Alone: Do projects by myself, without any significant amount of contact with others.

Knowledge: Engage myself in the pursuit of knowledge, truth, and understanding.

Intellectual Status: Be regarded as a person of high intellectual prowess or as one who is an acknowledged "expert" in a given field.

Artistic Creativity: Engage in creative work in any of several art forms.

Creativity (general): Create new ideas, programs, organizational structures, or anything else not following a format previously developed by others.

Aesthetics: Be involved in studying or appreciating the beauty of things, ideas, etc.

Supervision: Have a job in which I am directly responsible for the work done by others.

Change and Variety: Have work responsibilities which frequently change in their content and setting.

Precision Work: Work in situations where there is very little tolerance for error.

Stability: Have a work routine and job duties that are largely predictable and not likely to change over a long period of time.

Security: Be assured of keeping my job and receiving a reasonable financial reward.

Fast Pace: Work in circumstances where . . . work must be done rapidly.

Recognition: Be recognized for the quality of my work in some visible or public way.

Excitement: Experience a high degree of (or frequent) excitement in the course of my work.

Adventure: Have work duties which involve frequent risk-taking.

Profit, Gain: Have a strong likelihood of accumulating large amounts of money or other material gain.

Independence: Be able to determine the nature of my work without significant direction from others; not have to do what others tell me to.

Moral Fulfillment: Feel that my work is contributing significantly to a set of moral standards which I feel are very important.

Location: Find a place to live (town, geographical area) which is conducive to my life-style and affords me the opportunity to do the things I enjoy most.

Community: Live in a town or city where I can get involved in community affairs.

Physical Challenge: Have a job that makes physical demands which I would find rewarding.

Time Freedom: Have work responsibilities which I can work at according to my own time schedule; no specific working hours required.[3]

► How Your Values Are ◄ Exhibited

Identifying values is the single most fundamental process in a successful career search because every other skill depends on your ability to state your motives with clarity and some precision. In this section, I have outlined some specific methods you can use to crystallize your awareness of your values. Each method represents a different way of tapping into your values and is followed by an example of some results the method might produce. There are many more strategies for eliciting values than can be noted here. Simon, Kirschenbaum, and Howe, in their book *Values Clarification,*[4] have an excellent compendium of such strategies, many of which you can also apply to career concerns.

All methods for identifying values yield one or two essential kinds of information: (1) *past experience*—what you have already done in your life that you have valued, and (2) *future desires*—what you hope to do in the future that you would regard as highly rewarding.

Past experience is a rich source of your work values because your behavior is strong evidence of your preferences. Even if you are young, twenty years of personal choices can yield many clues about your prominent motivators.

Future choices are expressed in daydreams, fantasies, and plans, which cannot be verified by actual behavior. Hence, the values they reflect may be more tentative. Dreams, however, are powerful forces when they are vivid enough to be imagined in great detail. Often they are harnessed to your understanding of your past experiences. When you shape past values in the light of your presently unfolding and changing needs, you can forge a powerful vision of a desirable future.

Mattson and Miller, in *The Truth about You,*[5] assert that your key values can be determined by a thorough review of your peak life experiences—occasions or periods when you have exerted yourself strenuously, have performed successfully, and have been pleased with what you accomplished. These occasions can be studied for the presence of values, and, Mattson and Miller claim, your one or two most prominent values appear consistently in these life experiences.

EXAMPLE ► Won spelling bees at age twelve. Wrote essay on psycho-neurosis at age sixteen. Wrote and presented a show for children at age eighteen. Edited a sports section and wrote column at age nineteen. Wrote songs for a camp show at age nineteen. Edited book manuscripts at age twenty-four. Read poetry at age twenty-six. (Values: personal recognition, precision with words.)

I subscribe to the view that values are extremely important in career behavior because our culture is intensely dominated by a work/achievement orientation. An individual typically expends far more effort than the minimum required to earn a paycheck when it is possible to satisfy prized values. The individual climbs a personal Mount Everest not only because it is there, but also to satisfy a compelling personal need.

Because people's needs change with age, you may have some career aspirations that are linked only marginally to your past experiences. These desires can also be examined for the presence of consistent themes.

EXAMPLE ► I would like to: build bookcases, understand decisions made on the commodity exchanges, buy and sell antiques, study American folklore, collect historical anecdotes about the Civil War, raise farm animals for profit. (Key themes: interest in historical America, manual activities, and the farming business.)

Of course, these aspirations must be tested in the crucible of life experiences, but dreams should not be damped down by skepticism or taken too lightly. Your visions for the future are your assessment of your past, as you reject certain values and embrace others. Effective dreams grow from your being in close touch with past successes and especially with failures. The strongest drives often result from earlier disappointments or half-successes that were aborted by circumstances.

You may protest that dreams and values are fine, but few people get a chance to fulfill career fantasies in their lifetimes. Most of us are stuck, you say, with marginally satisfying jobs. Changing your dull job for someone else's will not help matters.

The mistake in this reasoning is in viewing jobs as finished landscapes. Of course, values will not magically appear once you have discovered them. And employers will frustrate your dreams. However, knowing what the dream looks like will help you piece it into your current situation. Finding even one source of value in a sea of boredom is a powerful antidote to a deadly job.

- If you dream of architecture but are only a mechanical draftsman, try designing your best attempts at floor plans during your spare time and ask the professional staff to evaluate your work.
- If you can barely tolerate your job but see no way out, find a source of stimulation incidental to the job that will allow you to endure it, such as joining the company bridge team, starting a local investment club, or organizing theater trips.
- If the only enjoyable part of your present job is public speaking,

but your boss lets you do precious little of it, look for another department that might want to borrow your services.

- If you want a job with complete independence, but the only available ones are too risky financially, decide how much security you are willing to surrender in exchange for some autonomy. Perhaps a part-time source of income where you have decision power will help you to tolerate submission in your regular job.
- If you love exercising control over budgets, but have little authority to do so, try seeking an outside source of funds for your organization (government grant, foundation money, or other) and then put yourself in charge if your proposal is successful.

In *Clarifying Values through Subject Matter,* Harmin, Kirschenbaum, and Simon outline the seven subprocesses that help people make value choices that are both personally satisfying and socially responsible:

1. *Choosing freely.* If we are to live by our own values system, we must learn how to make independent choices. . . .
2. *Choosing from alternatives.* For choice-making to have meaning, there have to be alternatives from which to choose. If there are no alternatives, there are no choices. . . .
3. *Choosing after thoughtful consideration of consequences.* We need to learn to examine alternatives in terms of their expected consequences. If we don't, our choice-making is likely to be whimsical, impulsive, or conforming. . . .
4. *Prizing and cherishing.* Values inevitably include not only our rational choices, but our feelings as well. In developing values we become aware of what we prize and cherish. . . .
5. *Publicly affirming.* When we share our choices with others— what we prize and what we do—we not only continue to clarify our own values, but we help others to clarify their values as well. . . .
6. *Acting.* Often people have difficulty in acting on what they come to believe and prize. Yet, if they are to realize their values, it is vital that they learn how to connect choices and prizings to their own behavior.
7. *Acting with consistency.* A single act does not make a value. We need to examine the patterns of our lives. What do we do with consistency and regularity?[6]

At the end of this chapter is an exercise that uses these seven subprocesses to help you determine your values.

► Values of Significant Others ◄

How do your family and friends feel about the career choices you are considering? How do you feel about their opinions regarding what kinds of work might be best for you? You are not likely to reject everyone else's values entirely, but neither must you be a mirror image of the people around you. How would your mother react if you told her you were going to become a motorcycle racer? a sewage inspector? a chicken plucker? Inevitably, people will try to influence your choice. Your job is not to ignore them but to take their thoughts and feelings into account, and then make your best decision based on your own judgment and preferences.

► Values-Clarification ◄
Exercises

The data for discovery of your values are all around you. Your values weave through the fabric of everything you do. The kinds of work to which you are attracted and the forms of play that exhilarate you are revealing. Those activities you regard as both work and play say even more about where your values lie. Building a toolshed, watching horror movies, plotting the course of a caterpillar, digging with your hands for seashells, listening for little harmonies in sounds of the night—any of these activities has value to the person who does it.

You can learn to interpret any of your experiences or imaginings if you nurture the simple habit of putting words, however imprecise they may be, to your feelings about events. If you enjoy having time to sit alone and ruminate, for example, you can say: "I value quiet." If you get excited about NBA playoff games, you can assume: "I enjoy the noise of competition." If you get a good feeling from seeing your words in print, you can put that into words: "I value recognition from others."

Here are a few exercises you can do to clarify your values further.

► Exercise One

You may find important clues to your career values in how you view the work of those closest to you. Unless you choose to, you need never feel obligated to carry on the occupation or profession chosen by a significant relative; however, you should notice which parts of that work appeal to you in a natural way and take this as evidence of your own preferences.

Try making a list of your family and friends, and put the occupation of each person beside his or her name. *Occupation* is here interpreted broadly to include the major way in which the person spends his or her time, including student and other nonpaid activities. Which single part (activity, task, subrole, duty) of that person's job do you find the most appealing? Try your best to find at least one part of the occupation that represents a value you appreciate. Identify the aspect of the job you would choose for yourself and the value it represents.

> EXAMPLE ► Friend, barber: meets many people (friendliness)
> Friend, carpenter: builds houses (body use/seeing results)
> Mother, schoolteacher: supervises class (decision making)
> Father, accountant: has steady income (security)
> Uncle, banker: handles money (responsibility)
> Aunt, dress designer: makes new designs (creativity)
> Minister: exhibits concern for others (compassion)
> Neighbor, treasurer: controls finances (responsibility)
> Neighbor, professor: keeps knowledgeable (learning/reading)
> Brother, coach: physically active (health)

Once you have identified all these separate values derived from the occupations of family members and friends, try making a composite occupation from the values you have identified. Be creative. Don't worry about whether such a career actually exists or whether you could enter it. Just try to stitch the values together into a coherent whole.

> EXAMPLE ► Values: friendliness, body use, seeing results, decision making, security, responsibility, creativity, compassion, learning, reading, health
> Possible composite careers: health director for a summer camp, physical fitness consultant for private industry, forester or range manager or other outdoor administration

► Exercise Two

Refer to the seven subprocesses of valuing on page 39 for this exercise. Use them as a framework to review your own activity of the past week:

1. Name one choice you made freely.

   > EXAMPLE ► I read a book about the history of the town in which I live.

2. Name another choice, this time one you made from among two or more alternatives.

   > EXAMPLE ► I went to the farm show rather than the stock-car races or the picnic.

3. What consequences did you consider in making your latter choice?

   > EXAMPLE ► I knew my friends would be unhappy that I didn't join them at the races and the picnic afterward.

4. Did you choose on the basis of your personal feelings, because you prized the activity you chose?

EXAMPLE ▶ I chose the farm show because I think raising animals is important and more enjoyable than tinkering with car engines.

5. Did you publicly clarify this choice?

EXAMPLE ▶ I told my friends why I could not join them, even though they did not fully understand.

6. Did you act on your value?

EXAMPLE ▶ I acted on my value by attending the farm show.

7. Have you acted consistently on this choice in the past?

EXAMPLE ▶ I regularly refuse to attend auto races because I do not admire what they are doing, and I attend farm shows at every opportunity, even if it means I have to travel fifty miles or do extra work around the house to compensate for my time away.

▶ Exercise Three

It is often even more revealing to witness an event with other people and then compare what each of you valued in it. By exploring the differences among you, you may see your own values in sharp relief, because others have seen the same event in different ways.

Choose another person with whom to do this exercise, a person who will help you focus on your values by participating in the exercise with you.

1. *Recall an experience that made you happy.* Recount to your partner an experience that gave you a good feeling, made you happy, or left you feeling better than when you started. Try to distinguish between something you *thought* was good and something that *felt* good inside. Your feelings are more important than your ideas in this case.

EXAMPLE ▶ I felt good about the summer weekend I organized for my cousins.

2. *Provide detail.* Describe the experience in as much detail as you can. What exactly did you do to make it happen? Try to remember as much of the sequence of events as you can, including not only what you did but also how you felt about it each step of the way.

EXAMPLE ▶ I arranged a preliminary meeting of the group at a restaurant during the winter to see if they were interested. We had a lot of laughs, recalled old times, and told stories. I told the most. Then I proposed a summer weekend and outlined how we would plan for it.

3. *Identify a value.* Of course there will be more than one value involved in the experience, but start by clarifying only one key value. What one aspect did you like about what you were doing? What seemed worthwhile about the experience? For what purpose did you expend this time and energy?

EXAMPLE ▶ I suppose the biggest satisfaction was doing something to keep a family and its bonds together, arranging an event that would make it possible for the cousins who were once close to revalidate a family tie. They all wanted to keep close, but would not do anything unless it was made relatively easy for them.

4. *Reach deeper.* Once you have stated a value to your partner, the two of you can take an even closer look by asking: "What in particular was satisfying about this?" It will seem you are repeating the original question, but you are actually reaching deeper to another layer of meaning. In fact, the question "But what did you really like about that?" might be asked several times until the deepest layer of meaning is reached.

EXAMPLE ▶ Well, I guess I like to be a catalyst, a person who brings other people together. I really enjoy recognizing a situation in which a group of people would like to fortify their bonds, but haven't been able to do so because of circumstances. I really enjoy being the person who makes it happen.

5. *Check with partner.* At one or more points in the process of describing your experience and identifying the values inherent in it, you should ask your partner to use his or her own words to help clarify what you were trying to say. Ask this person to restate in different words the value(s) you seemed to be expressing so that the two of you can arrive at the sharpest possible definition and label of your particular value.

EXAMPLE ▶ Partner: You seem to get a kick out of arranging things, giving people a chance to reach each other on an informal basis. Yes, you seem to have a definite preference for informality in the things you set up. You seem to believe that informality is the best setting in which to give people the freedom to get closer, enjoy each other better.

It is important to be able to place your own labels on your values and to derive and label these values by reviewing your own experiences. This exercise gives you an opportunity to practice examining your experiences and discovering values in them. This most basic form of value clarification can be used with any sort of experience, big or small. More importantly, it *should* be used with all sorts of experiences, because values may be revealed in even the tiniest of events. Your more enduring values are especially likely to be hiding in tiny, obscure life events because such events occur naturally and unconsciously without your thoughts, shoulds, or oughts intruding. These are the kinds of life experiences you can include:

- Teaching your little sister how to tell time
- Knocking over the bottles at the county fair
- Cleaning out your files till you know where every last item is located
- Losing the fourteen extra pounds you've been carrying for years
- Keeping a shell collection
- Walking barefoot in the rain
- Seeing how fast you can add up the restaurant check
- Reading every historical marker on your cross-country trip

Money

Money is America's most powerful drug.
—Philip Slater

Is there anything harder to ignore in career decision making than money? We have to examine money, because it affects every job you will ever consider. Inevitably, you ask yourself questions such as: I like that job, but does it pay enough? Can I afford to turn down that job? How much money do I want or need?

Like an umpire calling Go or No Go on every pitch an employer makes, money is always there in the background. We tend to think the job that pays the most is necessarily the best. For several reasons, it can be a mistake to simply go for the highest-paying job:

- Other forms of pay, present or potential, can outweigh starting salary. A discussion later in this chapter shows how you can measure economic gain in a variety of ways.
- Early in a career, the quality of learning is more important than earnings, because such learning will enhance your career market value in years to come. It is difficult to measure learning in the same way as money. Talk to those who have been in the field for a few years and ask them what kinds of learning most enhance your earning potential.
- If the job turns out to be something you don't feel (and you already suspect that from the start), you'll waste time and money later trying to redirect your career. It does not pay to grab a few years of good money and then leave a field to try something else.
- Starting salary, especially in an entry-level job, can be a poor index of future earnings potential in a given field. For example, advertising, publishing, and banking are industries that tradition-ally start people at low rates of pay. In part, this is a weeding-

out process. Those who stay and perform well earn significantly more before too long.

► What Kind of Relationship ◄ with Money Do You Want?

Money is like a passenger in your car every day you drive to work. You'd better decide how you're going to relate to this rider in the car pool, because it affects every decision you make. No two people relate to money in quite the same way. Some can almost ignore it even though they don't have a lot of it. Others seem obsessed by it. Most of us fall somewhere in between.

It helps to know how you will deal with money in your career, because you want your relationship to be a happy one. Here are several different kinds of relationships to money, from which you can choose, or you may want to define your own:

Comfortable and Predictable This is perhaps the most popular. In this relationship, you are saying that regularity of income is most important, that you don't want to face any great risks that your earnings will disappear anytime in the foreseeable future, as long as you do your job well. This relationship usually has less high-side potential, because you are not accepting much risk. It also has the danger of potential boredom. But, many people are happy with this relationship and would not trade it for any of the others.

Stormy But Exciting Money is always a factor in this relationship, because there is continual doubt about how much you're going to make. The thrill of competition is mixed with the risk of losing. In situations like this, people are usually shooting to "make a bundle" and are willing to accept the risks, in exchange for the challenge and combativeness. People who stay with this relationship usually win more often than they lose, but some even stay when the results are poor. They like the fun of the chase as much as the bottom-line earnings.

More Is Better In this relationship, money is in the driver's seat. Usually in some form of self-employment, this person wants to see the results of his/her efforts pay off directly in terms of economic gain. The harder and better you work, the more you earn. Sounds simple, but it requires talent, perseverance, and single-mindedness. Other gains, such as job satisfaction, new learning, or work relationships, may have to take back seats. The quality of the relationship here is a dollar count, easily measurable and very satisfying when it works well.

Unconscious   You would prefer to be completely oblivious to money. Some people manage this type of relationship well. No, they are not street bums or independently wealthy. They hold jobs or sometimes are self-employed. The key here is that they *do not think* about money. If you were such a person, you would concentrate on your work, be as good as you could be, and accept whatever earnings came to you. This is a pure state, one that is difficult to achieve. Many readers will think it is even a little ridiculous. Often a person has some kind of professional training or marketable credential to be able to ignore money completely. However, others do it too. This relationship requires the ability to say: "If I give my best to the work that suits me, the money will come."

What Won't You Sacrifice for More Money?

It has been said that everyone has his price. This rather cynical view predicts that every man or woman will do a particular something if offered enough money. Such a dictum could also apply to a career decision. Would you do any kind of work if the rewards were high enough? Some would answer yes.

What kind of undesirable work would you do if the pay were high enough—almost anything? You're not sure? It's a tough question. You'd like the money but don't know what you'd be willing to give up.

It is helpful to consider what you would *not* trade off in exchange for greater financial gain. Given the opportunity to earn a lot more than you are presently earning, which of the following would be unacceptable conditions?

- I would not give up the pleasure of the kind of work I am doing
- I would not live in an undesirable part of the country
- I would not work for people I don't like
- I would not take on significant risks of failure
- I would not disrupt my relationships with my family members
- I would not give up my relationships with colleagues/friends/etc.
- I would not give up the recreational opportunities I have available

There are many other possible trade-offs that might modify your desire to go for the most money available. Though it sounds simple to say "I would always go for the most money I could earn," you have probably already made certain decisions about the conditions of your work and life which are not tradeable. These factors are sometimes called "psychological income."

How Much Extra Incentive Do You Want?

How much do you want money to be on your mind as you go about your work? People who want the Predictable and Comfortable relationship often do not want any earning incentives at all, because then they may have to worry about how much they are making. Others may prefer to have secondary sources of income, things they do on the side. The more-is-better person wants an earning incentive every minute.

For those who earn a regular salary, the question might be: How much *more* (expressed as a percent of base salary) would you like to have the potential of earning, if you choose to work for it? Ten percent? Fifty percent? Such income can derive from work that is different from your regular job, or work that derives from your day-to-day job (such as consulting). Of course, the higher percentage you choose, the more additional hours of work and responsibility, and you risk that outside work will intrude on your regular job and place it in some jeopardy.

This is another kind of relationship to money, one that could be called "security plus incentive pay." This relationship has some of the nicer features of two different worlds, the secure job and the rewards of self-employment. In fact, small part-time businesses (often run by people who have regular jobs) are increasingly a part of our economic scene.

Is It Bad Enough to Get Out?

Some readers are nowhere near the blissful relationships to money that I have described. They have a precarious relationship to money without large potential gains. Either they don't have regular incomes, or they have regular incomes which are dreadfully low, or they have a lot of risk-taking excitement but little profit. For them, the question about money may be: Should I hold on to what I've got, bad as it is, or should I get out? Try answering these questions:

- Is your job low-pay without any prospect of change?
- Are you or your family suffering unacceptable discomforts?
- Are you not being paid what you believe you're worth?
- Is your pay unfairly low compared to others who do similar work?
- Do you feel deprived compared to others?

If you answered yes to two or more of these, you've probably started looking for a way out long ago. A yes to any one of these questions is sufficient reason to consider a different kind of work. Each of the above conditions represents a lot of potential unhappiness. Even if the search is difficult and does not immediately produce results, keep after it.

Being paid what you're worth is the most difficult to assess, because it includes your evaluation of how good your work is. Some people inflate their economic value, while others undervalue themselves. Nonetheless, it is important that you believe you are getting the money you deserve. If you feel otherwise, look for other employers or other fields of work.

► Money Is a Status Thing ◄

Let's face it. We rate ourselves all the time. "Where do I stand compared to my friends, relatives, and coworkers?" Everyone derives some of his/her self-respect from relative standing, or status, in the working world. How do you measure your self-esteem? If money is your primary index, then you'll want as much of it as possible.

Are there other ways you measure your self-esteem, or the status of your occupation? How about any of the following?

- The respect that my profession/occupation has among the general public
- The importance of the work I am doing
- The reputation of the organization I work for
- The academic credentials that I have earned
- The power of my position
- The relative excitement or allure attached to my field of work
- The value of my work to others
- My position of importance within my profession

Thus you can derive self-esteem from your work in many ways other than money earned. Certainly each of the above is a form of psychological income. Though you'd like to have more money, you can count your job or career success in terms of many of the above measures of status.

In some cases, the above factors will become even more important than earnings. If you were offered a different job with more money, you'd want to consider whether sufficient status would also be present. Money and other sources of self-esteem need to be weighed together in any consideration about possible change of work.

► Dealing with Money: ◄
A Three-Point Plan

I would recommend that you approach the question of money in any job or career decision in terms of three steps:

1. Act As If Money Did Not Exist   Initially, go for the kind of work you like. Try your best to ignore potential earnings when you are considering various fields of work. Choose what you think will stimulate you most, and go where you believe you have the most to offer. You won't be able to block money completely out of your mind, but do your best to keep it from being a guiding factor.

There are many who believe that this approach to career choice will net you the most money in the long run. By aiming at the kinds of work that fit you best, you will make maximum use of your talents and will thus be most successful, which usually means succeeding financially too. Entrepreneurs and professionals often say they got into their work to show that a particular idea (or product) would work, to prove the worth of the idea. Thus it is the challenge of doing something different, making a statement, or simply offering something that people need, which draws certain individuals to their businesses or their professions.

If you're seeking a salaried job, the "don't think of money" approach can still apply. Go for the work that appeals to you, and worry about money later, when negotiating the salary. Try to find the employers who will pay you the most for doing what you like to do.

2. Settle Your Self-Esteem Contract with Yourself   Is the job you are considering good enough for you? Don't take a job that you consider beneath you in terms of money or perceived status, even if it sounds like a good thing to do for the time being. You can't enter comfortably into a job if you don't have enough respect for it and it does not have enough respect for you. You can evaluate the self-esteem factor in any terms you want—salary, importance of the job, public visibility, contribution to others, etc.—just make sure it is there. The better you feel about yourself as you go to work each morning, the more energetic and productive your work will be.

The only reason to ignore the self-esteem contract, temporarily, is if you need money immediately and cannot avoid taking an interim job to make ends meet. In such a case, you should keep looking for the better job even harder once you have taken immediate employment. Otherwise, getting stuck in a low-status job can wear you down. Keep pursuing jobs that you believe fit your talents. Self-respect is a factor in every job. Make sure you get enough of it.

3. Resolve Your Relationship with Money   Okay, no more courtship or romantic notions between you and Money, such as "Money doesn't matter to me, as long as I'm happy." Money matters to everyone in a career, though perhaps in different ways. It's time for you to get serious about your relationship with Money, get down to the day-to-day prospects of living together. Will it be "stormy but exciting," or do you prefer "comfortable and predictable"? Perhaps you would like the "same time next year" approach—"each year Money and I will reunite to renew our acquaintance and see where things stand. In between, I don't want to bother with it."

However you want to handle the ties that bind you and Money, try to settle the matter so that you don't have to reevaluate your partnership every day. Too much thinking about money will detract from your interest in the job and may cause you to overlook other benefits you are gaining from your position.

Settling your relationship with Money is important, because it frees you from being obsessed by how others are relating to it. If you understand, for example, that "comfortable and predictable" is right for you, then you can be calm about someone else's pursuing "money at all costs" or "earn a lot, risk a lot." Every relationship is different, but yours is right for you.

► Career Decisions and Money ◄

Here are a few guidelines for evaluating how money may pertain to your choice of a job or career:

If the Pay Isn't Good Enough for You Now, Don't Expect That You Will Get Used to It   Don't take a job where you feel seriously underpaid, hoping that everything else will compensate. If you are unhappy about the pay before you even start, you're likely to feel worse about it as time goes on, and will eventually struggle to escape.

Don't Settle for Less   Even if other factors make low pay more tolerable, don't acquiesce to a situation you may regret later. Do everything you can to get paid what you think you are worth, or at least as much as the market will allow.

Potential Earnings Are at Least as Important as Present Earnings   Starting salary often does not correlate with what an experienced person earns in a given field. Be sure to weigh your prospects against immediate pay, and decide how patient you are about letting your earning potential develop. In some fields pay is deliberately low at the start, because it is considered a probationary period during which you are evaluated for future promise. How much do people earn who have been in this field for five years? For ten years? are good questions to ask.

Check the Reality of an Occupation Before You Decide for or Against It   You may get caught in stereotypes about the earning potential in a given field. A lot of people today avoid social services because they have heard "you can't live on that income." Well, perhaps the pay is low, but there are still social workers, and somehow they survive. There are also some social workers who do better, either by working in high-paying clinics and administrative positions, or by supplementing their paychecks with part-time private practice. If you're interested in that field, talk to social-service people; ask them how they manage financially and what they earn, versus your stereotype. Another common misperception is that architects make huge amounts of money. The 1987–88 *American Almanac of Jobs and Salaries* reports that the annual salaries of experienced architectural designers range between $18,000 and $35,000 per year,[1] less than some might imagine. Once again, check with a sample of these people to see if their earnings fit what you imagine them to be. When talking with practitioners, be sure to sample as broadly as you can. Don't limit yourself to one or two individuals, because their situations may be unrepresentative.

Consider Both Earning Potential and Degree of Risk A high starting salary may be less attractive if there is considerable risk that the job won't last. No job is permanent. Risk can be present in three areas: (a) The financial health of the organization you work for. If profit-making, is it doing well compared to the competition? Is there a history of laying off people? (b) The outlook for the industry. Is this organization in a field that has a good future? Check references such as the 1987–88 *American Almanac of Jobs and Salaries* for "Job Outlook" to see what is predicted for the industry of which that organization is a part. (c) You versus the competition. Are many people competing for your job? How much will you have to worry about your performance level in order to keep your job?

A degree of risk may appeal to you. In any case, risk is part of the equation in any consideration of initial earnings.

Look for Potential Secondary Sources of Income Before accepting the job that pays the most, consider whether your job options can produce other sources of income for you, either now or in the future. The knowledge or expertise that you acquire on the job may allow you to earn a part-time income on the side. For example, working as a government lobbyist may allow you to become a consultant. Or, working as a career counselor in a college may enable you to offer your services for résumé preparation on a private basis. A speech teacher for a public school may offer seminars for business executives who desire public speaking skills. Such secondary income can potentially outweigh the original salary, so consider this possibility carefully when choosing a job.

▶ A Formula for Evaluating ◀ a Job Offer

Here is a set of factors that can help you evaluate any job offer you may receive.

Value of a Job Offer = Starting Salary
+ Long-run earning potential
+ Possible secondary gains
+ New learning acquired
+ Quality of coworkers
+ Challenge of the job
+ Life-style considerations

Thus starting salary is just one of many factors that can determine which of your job possibilities is best for you. Each individual will evaluate the above factors differently, but it is important that none of them be overlooked.

On the Trail of Discretionary Income

Of course, money can be measured in different ways, but you still want to have some left in your pocket to spend after living necessities are taken care of. Economists call this "discretionary income." You want a decent starting salary, so that you can have some status and be able to negotiate your next job without having to bargain for a tremendous increase in pay.

Here's a way to deal with the importance of starting pay without letting it dominate your decision or dwarf all of the other factors that make a job offer good or bad. Develop two figures that you'll carry in your head whenever you negotiate salary for a job:

• Minimum = The rock-bottom dollars-per-year earnings that I need to feel good about myself, and to have enough discretionary income to satisfy my minimum needs. I won't accept a job that pays less than this.
• Maximum = The most dollars per year that I believe I could possibly be worth in this field (where I am applying) right now. This is the figure that I will ask for.

You will have to determine the minimum from personal considerations. It relates to what your friends are earning, how much money you like having in your pocket, where you perceive yourself on the status scale, and the minimum you believe you're worth.

The maximum will appear from the research you do about the field of work where you are applying. What do the best job applicants (with your level of education and experience) earn in this field, in the geographical area where you intend to locate?

Let your negotiations float between these two levels in each new job that you consider. There is plenty of room here for other factors (new learning, coworkers, etc.) to affect your decision. You'll probably try to get the maximum, but if other factors make an offer worthwhile, you won't feel bad about taking less. The minimum is always there to remind you how low (and no lower) you may go, in order to reach an agreement.

Skills

I believe there is no one principle which predominates in human nature so much in every stage of life, from cradle to the grave, in males and females, old and young, black and white, rich and poor, high and low, as this passion for superiority. Every human being compares itself in its own imagination with every other round about it, and will find some superiority over every other, real or imaginary, or it will die of grief and vexation.

—John Adams, 1777

Dear Howard:

I will surely never amount to anything. Lots of things I do are okay, but I never really get good enough at anything so that anyone sits up and takes notice. My dog runs faster than I do, my brother gets more girls, and every new idea I get has been thought of by someone else first. It would be nice to charge ahead carrying my banner into the world if I had something outstanding to offer, but mediocrity haunts me everywhere I go. To the talent-rich go the spoils, and the rest of us take what mud is left over.

Signed,
Destiny's Plaything

Dear No Destiny:

Modesty is truly the curse that kills a thousand careers. You would rather be put in prison than claim you're really good at something, so you sit around mooning about the few who seem to have exceptional talents and count yourself as one of the rejects on the slag heap.

Your modesty is the back door of your existence. It is the hedge against anyone who might come along and say you're really not as good as you said you were. You figure that if you don't claim to be great shakes in the first place, you can always slip out the back door you've conveniently left open for yourself.

Enough of this self-deprecation, protecting yourself against myth-ical judges who might appear from nowhere to compare you unfavorably with others. Behave as if you are permitted to use your better talents, regardless of how they compare with the next guy's. You really are better with your hands than most. And you can supervise people easily and calmly. And you take criticism well and have a lot of endurance. You're not so good with numbers, but you know enough to consult people who are. Go on, admit it. You've done certain things well before, and you'll do them again.

Modesty is all right in deference to the skills of your friends and respect for their right to have abilities too. However, modesty has no place when it disqualifies you from respecting yourself. Don't expect anyone else to notice your talents as well as you do.

Signed,
Howard

There is no putdown quite so devastating as the self-putdown. It sticks, because you make it stick. We prize modesty; the individual who is enraptured with his or her own accomplishments can be a pain. Yet strongly needing to present yourself as modest usually undermines your ability to acknowledge your own accomplishments. You become so worried that others may think you egocentric or pompous that you build a hedge factor into every victory or achievement so no one will accuse you of boasting. You use hedges. "I had a lot of help from my friends." "I couldn't have done it without old so-and-so." "It wasn't much; I certainly should have done better." "I was playing over my head, out of my tree."

You protect yourself from future criticism, but short-circuit your ability to derive praise from your achievements. Praise is the precious fuel that propels you to surpass yourself. You need not depend on the compliments of others or judge yourself by their opinions of you, but you must maintain (or regain) the capacity to congratulate yourself on a job well done. Remember—*there is no praise like self-praise.*

Recognition of your skills* is nourished by your own self-statements, your own ability to recognize your accomplishments and interpret them in terms of abilities that can be added to your personal tool kit:

- Once I acquire a skill, I will always have it to call upon.
- I will stockpile my skills for future use.
- I can detect one or more skills in everything I do.
- I won't be concerned about how long a task takes me.
- I will judge a skill by my own standards or satisfaction.

*Throughout the book, I use the word *skills* to denote those competencies that are important to successful completion of a career search. In this chapter, *skills* refers to all competencies that can be used by people in the widest possible variety of work settings and tasks. Thus, identifying one's marketable skills is a skill of the career search. I trust you will understand this double use of a most valuable word.

▶ Skills Inventory ◀

What is a skill? I have in mind any of the widest possible variety of attributes that represent your strengths, your key abilities, the characteristics that give you your greatest potency, the ways in which you tend to be most successful when dealing with problems, tasks, and other life experiences. There can be little doubt that you do some things better than other things. You are more comfortable in certain situations than in others. You consistently prefer particular tasks over all others. Your strengths reveal much of what makes you unique, a person who is different from any other individual alive.

Here is a sample list of skills found in a cross section of careers:

administering programs	evaluating programs
advising people	exhibiting plans
analyzing data	expressing feelings
appraising services	finding information
arranging social functions	handling complaints
assembling apparatus	handling detail work
auditing financial records	imagining new solutions
budgeting expenses	initiating with strangers
calculating numerical data	inspecting physical objects
checking for accuracy	interpreting languages
classifying records	interviewing people
coaching individuals	inventing new ideas
collecting money	investigating problems
compiling statistics	listening to others
confronting other people	locating missing information
constructing buildings	managing an organization
coordinating events	measuring boundaries
corresponding with others	mediating between people
counseling people	meeting the public
creating new ideas	monitoring progress of others
deciding uses of money	motivating others
delegating responsibility	negotiating contracts
designing data systems	operating equipment
dispensing information	organizing people and tasks
displaying artistic ideas	persuading others
distributing products	planning agendas
dramatizing ideas or problems	planning organizational needs
editing publications	politicking with others
enduring long hours	predicting futures
entertaining people	preparing materials
estimating physical space	printing by hand

processing human interactions
programming computers
promoting events
protecting property
questioning others
raising funds
reading volumes of material
recording scientific data
recruiting people for hire
rehabilitating people
remembering information
repairing mechanical devices
repeating same procedure
researching in library
reviewing programs

running meetings
selling products
serving individuals
setting up demonstrations
sketching charts or diagrams
speaking in public
supervising others
teaching classes
tolerating interruptions
updating files
visualizing new formats
working with precision
writing clear reports
writing for publication

► What Good Are Skills? ◄

Why should you examine your skills? Aren't people who have been around for a while aware of their strengths and weaknesses? If a person cannot assess himself accurately by now, isn't it a little late to wake him up? A resounding no in answer to these questions. The plain, unvarnished truth is that almost all of us are blithely unaware of many of our key personal strengths. The Johari Window[1] (Chart 2) proposes four areas of self-knowledge; only one area is available to both self and others.

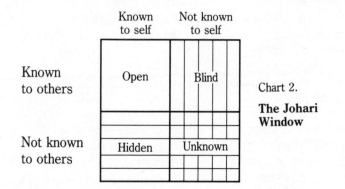

Chart 2.

The Johari Window

I propose that a similar statement can be made about skills and, further, that the largest proportion of this Johari Window for skills is the "unknown" area, where skills exist, but are known neither to the person who possesses them nor to others acquainted with him or her. Why is this so?

We Have No Vocabulary for Skills   Most people have a severely limited set of words to use when they try to describe their strengths. Thus, vocabulary must be created in order to make the task of skill naming easier. The skills inventory in this chapter serves this purpose. It is not an exhaustive list, but simply suggests a sufficient number of skills labels to allow people to talk about their strengths with the beginnings of a common language.

Skills Are Trivialized   Have you ever done something well, but then immediately thought to yourself: "What good would that possibly do me? That talent is useless, surely not relevant to anything in a career." Everything is practical in some special context. You should learn not to trivialize your assets, but to imagine contexts in which they might be useful. If you are a whiz at sorting mail quickly, determining its contents, and filing it appropriately, imagine someplace (other than the post office) where that skill would be useful (purchasing office of an organization? complaint department of a store? assistant to Dear Abby?).

> EXAMPLE ► Ever since I can remember, I have liked writing slaphappy, funny letters to my friends and relatives. They seem to pour out of me naturally, the more ridiculous the better. Well, it turns out that I have adapted this skill to my work as a claims representative at the insurance company, where I maintain the "personal touch" with those who file claims by writing to them in my own fashion, which they get a kick out of.

Skills Develop Late in Life   In contrast to the few highly noticeable skills that emerge early in life (musical talent, artistic talent, or mathematical facility, for instance), most skills come along much more slowly and are infinitely more difficult to recognize when they appear. Many of them relate to ways of interacting with other people (a talent for organizing other people into smoothly functioning units, a talent for persuading others to do things for you, a talent for explaining difficult concepts to others in clear, everyday language). Such talents do not ordinarily merit the status of "genius" and do not prompt standing ovations when displayed to the population at large. Nonetheless, they are strengths worth applauding because they move people and even mountains at times. Such skills may not become apparent until the age of thirty, thirty-five, or even forty-five, but they can be seen as they grow gradually into potency.

We Put Ourselves Down   It is probably only a minor exaggeration to say that we live in a putdown culture, a social structure in which claiming that you possess an extraordinary talent (especially one people have difficulty labeling) is an open invitation to ridicule. It is far easier to say "Oh, I'm not really that exceptional" or "What good could that talent possibly be?" than to value a skill and talk about it easily, even among friends.

However, the quieter you keep about your strengths, the more easily they tend to fade into the woodwork and become invisible even to yourself.

► Put Your Worst Foot ◄ Forward

I believe everyone feels that some skills are more reputable or desirable than others. If this is true, then many of us probably suppress our talents because we suppose that others would think less of us, or even laugh at us, if they knew we possessed these attributes. The happy message of skill identification is that any skill is worth crowing about, and the so-called status of a particular skill has little meaning when it comes to getting a job done well. For a moment, take a sneaky sideways glance at one or more of your own attributes that you believe are prominent, but somehow a little less than desirable in the eyes of others. Do any of these skills belong to you?

- *Compulsive.* I do everything in the same order, according to schedule.
- *Confronting.* I cannot help being very direct with people, saying exactly what I feel regardless of the consequences.
- *Talkative.* I have an overwhelming desire to talk, even though I know others would like me to shut up for a while.
- *Nosy.* I cannot restrain myself from nosing into everyone's affairs.
- *Persnickety about detail.* I leave no stone unturned, cannot rest unless the last crumb is picked up, the last note jotted, the last word said.
- *Antisocial.* I prefer to do most of my work on projects that let me be by myself for long periods of time.
- *Loud.* I can usually be heard by most of the people around me when I am talking and have a habit of speaking louder than normal conversational level, whether to an individual or in a group.
- *Dull, methodical.* My work has always been described as unexciting, proceeding at an even pace, so steady as to have no highs and lows at all; I purposely maintain an even pace so I will not have to deal with uncertainties.
- *Offbeat.* I prefer to do things the wrong way, or at least the crazy cockeyed way, so I don't fall prey to dullness, so I can build some adventure into what I do. No one knows what to expect of me and it bothers them, but I don't care.
- *Slow.* I am slow as molasses in January in every task I undertake, but that is all right with me. I enjoy consuming a lot of time so I never need to feel pressured by a deadline.

Is there any doubt that every one of these personal styles has been denigrated, ridiculed, or sneered at by many of your friends? If you are a closet practitioner of one or more of these traits (or skills), remember that you will benefit far more by acknowledging your particular traits, valuing them, and searching for contexts in which they are marketable than you will by trying to alter these traits simply to evaluate yourself on a mythical status scale.

Here are some examples of how "low-status" skills can be used successfully in job contexts:

- The *compulsive* person keeps perfect and orderly records of all calls, correspondence, visitors, and intrusions (birds flying in the window, etc.) in his department.
- The *confronting* one has an excellent record in approaching bank customers who have borrowed money and failed to make payments on their loans.
- The *talkative* individual is the best person we have in greeting new people in the community, making them feel wanted, engaging them in conversation when they feel shy.
- The *nosy* person hangs around enough bars, courthouses, barbershops, and shopping malls to hear about things before they even happen; that's why we couldn't be without her as a news reporter.
- Mr. *Persnickety* shines all the pots himself before leaving at night, makes sure no chair is out of place, and sees that all supplies are replenished; we need him as kitchen manager, even though he drives the staff buggy at times.
- Ms. *Antisocial* works over there in the corner, reading stacks of old manuscripts; someone has to do it, and I'm glad she prefers this to buzzing around the library making idle conversation.
- *Loudmouth* can be counted on to liven up a new group of people who are having difficulty talking to each other. That is why we use him as a greeter for tours of visiting firemen; whenever he wants to announce a departure or a change in plans, he has little difficulty getting the group under control.
- The *dull, methodical* one takes care of the tremendous flow of paperwork in this department by subjecting it to careful and systematic attention; we know that no important document will be missed, nor will any schedule be ignored.
- The *offbeat* person provides the unusual whenever we need it to promote a new idea to our membership; she is creative and knows how to catch people's attention, even if the other staff members think she's a little nutty.
- The *slowpoke* takes care of difficult mechanical tasks that carry

risks of overload or mechanical error; he's patient enough to work a task to death just so it will be done correctly.

▶ Transferable Skills ◀

Sidney Fine[2] has identified what is probably the single most important concept in viewing how personal skills are usable in career development. Skills that have potency in career contexts are not limited to being useful within a single kind of work, occupation, or vocational setting. On the contrary, most skills valued in work have the virtue of cutting a wide swath across many occupational boundaries. For example, the ability to write effectively and in clear language is valued highly in private industry, government agencies, educational institutions, and nonprofit organizations alike. In fact, most of the skills that are important in any responsible job have a similar virtue: they can be applied in a wide variety of work contexts to a wide variety of tasks. They are *transferable*.

Fine distinguishes among three broad categories of skills: functional, adaptive, and specific. The first two categories—functional and adaptive—contain all the transferable skills. Adaptive skills can be distinguished from functional skills because they usually refer to personality traits, characteristic ways of behaving. Adaptive skills tend to develop earlier than functional skills, yet they may not be valued or even noticed until the individual has done many years of career exploration. Adaptive skills, like functional skills, are eminently transferable.

Adaptive skills refer to those competencies that enable an individual to accept and adjust to the physical, interpersonal and organizational arrangements and conditions in which a job exists. Included are punctuality, grooming, acceptance of supervision, care of property, getting along with others, and impulse control. . . .

Functional skills refer to those competencies that enable an individual to relate to Things, Data, and People (orientation) in some combination according to their personal preferences and to some degree of complexity appropriate to their abilities (levels). . . .

Specific content skills refer to those competencies that enable an individual to perform a specific job according to the specifications of an employer and according to the standards required to satisfy the market.[3]

Adaptive and functional skills are frequently coded in specific content language. That is, the word you use to denote a skill that seems highly specific to your job obscures the fact that the skill is eminently transferable. If you are an accountant, for instance, and regard yourself as good at being an accountant (content-specific), you may fail to recognize that you are effective working with numerical data, handling detail, or adapting to peaks of the seasonal work load.

In addition, the work attributed to a specific job title can be accomplished well by two different people who possess different functional and adaptive skills. An effective administrator, for example, might possess these skills in abundance: handling financial data well, diplomacy with other staff members, flexibility in decision-making routine. A different person, also effective in the same position, might possess these skills: planning for new programs effectively, supervising other people's work effectively, training new employees well. Admittedly, a good administrator would possess some minimum level of all these skills; however, two different people might emphasize some of the skills much more than the others. Thus, as you evaluate your work, you must ask yourself "What did I *do?*" rather than "What was my title?"

Let's take a look at how skills are transferable. Say you aspire to be a bank officer. You list the skills you believe are most crucial to effectiveness in the role of bank officer:

Being careful with money   Working patiently
Analyzing numerical data   Making financial decisions
Dealing with the public   Reading detailed reports
Anticipating community needs   Supervising others

Of course, the above list might be different if you knew a bit more about what bank officers do. However, for the purpose of this example, ask yourself: If I were to take away the title of bank officer from this list, would the skills listed indicate clearly that it is a bank officer we are describing? The answer is a clear no. The skills noted are either functional or adaptive, and they are clearly transferable. They might be applied to any of numerous other occupations.

When a person asks you (or you ask yourself), "What can I do in my life that will improve my chances of advancing in the world of work?" don't concentrate entirely on the specific content skills available from formal programs of educational credentials. Talk about the transferable skills that can be acquired anywhere:

- *Communication skills.* Writing reports, essays, and correspondence in plain language; speaking effectively to individuals and to groups; listening carefully and empathically whenever necessary; portraying ideas clearly and imaginatively.
- *Thinking skills.* Defining a problem cogently; evaluating alter-

native courses of action critically; creating divergent solutions to a problem when more than one answer is possible; shaping new ideas in the context of old circumstances.

- *Human relations skills.* Interacting cooperatively with superiors, subordinates, and peers; communicating orders, instructions, and feelings with openness, genuineness, and understanding; delegating tasks in ways that show respect for the other person and receptivity to his or her ideas.
- *Valuing skills.* Being able to view and assess an area of work activity in terms of the effects it will have upon human welfare; making and enforcing decisions in terms that will maximize such welfare.
- *Research skills.* Discovering and identifying people who have information that is relevant to a task or a problem; identifying resource materials necessary to the solution of that problem.
- *Interviewing skills.* Acquiring information from people when they are reluctant to divulge it or when information is difficult to reach; generating trust in such situations, necessary for future contacts.
- *Planning skills.* Being able to sense an idea whose time has come, to move toward work modes that capitalize on this idea, and to sell the idea to appropriate people.

► You Can Acquire New Skills ◄

Even though we have focused skill identification on what you have done before, new experiences will occur that will add to your stockpile of skills. Furthermore, you can be deliberate about choosing future activities that will nurture *new* skills. It is a deadly mistake to assume that your skills are fixed, that you are unable to acquire new talents. Most skills people bring to the work marketplace are ones they have nurtured and practiced in their informal, nonpaid lifetime of experience. Many of the most powerful skills are developed by accident, in the name of just plain fun, for purposes other than their current use or perhaps even for opposite purposes (as when former criminals bring marketable skills to their work as law enforcers).

Here are a few hypothetical and whimsical examples of people whose job-related skills were cultivated in contexts far removed from the marketplace:

EXAMPLE ► Organized Orville is chief steward at the Roney Plaza Hotel, which serves a thousand people nightly. He stocks the entire place every week by keeping track of drinks served, glasses washed, dollars spent, table napkins needed, etc. Orville's talent for detail is compulsive. He used to inventory his father's toolshed, his mother's cupboard, his uncle's auto parts store, and anything else in sight, just to keep himself amused when he got home from school.

Oratorical Olive is chief spokesperson for the United Fund of Jivetown. She promotes social services everywhere, raises funds with in-person appearances, and speaks to community groups at the drop of a hat. Olive grew up making speeches at the dinner table, imitating the politicians while they droned away on TV. Olive was applauded by the family, encouraged to speak out no matter what people thought. She ran for school offices just to get the chance to make more speeches.

Dignified Dan is maître d' at the Sans Souci Restaurant. His cultivated speech, attention to formality, and sensitivity to the subtle needs of his guests make Dan a natural for this position. Where did he acquire this skill? Dan's years on the stage in comedies of manners were not wasted, nor were his trips to Buckingham Palace with an uncle of royal lineage.

Persuasive Paula is a lobbyist in state government. She twists tails of tigers, bends ears of elephants, and tweaks legislators' noses when necessary to get their attention. Paula learned on her block as a six-year-old that bargaining is done best by tone of voice, persistence, and attention to the individual ego. She learned long ago that peanut butter and jelly can be traded for roast beef if the proper words are applied to the bargain.

► Six Cardinal Rules of ◄ Skills Identification

As you become accustomed to identifying your skills in your daily routine, keep in mind these six rules.

Compare Only with Yourself   Avoid at all costs having to compare your level of talent with others'. Your only consideration is that your skill rates highly within your own private system. Which activities do you perform better than other things? The only relevant comparison is internal.

Be Sure the Skill Is Fun   A skill is really not worth calling attention to if you hate doing it. Only those activities you both enjoy and do well matter for future reference to your work. Count only those skills that wear comfortably on you when you are using them, ones you smile about when you anticipate doing them.

Look for Evidence   Make sure you are talking about actual life experiences, not just something you wish had happened. The only credible validation of a skill lies in a real experience; something you did cannot be taken away from you. If you have evidence of a skill, you cannot be argued into denying it by superficial criteria such as test scores, interest inventories, or other externally generated data.

The Function, Not the Title   Make sure you are talking about what you actually did, rather than any title you may have carried. Titles and labels of positions often do not reveal functions especially well. Camp counselors do not always do a lot of "counseling," for example.

Label It Yourself   Even though you will get some help with the vocabulary of skills by referring to the skills inventory on preceding pages, you should ultimately call the skill by its rightful name. Your own descriptors are more accurate than any label I have suggested. Since you are in the best position to describe the function as it really was performed, don't hesitate to use the words you feel best reflect exactly what you did.

Focus on Irrelevant Experiences   This rule may startle you a bit; however, I suspect you will instinctively look for those life experiences that seem somehow more important to you and will ignore those that seem irrelevant. Hardly any life experience can be called irrelevant. I insist that some of your most special and powerful skills can be found in the life experiences you would dismiss out-of-hand.

▶ Five Ways of ◀
Identifying Skills

There are several different ways you can tap into your particular skills. You should try using all of them at one time or another, because each method may elicit strengths that had eluded you before. Moreover, you can use one method as a check against another, to discover whether the same skills are being identified by different approaches.

From Personal Achievements   This method is detailed in the exercise at the end of this chapter. It asks you to describe an experience that made you feel good about what you did and satisfied with your behavior by your own standards, not anyone else's. Is it difficult for you to imagine you have done anything well? Then try something really tiny, a skill you bet is no good to anyone.

> EXAMPLE ▶ I wrote a short verse for my daughter on her sixteenth birthday, making fun of her talents, yet extolling them, to the tune of "Wizard of Oz." (This skill with words and music and sensitivity to an individual's traits bodes well for your ability to express yourself creatively.) •

A Happy Role You've Occupied   If you still have difficulty thinking of things you did that were successful, try remembering any position or role you held that made you feel reasonably satisfied with yourself. Boy

Scout leader, organizer of the kitchen on camping trips, keeper of the keys, leader of the drinking games at parties, editor of the social section of your school paper, the one who restores order when things get out of hand—any role has its attendant skills that enable you to perform the role successfully.

> EXAMPLE ► I was always the one who kept the group calm when something went wrong, by telling stories, creating a little foolishness, and generally getting people's minds off the trial of the moment. (Interpersonal skill, timing as a skill, perception of tension, and so forth.)

A Peak Experience You cannot think of anything you would call a peak experience? You say just getting out of bed each morning is the peak for you, and everything else is anticlimax? A peak experience need not refer to a high-level accomplishment. When was the last time you laughed really hard? Which single moment of the past week would you most like to repeat? Whom did you meet recently who sticks in your memory?

> EXAMPLE ► I heard this fellow talking at the grocery store about his life at home in Maine. I'll never forget his regional accent and way of expressing himself. I guess I just have an ear for speech, a fascination with it, and some talent for imitating it.

Skills Inventory Use a skills inventory (pages 57–58) to help you recall experiences from your memory bank. As you spot a skill you have used before, you should be able to remember when you used it. Run through the inventory, checking off skills as you go, and let your memory make the connections.

Ask Your Friends Your family, friends, and acquaintances see attributes in you that you may overlook yourself. They may even be more likely to notice the skills that are shady but nonetheless marketable. Others will probably tune in to many of your adaptive as well as functional skills, because they are receivers of your personal traits every day.

> EXAMPLE ► You are really good at getting out of doing things. You have a talent for making other people smile. You are a champ at nagging people to get things done.

► The Curse of the Single ◄
Outstanding Talent

People born with a great talent, and many of those who depend on a single prominent skill, often get themselves into deep trouble. They depend heavily on the single great ability to surmount any crisis and gain approval from others, and in general they expect the talent to compensate for any other shortcomings they possess. In fact, highly talented people are so hugely rewarded for their abilities that it becomes all too easy to rely on the talent and neglect everything else.

The biggest basket cases in career planning are professional athletes whose talents have dwindled with the years, college professors who have been denied tenure, beautiful women whose physical charms have faded, artists who haven't found an immediate market, and others who have depended on a single talent for many years. Their problem can be stated simply: It is not necessary for them to build other skills as long as the one big talent is working for them, drawing acclaim and winning temporary rewards, so by the time the one big talent fades, a vocational rigor mortis, known as learned helplessness, has set in. The talented one has been fussed over, catered to, and provided for. The whole idea of struggling along like us working stiffs has been anathema. Bill Bradley writes in *Life on the Run* that the end of an athlete's playing career is a death in every sense but the physical. We no-talent folk look for a skill to perfect that will answer all our prayers, solve all our career worries, and be always in demand. If you get too good too quickly with a particular skill, beware of the same perversity that afflicts the one-talent person who suffers decline after a brief period in the sun.

- A supersalesman who ignores management skills suffers when the time comes to direct the efforts of others.
- A whiz accountant who handles the numbers like a Ouija board finds his numerical skill small comfort when he learns that interpersonal skill is necessary to deal warmly and effectively with clients.
- A dean of students who can establish friendships on a personal basis with everyone enrolled finds to his dismay that planning skills have eluded him because he was too busy prowling the dormitories and making friends.

To become very effective with a single skill is to become drunk with power. For a time, this skill seems to work in every circumstance, people reward you for it, and there seems little need to waste time with other matters. Read on, however.

► The Hidden Charms of ◄ Multipotentiality

Artur Rubinstein was known as the King of the Wrong-Note Pianists. There are probably scores more technically competent than he, but he brings an extra dimension to the stage, a sensitivity of interpretation and a personality that sparkles and breathes life into his music. People prefer him to the pianistically perfect drone who lacks the twinkle and personal magnetism. Rubinstein can also talk with the best of them, charm folks away from the keyboard, swing at parties; people appreciate this dimension of his talent too.

It would be extremely difficult to find a career that depends entirely upon a single talent. One might think of artists first, but Rubinstein and others dispel this notion. The blessing of calling upon a cluster of abilities instead of just one is that almost every career imaginable demands a cluster of different skills. Being a social worker, for example, involves helping others personally, researching sources of community information, writing reports to public agencies, and recruiting unpaid volunteers. A carpenter must be able to handle materials, measure with precision, and visualize space requirements. A store manager has to relate effectively to customers, organize the ordering of merchandise, and create effective visual displays. A secretary prepares written materials neatly, deals with the public, and develops a careful filing system.

The curse of multiple demands is also its blessing because you are never required to be flawless in a single category of skill. It is the cluster that counts, not the single outstanding strength.

EXAMPLE ► John was a young man whose transferable skills included the ability to supervise other people, the ability to mix social life with promoting ideas easily, the ability to manage money, and a good sense of what kinds of leisure activities people enjoy. He had studied biology in college and had cultivated an interest in scuba diving. It occurred to him that the scuba background should not go to waste and that he might train a group of people to provide weekend lessons to vacationers. "Rather than get a real job, I decided to fool around in the sun for a while and see if anyone would pay me and my friends to teach them scuba." So he flew to the Bahama Islands without delay, rented quarters, and started the first of weekend excursions for scuba devotees. John's Underwater Explorer Society is prospering today.

The contest between multiple talents and a single outstanding talent is a modern-day version of the tortoise-versus-hare contest. The single-talent person gets off to a blazing start, then is outdone by the industrious but nonflamboyant person who parlays many marketable skills into a winning combination. You need not regret your lack of a single prominent skill; your future success hinges upon your unique cluster of modest abilities that, when combined, are highly marketable.

► Skills-Identification ◄
Exercise

Remember that a skill can refer to any particular way you have of doing things. If you like working by yourself for long periods of time, if you're a hard-core compulsive who gets a thrill from absorbing detail, if you operate by conning people rather than overpowering them with logic, if you like to read a lot, if you do things the wrong way but they turn out right—all these activities are legitimately called skills here. Stick to your ways as long as they work for you, and don't worry about skills other people seem to have.

Do this exercise with a partner, a person you see on a regular basis and with whom you feel comfortable talking about yourself.

1. Identify an experience. Recall a particular experience you had within the past two weeks, one from which you felt some source of satisfaction.

   EXAMPLE ► I cleaned out and organized the materials closet in my office.

2. Describe in detail. Tell in the simplest possible terms what you did from beginning to end of this experience. Try not to skip steps, ignore the obvious, or summarize detail that deserves a closer look.

   EXAMPLE ► I pulled everything out to the open floor, threw away 30 percent of it we no longer needed, rearranged each thing according to the time of year it is used, created labels easy to see, made room to walk in and out easily, and left two or three open shelves for future acquisitions.

3. Use checklists. Refer to the skills inventory (pages 57–58) as a starter method for identifying some possible skills that were involved in what you did. Don't be wedded to these labels; simply use them to jog your memory about abilities you had to employ in this activity and as a stimulus for further information.

   EXAMPLE ► Possible skills labels include organizing data, displaying, handling detail, or even physical activity.

4. Look under the surface. Your first description of skills will probably be somewhat superficial. You will probably use a label that is convenient for talking about the skill, but hides some of the meaning in what you did. Many of the labels in the skills inventory (pages 57–58) will be too superficial for your purposes. Looking under the surface label requires using your own words to describe what you did.

EXAMPLE ▶ I looked through every item in the closet to assess whether we have used this very much in the past year (evaluating), then put it in a different place so it would be located with other items used in the same way (classifying).

5. Generalize to a broader skill. Just as a surface skill label can be examined more closely to discover a more detailed talent, so can a detailed skill label be scrutinized so it reveals a talent that is broader in its implications. The words you use to characterize a skill may distort its larger importance or realm of application.

EXAMPLE ▶ My ability to winnow out the materials that are not helping us from those that have utility is really a talent for patient reexamination of a total operation, an ability to view all our necessary activities simultaneously and then anticipate what our future requirements will be. This ability is really one of planning or organizing for future action and being able to conceive of a long time span without needing a narrative of the past year's activity on paper. Abstraction of present and future needs seems directly involved in what I did.

6. Check for meaning. Lest you get carried away with generalizing your skill to too wide a perspective, use your trusted companion to help you assess the most accurate label for the skill(s) you have identified. Compare your own words describing the skill with your friend's, and do your best to reach agreement about how best to characterize this skill before you move on to another one. You are the final judge of how to label the skill, but be willing to rely on the independent view of your friend.

EXAMPLE ▶ I guess we agree that the skill can be best described as reviewing large amounts of material quickly, being able to assess the utility of the materials in light of organizational objectives, and translating these needs into an effective display for future use.

4

Creativity

Dear Howard:

Now I know where that term *pigeonhole* came from. Every job I look at has one requirement after another, so you can't figure out where there's room for yourself. Nothing but pigeon droppings left over from the guy who was there before. Every job might as well be a cave or other dark hole in which rodents secrete themselves, because I sure can't find any light for myself. Is there any elbow room in a new career? Is there a place for the real me?

Signed,
All Boxed In

Dear Foxhole:

There was the man who asked, looking up at a ten-ton behemoth facing him in the jungle: "How do you eat an elephant?" Came the reply from the wise old witch doctor: "One bite at a time." You may feel a new job or career is as big as an elephant and twice as formidable, but it can be digested one bite at a time. The creative process begins when you recognize that you are different from the person who did the job before you. Within the limits of organizational needs, the person makes the job; the job doesn't make the person.

Creativity is the accountant who recognizes that a filing system has been frustrating the office staff and does something to reformulate it. Creativity is the social worker who figures out that home visits might better take place outside the home, if the outside location keeps the family members from wrangling as they habitually do on their own territory. Creativity is the bus driver who notices

72

a change of traffic pattern in his daily circuit and recommends a new route to his supervisor.

Creativity is also realizing you have a talent that's not been used lately and figuring out a way this talent can help you do your job better. People are bigger than job descriptions. Creativity is remembering that you have more abilities than can possibly be used in a single job and slipping in a new role when the job description isn't looking.

Creativity is also piecing together your various talents and traits into a new and previously unimagined whole. I know a woman who has theater background, an interest in antiques, and is very handy with figures. She dreamed up the idea that such a diverse collection of skills and inclinations could be combined in developing financial data (figures) for an antiques business and using dramatic presentations to attract customers to the shop. Most other antiques dealers sit on their haunches, but Sadie brings her "dead" things to life and sells them between gigs.

Signed,
Howard

All your carefully collected values and skills are destined to be lost, scattered like the pieces in a jigsaw puzzle, if you cannot put them together in creative and imaginative ways. Isolated attributes make little sense if they float in space by themselves, not hinged to any coherent whole. The ability to be creative with yourself allows you to infuse any job with a style of your own, allows you to take a seemingly senseless, unrelated collection of traits and attributes (your own values and skills) and weave them into a coherent pattern.

▶ What Is Creativity? ◀

Ellen wanted all her life to be involved with cycling in some way, but recreation jobs seemed few and far between. So she poked around looking for work in state or local government, hoping someone might sponsor bike trail legislation that would trigger some new employment. She canvassed every bicycle club, volunteered her time to map possible new trails, and started a part-time repair shop on her own. One day a state legislator brought his children's bikes for fixing; Ellen rattled on about her plans for the future, and the legislator told her she should bring her ideas to the Community Service Department. Ellen discovered that, lo and behold, this department wanted a combined researcher/promoter for bicycle resources and two weeks later found herself writing grant proposals to the federal government to acquire funds for her favorite community service.

Brian was a college minister who, weary of the campus routine, decided to pick up and leave on a long trip. He toured forty-two states, exploring every new life-style he could discover. His travels led him to the Personal Growth Center in Arizona, where he took a job as a dishwasher. He used his mechanical skills to fix the dishwashing equipment when necessary and his ministerial skills to develop relationships with the people in permanent or temporary residence at the growth center. This center had not thought of assigning itself a ministerial role, but Brian created it, relating to life crises as they occurred, providing gentle counsel to all members of the group—and supervising the dishwashing after every meal.

Creativity is really several different animals called by the same name. It is, first of all, combining diverse elements. Your ability to be creative in your work can perhaps best be demonstrated in your efforts to pull together values, skills, and traits that seen unrelated. What do you do with mechanical ability, a love of the outdoors, a desire to work with numbers, and a passion for furniture? Perhaps you investigate forests for future timber crops, count the trees, set up an inventory system for manufacture of furniture.

Creativity also means changing horses in midstream. The metaphor is a caution against giving up one work style for another, but when you think about the process—getting off one horse and mounting another in the middle of the water—it sounds like a lot of fun. Creativity is a way of periodically wiping the slate clean and asking: What if this job had never been done before? Whoever invented the ball-point pen had watched too many fountain pens spill too many times on too many pairs of pants. Imaginative people never want to do the same job the same way twice and are willing to risk falling off a horse or two in the process of figuring out a better way to negotiate the stream.

Creativity also involves taking new skills off the old shelf. Since the person is always larger than the job, we can assume you are forgoing the use of certain skills because the job does not seem to call for them. But wherever there is a job that might be done better, there is an opportunity for a new skill to be introduced. Which of your favorite little talents have you not used for a while but would like to send into the game? Writing is fun for you? You like to build things? You really get a kick out of interviewing people? Assume that you have the power to rewrite your job description at least a little, because you do.

We have become accustomed to thinking that creativity refers exclusively to the fine or performing arts. In the context of the work search, however, I call *creativity* all forms of thought that focus on the production of ideas rather than on the solution of problems. In its fullest sense, creativity here means *divergent* rather than *convergent* thinking. I assume there is always more than one solution to any career problem and expend my energy toward developing new ideas before becoming concerned about the direction the individual will take.

▶ Stimulate Creativity ◀
Through Wrongheaded Thinking

The more we submit career decisions to logical, analytical thought processes, the more such decisions seem to elude us. Hence, our solutions may lie in thinking *illogically*, or at least not deductively, so that we do not expect answers to flow in an orderly way from the gathering of data about the self.

Wrongheaded thinking encourages a plentiful stream of ideas, images, possibilities, and random meanderings. If we can accept that career development is more a creative than a scientific process, we must be most concerned about teaching you to think freely and imaginatively, like an artist, rather than strictly and deductively, like a scientist seeking a natural law.

What I call imaginative or nonscientific thinking will be recognized by scientists as the hypothesis-generating stage of scientific discovery or problem solving. Fresh, original ideas always precede scientific rigor. It is these that are most lacking in career awareness. The individual who cannot decide what to do gropes for the nearest alternative, not yet having learned ways to generate many career hypotheses.

Wrongheaded thinking suspends judgment and thus frees you from conducting a pseudoscientific analysis of your possibilities when your sheaf of ideas is embarrassingly thin. For example: "I have good mechanical ability, therefore I must study architecture or become an automotive designer."

Several key propositions are central to your having the power to roam freely in designing possible career futures. I urge you to accept and practice all these propositions in order to accumulate a rich collection of ideas that you can sort, compare, and validate when the time for making choices can no longer be delayed.

The Rigidity of Words   Recognize initially that the words we assign to career matters—occupational titles, names of skills, and so on—may do more to bind and hinder our thinking than to assist it. Words are symbols that denote classification, and any classification restricts thinking. If we call a person an accountant, does that mean all he or she does is "account"? Of course not. An accountant manages, counsels, analyzes, writes, and performs a hundred other functions. Does your title adequately represent what you do? Do other people who have the same title as you perform the same functions or carry out their responsibilities in the same style as you? I doubt it. You must begin with a healthy measure of caution about what words mean when you are selecting a career direction.

Thinking Visually   Richer and more descriptive insights will occur as you begin to use pictures and symbols instead of words to describe your career hypotheses. Is your career a cyclone? A treasure hunt? A comedy of manners? A Noah's ark? I have often thought of my own career of counseling psychologist as a pinball machine, in which I bounce crazily from one standard activity to another, never being absorbed into a particular place. The pinball describes the process of my career; a kitchen blender characterizes the content of my work, a bubbling mixture of psychology, education, marketing, and applied mathematics. Visual imagery allows you greater use of fantasy and far greater latitude in portraying your own set of objectives and the environment in which you desire yourself to be. If you can picture your career—where you are, what you are doing, by whom you are surrounded, and other odd details—you will have a fuller version of what you hope for yourself than you can attain simply by attaching your wishes to one or two sterile words that carry nothing more than abstract meaning.

Irrelevant Data   If it is true that the obvious things we know about ourselves may be misleading (Should I be a politician because I have a gift for giving speeches?), then perhaps the missing pieces of our career puzzle lie in the darker corners where we would not immediately look. The little irrelevant things we know about ourselves may provide the best clues. If, for example, you are a social worker by training and inclination, but spend your spare moments in political campaigns and reading about new legislation, perhaps you belong in politics more than the person who has oratorical skills. If you devour stock market data when you are supposed to be preparing lesson plans, this may be a clue for your future involvement. Any activity that commands your attention is relevant, no matter how separated it seems from your professional training or visible career history. Stamp collecting or an abiding interest in psychotic murderers—either may be a missing piece in your career puzzle.

Lateral Thinking   DeBono, in *Lateral Thinking*, characterizes vertical thinking as digging in the same hole deeper and lateral thinking as digging the hole in a different place. "Lateral thinking . . . has to do with new ways of looking at things and new ideas of every sort."[1] Lateral thinking raises questions without immediate answers and freely permits the individual to be as *wrong* as he or she wants to be. Lateral thinking allows rich interpretation of one's work. You may insist that a waitress is a waitress by anyone's definition, but a waitress in Studs Terkel's *Working* likens herself to Carmen, who dances fluently and exotically while her audience throws coins. Vertical thinking encourages objectivity, an agreement among observers about what is being observed. (It is nearly impossible to have such objectivity in your perception of your career; hence, lateral thinking is more suited to your interpretation of the work you choose for yourself.)

Reversals   You will increase your creative insights about your career by often doing what is not expected, by perhaps doing the opposite of what seems most obvious to do. Reversal thinking encourages you to turn a situation around or inside out in order to gain a completely new perspective. For example, to reveal what is most salient about your work, take a close look at your play. To discover your areas of strength, examine your most extreme weaknesses. To isolate what you really like best, identify the things you dislike the most. A clever reversal uncovers a new reservoir of data. Reversals can also be used in different ways. Suppose you took an obvious function, such as counseling, and asked: "How might a counselor do the work by being the object of counseling rather than the provider of it?" The answer might be a counselor who devises a new therapeutic process enabling people to counsel each other. Reversals are necessary to counter habitual thinking, at the risk of proffering ideas that may seem ridiculous. Whether a reversal yields right or wrong answers is beside the point; what are needed are new viewpoints and ideas.

The Arrogance of the Dreamer   Perhaps the more outlandish a goal, the more power it has to propel you and help you endure the misgivings and misunderstandings of those around you. A ridiculous goal provides direction for you and establishes incentive; an ordinary goal probably bores you. If you are not daring and arrogant enough to suggest a goal that others will view with skepticism, then your goal is probably not imaginative enough. Unless your goal offends someone, you have probably not succeeded in departing enough from what is already known. Welcome criticism and defense of present standards as signs that you have begun to say something new and that your career hypothesis is worth further investigation.

In *Your Creative Power*, Osborn[2] tells us three characteristics to develop in divergent, or creative, thinking: (1) strive for quantity of ideas, (2) defer your judgment—when being creative, do not be concerned about quality, and (3) make sure your ideas are as wild as possible. You must allow no critical judgment about the value or quality of your ideas to interrupt the creative process. Any and every idea is okay in the brainstorming stage; judgments of quality and worth are postponed until a later time. In the words of Blake, the poet: "The road of excess leads to the palace of wisdom. . . . You never know what is enough unless you know what is more than enough." George Bernard Shaw used to look at the title of a book and then write a full outline for the book before opening it up to read. He didn't want the book to disturb his creative powers for imagining what might happen in the volume.

► Nine Creative Processes ◄

It may help you to know there are ways of thinking creatively—not formulas designed to reduce the creative process to a technocrat's delight, but nine excitingly different ways of shaking up your thinking, looking at an old situation in a new way.

Here is a summary of some of the questions to ask about a situation in order to stimulate ideas:

Put to other uses? New ways to use as is? Other uses if modified?

Adapt? What else is like this? What other ideas does this suggest? Does past offer parallel? What could I copy? Whom could I emulate?

Modify? New twist? Change meaning, color, motion, sound, odor, form, shape? Other changes?

Magnify? What to add? More time? Greater frequency? Stronger? Higher? Longer? Thicker? Extra value? Plus ingredient? Duplicate? Multiply? Exaggerate?

Minify? What to subtract? Smaller? Condensed? Miniature? Lower? Shorter? Lighter? Omit? Streamline? Split up? Understate?

Substitute? Who else instead? What else instead? Other ingredient? Other material? Other process? Other place? Other approach? Other tone of voice? Other power?

Rearrange? Interchange components? Other pattern? Other layout? Other sequence? Transpose cause and effect? Change pace? Change schedule?

Reverse? Transpose positive and negative? How about opposites? Turn it backward? Turn it upside down? Reverse roles? Change shoes? Turn tables? Turn other cheek?

Combine? How about a blend, an alloy, an assortment, an ensemble? Combine units? Combine purposes? Combine appeals? Combine ideas?[3]

Let's take an example and show how each of these creative processes would operate. Let's assume you have a job that doesn't seem creative at all. You're a claims examiner for an insurance firm. Here is an example of how each process could function in your situation.

- *Put to other uses.* Can I arrange the claims files for other purposes? By last name, by type of accident, by geographical location, by year of policy, and so on?
- *Adapt.* How can I adapt my work as a claims examiner to another position within the insurance company? My skills in dealing with the public, corresponding, handling detail, and organizing files are transferable to other contexts.
- *Modify.* How can I take an essential procedure and modify it to work better? I have to file the claims in order of their occurrence,

but will change the system to record also the dates the claims were filed, so that we can correlate type of claim with length of delay in reporting.

- *Magnify.* How can I magnify my passion for working with statistical computation to make it a larger part of the job? I can figure out how many claims were handled for how many dollars in each of the categories, or tabulate the environmental conditions that precipitated each accident, or figure the number of miles between home and accident for the actuaries.
- *Minify.* What detail in my work might be reduced to the smallest possible importance? If I can reduce the exchanges of correspondence until I have thoroughly researched each claim, I will save both myself and the claimant a lot of needless communication.
- *Substitute.* If I wanted to substitute a special skill in my daily routine, how would I do this? I can substitute my conversational ability for the painstaking correspondence I labor through by talking with claimants before writing to them, so they can understand what we are doing without my having to write it in great detail.
- *Rearrange.* Is there some way I can rearrange the sequence of contacts between myself and the claimant so that there are fewer steps each of us has to complete?
- *Reverse.* Is there some aspect of my work that is so boring or distasteful that I would like to reverse it? I have always hated answering the phone, so I will try calling the claim filers before they interrupt me, so I can answer their questions and then get on to my other paperwork.
- *Combine.* Which of my responsibilities can I combine without sacrificing effectiveness? I have papers to process, reports to write, and people to notify. I will design a form that can be used both to notify the claimant and to serve as entry into the monthly report, so that one need not necessarily duplicate the other.

▶ Creativity-Stimulating ◀ Exercises

Here are a few mental devices that will stimulate your creative, lateral, or divergent thought processes and enable you to postpone vertical thinking, or problem solving, until you have generated a large number of possible alternatives.[4]

► Exercise One

1. *Challenge assumptions* Identify a key assumption in your present idea and test whether the assumption can be violated, eliminated, or otherwise altered.

    EXAMPLE ► Must all accountants work with numerical data? Is it possible they might work instead with pictures (of financial records) or computer languages that would eliminate the need for numbers?
    Must all counselors counsel? Is it possible that counseling service can be provided *indirectly* through the management of resources, training others to do direct service, creation of self-help materials?

2. *Fractionate* Break your work idea into parts, examine each part and discover which you like best. Or fractionate a nonwork experience to look for new data.

    EXAMPLE ► What parts of being in a fraternity/sorority did you like when you were in college? The socializing, the philosophical bull sessions, being forced to live together, the group tasks, the identity, the adventures?

3. *Analogy* The analogy or picture or metaphor can help you envision what you are trying to accomplish. Use words to create a picture of your situation.

    EXAMPLE ► I have often thought of an individual's career as "stable as a hog on ice." I also like to picture self-assessment as "sorting out the pieces in a jigsaw puzzle."

4. *Random stimulation* In this variant of creative thinking, one uses an artificial device to prod and jiggle the collective memory bank. DeBono suggests looking up words randomly in the dictionary or wandering around a room or open space to expose oneself to a variety of stimuli without looking for anything in particular.

    EXAMPLE ► I tried the random word approach, came up with *wench* and *lobby*. I related these to career planning by wondering whether there could be special methods for women and musing about the political dimensions of the work-search process.

5. *Force relations* Osborn suggests that you take highly dissimilar concepts and try to force them into some sensible connection or find a common ground between them.

    EXAMPLE ► What do an engineer and a seamstress have in common? (Work with precision.) What do an oil rigger and an antiques dealer have in common? (Patience.)

6. *Deliberate exaggerations*   Take a normal, common work situation and stretch it to an unusual degree. See what ideas occur.

EXAMPLE ► Sell insurance to dogs, cats? (Pet insurance.)
Education as total deprivation? (Wilderness experiences such as Outward Bound.)
A camera as big as all outdoors? (Radar.)

7. *Alphabet system*   Use the alphabet to generate ideas by hooking your problem to each single letter in turn, and see what results.

EXAMPLE ► What kinds of employers might want a person with numerical skill?
Actuary, accountant, bookkeeper, computer programmer, credit manager, and so on.

8. *Attribute listing*   Brainstorm as many attributes as possible about a given occupation (the same procedure can be used to describe a person) in order to generate data relevant to the decisions you might make about this occupation.

EXAMPLE ► Attributes of the work of an insurance salesperson: social, financial, personal, abstract-intangible, future-oriented, risk-related, numerical.

► Exercise Two

Find a relationship between a past experience and a future aspiration by using one of the nine creative processes outlined on pages 77–78.

EXAMPLE ►
1. Rita is a program director for the local YMCA. She would like to get involved in the retailing business.
Creative process: adapt. Rita can adapt her experience in promoting programs and services to the task of learning how to promote merchandise to customers.
2. David has done a newsletter for his Hebrew school synagogue group. He would like to do personnel work with college students.
Creative process: magnify. David can attempt to magnify his writing and data-gathering skills into a research and program development position with a large university student personnel staff.
3. Phil has done numerous bake sales in his neighborhood. He would like to become involved with a community arts program.
Creative process: substitute. Phil can substitute a different artistic skill—such as handicrafts—for that of baking and apply his manual and creative skills to developing new programs of this kind.

5

Decision Making

It doesn't seem fair that you have to choose one right career from among the thousands which are possible. It's like being in an enormous candy store where most of the candy-bar wrappers are blank and you cannot tell what is inside them. Even when you begin looking into career possibilities, it seems as though the more you know about them, the harder it is to make the final choice. You quickly begin to suffer from "information overload."

You can review your values and skills till the cows come home, but how do you add them up, especially when not all skills and values are of equal importance? One career brings the most money, another offers the most independence, another uses your most prominent skills, another capitalizes on your people skills, and a still different career offers you the most free time. And so it goes. Every way you turn, a different career choice seems like the right one. The more you know, the less you know. How's a person to decide? Even when you feel fairly comfortable in comparing the careers you know about, you still worry that there are other fields you have not heard about that might be even better.

Your choice of a career direction could be the key to using the rest of this book effectively, because the more enthusiasm you have about your career path, the more likely you will stay involved with the job search, charge hard toward your goal, and be persistent in rooting out opportunities. The more lukewarm you are about your career direction, the more likely you will short-circuit the job-search tasks and do them poorly, succumbing to apathy and a belief that "the right job just won't turn up for me."

How does anyone know what his/her "right" career might be? There are thousands of options, one person, and one lifetime. We can't do them all on a trial basis. Even if we could, there would be several hundred new ones created each year.

You may wish someone would come along and say "Here, take this job, it's a good one," but you know that other options are available, so you keep looking for a solution.

People made good, satisfying career choices long before there were career counselors, job-search experts, or books like this one. Chances are no one helped your parents make their career choices, but they probably did all right. So, why should we be so worried? What's the big deal when many people seem to land in good jobs and careers on their own?

Most people find steady employment, and some stay in their jobs or careers for the majority of their lives, but that does not mean they are satisfied or their abilities are fully utilized. Unsuccessful career choices are revealed by an abundance of work-related illnesses, and by endless stories of job boredom and disillusionment. Each of us has friends or relatives who have endured work lives of great regret, yet did not know what they might have done to prevent it.

Also, times are different today. Career counseling did not come along as a profession by accident. With increased freedom of choice have come increased technological complexity, a far greater number of college graduates competing with each other for the same jobs, and the ever mysterious relationship between college major and career potential. (How does a philosophy major become a business executive? Or, how do we explain the fact that biology majors become lawyers?)

While it is always possible for you to change your direction, you still want to make a good choice initially, to do your best to find a job that will develop into a career commitment. Time is passing. You don't want to experiment and dawdle around forever.

So, what's the magic answer? Perhaps you would like me to tell you there is one best approach to career decision making, but I cannot do that. Because people make decisions in different ways, there appear to be several viable approaches to developing a career direction. Each has its merits and its drawbacks. I would recommend that you consider all of the following approaches and choose one or a combination of them that is right for you. In all likelihood, you will benefit most from a combination approach, since each of these has its own deficiencies, and you will want to merge the best features of all of them.

► 1. The Psychometric ◄ (Testing) Approach

Since the days of the early IQ tests, we have encouraged the belief that tests could measure and predict human performance. Many have searched for tests that would predict career satisfaction and success. Though tests such as the "Strong-Campbell Interest Inventory" and the "Self-Directed Search" are psychometrically sound (reliable and internally consistent), even the best psychometric instruments have limited ability to direct a person to careers that have the highest probability of success and satisfaction. The worst of the tests have little validity at all.

By seeking expert advice, the career seeker shakes off the more arduous task of self-assessment and firsthand exploration. The hope that an expert and his/her tests "know what careers are right for me" is enticing. I do not recommend this approach, because it will give you false answers and will discourage you from gathering your own information and relying upon your evaluation of yourself and the various career options.

Standardized testing can have some merit and be helpful to you, if the counselor who gives you the tests explains the limits of their validity. In such cases, test results are used as points of discussion, and are sometimes helpful in suggesting previously unknown career options.

No matter how seductive and expert the results of a test may seem, do not let these results or profiles prescribe the kinds of work you should enter. Tests cannot measure all of the factors that are important in your decision process, nor can they combine these factors in any valid way.

Standardized tests are typically available in high school or college career centers, community career centers, or from private counselors. The fees are sometimes reasonable and sometimes quite expensive. If the costs for testing are $50 or more I would urge the reader to proceed with caution and check the reputation of the agency closely.

If they are available, I would recommend interactive computer-based career decision-making programs as a superior form of standardized instrument. Programs such as DISCOVER (American College Testing Program) and SIGI (Educational Testing Service) use self-assessment methods to help you generate career options. Instead of being prescriptive, as many standardized career tests are, these computer software programs allow you to generate a wide variety of equal-appearing options, based on your answers to various self-assessment questions. You can change your answers to the questions, and thus get different lists of career possibilities. Such computer programs put you in charge of deciding the career options that you want to explore, and encourage you to let your decision process develop at its own speed. SIGI, DISCOVER, and similar software programs are thus superior to standardized tests, and you need not rely upon test profiles that seem to tell you the careers you should enter.

▶ 2. Take What Comes Along ◀

Using this approach, you would make your career choice according to the jobs or opportunities you happen to hear about. You go about your business, stay in touch with people, keep alert to what other people are doing, and respond to a good career option when it crosses your path. Many people make their career choices this way, because they assume it is impossible anyway to know about everything out there, so "might as well just take into account what I know about and not worry about the rest." They prefer to think, "If something is that good, I'll hear about it."

This approach is usually maligned by professional counselors and people who write career development or job-search books, because we believe that individuals should investigate as many options as possible, and that reacting to "what comes along" shows an unwillingness to break out of one's normal routines. By thus being in a rut, the individual is seen as unlikely to learn about new career opportunities.

However, the "take what comes" approach is not necessarily all bad. The person who adopts this seemingly casual attitude is often very aware of his/her environment, continually in the process of reviewing possibilities, and would prefer not to have his/her daily life interrupted by elaborate job exploration.

This approach is a form of intuitiveness, and may be consistent with how the individual makes other decisions effectively. Such a person might say: "I'll know it when I see it, so don't bug me about looking all over the place trying to find it."

The "take what comes along" approach works well if you are an out-and-about type of person who gathers information from your environment in a natural way and have a strong, clear concept of what you like and don't like. It works less well if you use it as an excuse to hide from opportunities and are not sure what you want.

I probably would not tamper much with this approach if you are reasonably confident about its results, if this is the way you usually approach key decisions, and it has worked for you before. Many people handle their lives this way; they deal spontaneously with decisions and get good results. However, if you are at all unsure about your decision making, I think that "take what comes" should be supplemented with either the "Exhaustive Self-Assessment and Career Exploration" approach, or the "Career Decision-Making Matrix" approach, or both.

► 3. Exhaustive ◄ Self-Assessment and Career Exploration

This approach is widely recommended today as the treatment-of-choice, especially for job seekers who want to take responsibility for getting the best possible employment. Richard Bolles's best-selling *What Color Is Your Parachute?* and many other self-help job-search books, including this one, recommend this method. It involves (a) a thorough review of your skills, values, interests, and preferred work environments, and (b) systematic investigation of career options, preferably on a firsthand basis.

This approach encourages and teaches you to compare careers based on how well they fit your prominent skills and needs, and thus gives you a great deal of control in the decision-making process, especially if you are painstaking in the self-assessment and exploration processes. In addition to teaching specific ways of gathering information about yourself and career options, this approach also teaches the broad virtue of self-reliance, and enhances confidence in your own powers of evaluation.

Notwithstanding its numerous merits, this approach can be both exhaustive and exhausting. Even under the best of circumstances, it takes a lot of time to do properly and may leave you worn out and confused. Some individuals are not sufficiently introspective to do either detailed self-assessment or evaluate the results of numerous information interviews. Others simply have little patience with setting up many meetings and keeping records of people they have met. Once begun, the process of skill identification and value clarification can be very detailed, and the field survey of every job you're considering can consume many hours and a great deal of energy.

The key principles of the self-directed job and career search should be embraced and strived for, because it stresses initiative and self-direction, but readers should feel free to supplement or modify it with other methods.

This model also assumes that career choice is entirely a conscious process, one in which the individual can summon all the key factors into his/her mind and incorporate them into a decision process. Other approaches allow for unconscious factors in career choice and unconscious movement toward career goals. "Unconscious" means that you don't know exactly why you are doing what you're doing, but it's all right because you are trusting your internal radar. The "take what comes along" approach is one of these latter, and the intuitive approach, which follows, is another.

▶ 4. Intuitive Approach ◀

Many of our best life choices are made without a lot of conscious deliberation. Choices of personal interests, types of cars, vacations, friends, and even mates are often made by instinct, according to what "feels right." We trust our inner judgment.

Unlike the "take what comes along" approach, in the intuitive approach you investigate the options, but the final decision is from your gut, an instinctive movement toward the option that feels the best.

The intuitive approach to decision making is often criticized because it is not rational, not organized, and does not seem to account for all of the factors involved in a decision. However, that assessment is unfair, because the intuitive decision maker does account for many factors and has an internal weighing system for putting them together, even if he or she cannot describe in precise terms what this system is.

The drawback to intuitive decision making is that it can make a person lazy. You can forget to gather information or explore key factors about career options, relying instead on your inner judgment. You can become so negligent that a career choice can degenerate into blind guesswork, like picking horses in a race according to the colors of their silks.

The intuitive approach has merit if you will investigate how your career options compare in terms of nature of the work, skills required, work setting, and other factors important to you. Once having gathered such information, you can decide how to mix these factors in your overall decision.

If it feels right, go for it. Ultimately, every decision must be an intuitive one, because you must trust your own best judgment rather than anyone else's, and because there inevitably will be factors in the decision you cannot put your finger on. But, don't become a crystal ball reader. Gather as much information as you can stand, using the simple and enjoyable principles of Detective Work (pages 103–108), and then assemble it all in your internal master processor for final judgment.

▶ 5. Career Decision-Making Matrix ◀

For the person who is unsatisfied with the fluid, subjective nature of the intuitive approach, and wants more orderliness and a decision-making system to use, there is another way. Here is an approach that is especially good when many factors are involved in your career decision, and you find yourself swinging back and forth between various alternatives.

Using a Career Decision-Making Matrix (CDM matrix) allows you to enter both your *knowledge* and your *feelings* about various career possibilities into a system that compares all of these variables according to numerical ratings. Sounds intricate. Sounds complicated. It's easier than you think, and all of the numbers are rated by you. It's a game that lets you weigh career ideas against each other without being bound by the results.

Why use a CDM matrix? Why pull together many factors and rate them? Because it won't do to simply say that one career is "better" than another. One may offer more dollars, but another offers more challenge or more interesting work. A third career may suit your life-style better because it lets you live nearer to the lake. So, it gets confusing. Here is a way to put all the factors in one place, rate them, and emerge with numbers that "score" each career versus the others.

Let's not pretend that the scores are final or contain some higher wisdom about where you should go with your career. That would be too easy. But numbers are fun to play with, and they may give you some ammunition for favoring one career over another if its rating is higher. So, get out your career options and let's play the game. Here is an example:

▶ **Career Decision-Making Matrix**

1. Enter names of three *careers* you are considering.
2. Enter four *values* that are very important to you in a career. These can be any factors that you must have in a career for it to be satisfying to you. Examples can be money, independence, creativity, outdoor work, etc. You can refer to the Values list on page 35 for help in choosing these, but you need not limit yourself to this list.
3. Assign *weights* from 1 to 10 to each value, according to its relative importance. If, for example, competition and money are two of your key values, and competition is more important than money, you might give competition a weight of 8 and money a weight of 3.
4. Estimate how well you believe each value will be satisfied by a particular career, using a scale from 1 to 10. Let's call this your *rating*. Enter this number in the appropriate cell of the matrix. For example, if you believe you would have a lot of independence as an accountant, then you could enter an 8 or 9 rating in that cell. Make these ratings based on your best information, even if you are guessing.
5. Multiply each rating by the weight for that particular value. Let's call the result of this the *weighted rating*.
6. Add the weighted ratings for each career, to get a *total*.
7. Compare the totals for the three different careers.
8. As you get better information about each career (based on your detective work), reevaluate your ratings and recompute the totals. It's a good idea to rerate the matrix every few weeks.

Career Decision-Making Matrix

		Accountant		Psychologist		Carpenter	
Wt	Value						
6	Profit, Gain	9	54	8	48	6	36
9	Physical Challenge	1	9	2	18	9	81
4	Time Freedom	8	32	5	20	7	28
7	Independence	8	56	9	63	7	49
	Total		151		149		194

What Do These Numbers Mean?

Is the "winner" of the CDM the career you should go into? It looks impressive. In the example above, "carpenter" seems to have a clear edge over "accountant" and "psychologist." Numbers don't lie, do they?

The "winner" of the CDM may be the career you want, but the results may be misleading too. Here are ways that the results of the CDM could change:

1. You might learn more about how each value is present in a career, and thus change your ratings. For example, you might discover that accountants don't have as much independence as you thought, and lower that particular rating. The rating in each cell depends greatly on your knowledge and familiarity with a given career.
2. You might decide to change the relative importance of the values, thus changing their weights. For example, if the author of the above example decided that physical challenge was less important than he/she once imagined, and weighted it 4 instead of 9, that would alter the totals dramatically.
3. You might add other values that you had not thought about before, and perhaps drop other values from your top four. In the above example, the author might substitute creativity, security, and intellectual challenge in place of Profit/Gain, Independence, and Physical Challenge. The results of this matrix would be entirely different.

Since the numbers cannot be counted upon for final judgments, what should you do? Go back to the intuitive approach, or exhaustive self-assessment and career exploration? Eventually, the intuitive method will carry the day for you, because you want to trust your instincts and your ability to process all the factors affecting you. But for now, the CDM, though it is imperfect, is a good tool for you to use because: (1) It brings many factors into one place, thus helping you to summarize your feelings about career options; (2) It reminds you of the factors you need to know more about (Where cell ratings are weak—based upon limited information—you need to use various Reality Tests [see pages 92–102] to help you make ratings that are based on sounder knowledge); (3) The CDM game may be organizing your intuition, helping you to see why you are leaning toward a particular career.

Are You Rooting for One Career to Win?

If the results of the matrix agree with what you hoped and expected, then you're happy with the game. But, what if you were hoping that one career would "win" and a different one did? If so, go back and look at your values, weights, and ratings again. Put in one or two different values and perhaps remove one or two of the original ones. Change anything else you may have had doubt about. Then, rescore the matrix.

If the horses change position, you have probably uncovered something that is important to you. Keep shuffling the factors in the CDM game until you get results that you like, that is, work the game until the right horse wins. The "right horse" probably represents your intuitive preference for a certain career. When the CDM supports your choice, it gives your intuition strength, because it helps you to see the factors underlying your preference.

The CDM can also have the reverse effect. The results of the game can change your mind about your intuitive preference. In the example above, the author may have not realized how much he/she liked carpentry until looking at the number totals. The numbers can reveal feelings that were previously vague and unformed.

The CDM is a fun tool to use in combination with the intuitive and firsthand exploration approaches to career decision making. Whenever you are not sure how to assess some new information you have obtained, plug it into the CDM game, and see if the horses change positions.

The CDM will be a helpful companion during the detective stage of your job search. Make up several blank copies of the matrix and use one of them whenever you think you have gathered enough new information to produce new scores for your career alternatives. Run the horse race again, and see who wins this time.

► Conclusion ◄

Career decision making is an art, not a science, and the artist's brush will forever be in your hands. While the methods in this chapter give you some idea of how different people make career choices, they do not relieve you of either the pleasure or the responsibility of designing your own life's work. The good news is that you can be what you want to be, and you'll be happy if you choose according to what is most important for you. The only way to lose the career decision-making game is to let someone else choose for you.

Some will ask about aptitudes: "What if I do not have the talent for the careers that I want?" Yes, of course, we can't have any career just by wishing it, and you have to work within your abilities. This sequence is important:

1. Identify the career you think you want.
2. Do the Detective Work necessary to determine how your abilities match what is required.
3. Give yourself the benefit of the doubt. If you *might* have a chance at growing into a particular career, that is, you think you can develop the abilities needed or acquire the knowledge through diligence and experience, develop a strategy for working toward that end. Don't disqualify yourself without some reality testing.
4. While you are checking out the career where you're not sure about your aptitudes, explore other careers as well, where your abilities seem appropriate. Reach for the most challenging career you can imagine, while you have a steady one waiting in reserve.
5. Be open to creating a career that does not yet exist. In some cases, not so rare, individuals dream of careers that need to be invented. Give yourself that freedom, if you want it. If you can form a picture of it in your mind's eye, you just might make it happen.

6

Reality Testing

One thorn of experience is worth a whole wilderness of warning.
—David Campbell,
If You Don't Know Where You're Going,
You'll Probably End Up Somewhere Else

Most people look for new employment as though they were walking the plank—blindfolded, hands bound, last rites on their lips, hoping everything will work out okay. You are leaping into the dark unknown if you choose to enter and make a commitment to a field of work you have never even sampled. I admit that there are numerous such adventurers among us, but their existence does not validate the ways in which they arrived at their chosen profession: "Oh, I just fell into it, gave it a try, and it worked out okay"; "I heard what my neighbor said about it, and it sounded good, so I signed up"; "Nothing better came along, so I figured what else could I do?"

Reality testing is any method of personal research in which you can gather data and be involved in the actual work activities at the same time. By both doing and observing, you have the unique opportunity to look upon the work as insider and outsider at the same time, to sample the wine before opening the bottle.

Probably the most common mistake people make in job hunting is to disqualify themselves before the horse race even starts. Perhaps the universal fear of failing or discovering the limitations of one's abilities leads people to say: "Oh, I could never succeed in that field." "There's just too much competition there." "They'd never want a person like me."

Better not to know your limitations than come face to face with them? Maybe it all goes back to our fear of speaking in school classrooms, lest we look foolish or say something wrong. Whatever the reason, it doesn't take much to throw a job hunter off the track. Other people are quite willing to add to the chorus that says: "Be careful before you enter the field of work."

"Be realistic," they say, which usually means, "Be practical, be safe, choose a job or career that you are sure of doing okay in." How can anyone be *sure* of what will happen in a job? Outsiders don't bother to answer that one.

Reality is in the eye of the beholder. One person's minefield is another's career adventure. Sometimes the cautions of others are translated to mean: "Do what I think you ought to do." The problem with "reality" is that others are always defining it for you. Their information can be helpful but it can also contain bias. You must take care not to make their opinions your own.

▶ There's No Substitute ◀ for Reality Testing

Do you let anyone else pick your social companions, your friends, your automobile, or your bedsheets for you? I didn't think so. A job or career is equally a personal decision, where personal taste must rule.

If anyone else talks you out of a job or career, you will never know if they were right or wrong. Others' viewpoints are no substitute for your firsthand experience. The person who says "Museum work is a tight field. I would avoid it if I were you" may be right about its competitiveness, but may not know that (a) You have talents uniquely suited to that field; (b) You have a special area of knowledge (e.g. your archeology background) that would be attractive to museums; (c) You have enough desire that you are willing to work for low pay to acquire experience. Furthermore, they may be turned off by their own failed attempts to get museum work, or they may know people in that field they do not like. Other people's biases can come from a hundred different directions, and seldom should they influence you.

You might say: "Of course I will make my own decisions. What made you think that I would not?" Forgive me for underestimating you. My concern is that you gather as much information as you can firsthand, from experience, from talking with people in the field, from personal observations of the work you are considering. Because all this takes time, you may be tempted to skip it and rely on an "expert" to tell you the best field for you. There are plenty of such experts around who are only too willing to tell you what they think the Truth is—psychological testers (the Truth about you), labor market forecasters (the Truth about where the jobs will be), futurists (the Truth about where the world is going), etc. Such experts have not been notably accurate over the years, and there is little reason you should rely on them to help you make a career decision.

Why Reality Testing Is Good for Your Health

It Keeps You from Making Premature Decisions Everyone is dogging you to make up your mind. It seems like you're the only one left who is still debating with yourself about what to do. As you tell people "I don't know yet," the pressure builds. Reality testing allows you to keep people at bay, giving you time to think things over. Reality testing also makes sense to other people. They may even wish they could be as careful and forward-thinking as you.

It Keeps You from Being Eaten Alive by a Career Stereotype Stereotypes are voracious. They chew up individual differences and spit them out. They are ruthless; they allow no room for individual deviations. A career stereotype insists that you see a job and its inhabitants in a certain way—an engineer as a thing-oriented noncommunicator, a public relations person as a glad-handing fast talker, or a social worker as a weepy do-gooder.

Without reality testing to save you, you may be trapped in the jaws of a career stereotype and not get away. Let's suppose you want to be a news reporter, but you imagine they all are hyperenergetic and aggressive, and you don't want to be like that. Thanks to reality testing (talking with some of these characters), you find out pretty quickly there are plenty of reporters who shatter the stereotype. Thus, you can see there is ample room for you.

An Ounce of Reality Can Equal a Pound of Self-Assessment Just when you have done a lot of self-assessment, and think you have yourself all figured out, you can do a couple of reality checks and find out:

> I can understand those stock market terms and work with those numbers better than I thought; they're not so hard, and I'll get even better with practice.
> I don't really like the pace and life-style of advertising people; it's even worse than everyone told me.
> I thought I would like people well enough to run a restaurant, but now that I see what you have to put up with from the public, I'm not so keen on it.
> Now that I see what a technical writer does, I realize I could do that without much trouble, even though I don't have an engineering background.

It is easy to overestimate or underestimate ourselves. It's better for you to find out now what your possibilities are than to say years later, with perhaps an ocean of regret, "I could have been a good ———."

Reality Testing Is Not for
Everyone or for All Situations

"If I had known what this job was like before getting into it, I never would have gotten into it."

How many times have you heard someone say that? And they have a good point. The reality of a field of work—its many problems and complexities and difficult people—might scare a person away if he/she looked too closely before deciding to enter. Sometimes it is better *not* to know everything when you are ready to take a big step.

Is it all right to take a risk when you know little about the field and are not willing to investigate it? Well, only so long as you can handle the consequences of whatever happens and can learn to "fail forward."

Judy had wanted for years to quit her job as a bank examiner and become an independent financial consultant, but said: "Every time I look at what becoming a consultant would be like, I see too much—my husband's modest income, the competition I would face, my two growing children and their needs. I think I am going to have to hold my nose, shut my eyes, and jump."

Jumping can be a lot better than standing over the water, trying to decide what it will feel like, or the discomfort of getting yourself wet one body part at a time.

There is also a limit to how much can be known about a work situation before you actually enter it.

- How can Emil know the future of rowing and boating in Austin, Texas, when he builds his boathouse? He makes an educated guess, but only the future will tell whether regattas become a tradition and participants flock to the sport of crew.
- How will Margie, who has been in the private sector for several years, know the politics of working in state government before she takes the job as a coordinator of training? She has some idea of the problems, but will only know the full story once she is there.

Using the reality-testing guidelines below, you can cut down the number of surprises waiting for you when you change careers, but much will not be as you expected and you will decide then how long you want to stay. "Ya pays yer money and ya takes yer chances."

Reality testing is most needed by people who would eliminate themselves from trying a career if they did not investigate it. You may not be one of those people. You may be impatient about looking into a job and just want to try it, come what may. The following guidelines are useful for many, but if they just slow you down, move ahead at your own pace.

Reality-testing a career is easy and it is fun. There is no reason why you cannot gather data firsthand about any job or career. Undoubtedly, you are already doing some of this on your own. Perhaps reading this section will enable you to say: "Ahh, I have been doing this right all along." If so, keep up the good work. Here are some key guidelines for reality-testing job or career ideas most effectively.

1. Allow the Career Idea to Get Born Before Evaluating It

Most failures of careers are failures of imagination.
—Leona Tyler

While you are cooking up a great idea for a career, do not allow reality to intrude. Let your imagination have its full play. Cultivate the idea of "what I most want to do" in your mind's eye. Get a clear picture of your possible future. Follow yourself around. What tasks are you performing in the course of a working day? What people are you interacting with? What are your best moments?

Does all this sound too fanciful? Creating images is nice but perhaps a little ridiculous? Are you worried that this is just a fun exercise that will shatter when it sees the light of day?

That sort of fear and wariness is exactly what keeps people from having good ideas in the first place. That is *why* career ideas must get born before reality-testing them. So what if the thing doesn't fly when you let it out the door? That's something you can find out later, without serious consequences. A career idea needs room to breathe. Do not suffocate it by judging the outcomes before it even has a chance.

2. Any Career Idea, No Matter How Farfetched, Competitive, or "Unrealistic," Can Be Tested—by You

Reality testing focuses on two key questions:

1. Am I good enough to make it in this field?
2. Is this field what I think it is—will I like it well enough?

Here are the key ways you can reality-test by yourself to answer these questions. Use all of these if possible. These reality tests are listed according to the easiest first, so you may want to start at the top and work down.

Observe the Work Being Done Follow the person around. Watch the person at work. Ask yourself: Could I do that, with sufficient training and experience? Be careful in evaluating yourself here, because you could be intimidated by watching people who are very good at their work. You could be overwhelmed by their seeming expertise. They could even be showing off for you, letting you see their best side, not showing you the situations where they perform less well. In general, though, firsthand observation will give you some idea of the ability required. Don't render a final judgment on yourself yet. Move on to other reality tests.

Simulate the Experience   Often you can reality-test yourself for a particular field of work without actually entering that field. This may be necessary for careers where you cannot get immediate experience. For example, you cannot get part-time or volunteer experience as a company executive, practicing physician, or courtroom lawyer without the necessary training and experience.

A simulated experience is one in which you test the skills and temperaments needed in the real career. For example, you can test the verbal skills of lawyering by joining college activities in which you speak a lot and argue for your point of view. You can test the leadership skills of company executives by getting involved in the management of a community program or campus organization. You can test the physical and analytical skills of potential doctoring by working in science courses and giving personal attention to your own body. The examples are numerous: future psychologists and counselors are usually tested in simulated experiences such as camp counseling or informal conversations with friends; would-be architects try their hand at building things or designing rooms in their own living quarters.

Read about It   An easy way to reality-test a job or career you know little about is to read about it in one of the many career reference books that exist. The *Occupational Outlook Handbook* and many other career references provide concise information about a particular field—nature of the work, methods of entry, types of qualifications required, job outlook, and places of employment. Your local colleges or universities will be likely to have these references, and will usually let you read them even if you are not a student there. Libraries also have many of these career books, and a reference librarian can help you find them. As you read about a field, if you find your enthusiasm growing, you can move on to the next reality test.

Talk to People in the Field   We tend to stereotype fields of work. All lawyers are regarded as highly vocal and argumentative. All accountants are perceived as reclusive, numbers-oriented people who seldom interact with others. All musicians are perceived as wild and disorganized characters who live by their feelings. Such stereotypes may not fit how you perceive yourself, and may discourage you from considering a field of work. Talk to a wide sample of people in this field before you make your judgments. Check out if you like them, and see whether your own personality could fit in that environment.

Even more important, talking to people in the field will enable you to reality-test whether the challenges and problems of that field appeal to you enough to weather the preparation you must go through. People who work in a career can tell you things that you will seldom find in career books and references, which tend to either glamorize a field or talk about it in emotionally neutral terms. People can tell you both the joys and frustrations of that kind of work from their own experiences. Be careful to sample broadly, because everyone is biased by his/her particular job, personality, or life situation. Talk to both successful and unsuccessful people. Ask them about the good points and the bad points. "What keeps you in this field?" "What are the most exciting challenges in this field?" "If you were ever to leave, what would drive you away?" are good questions to ask.

Firsthand Experience   Firsthand experience will be the best reality test for finding out whether you like a field enough to make a commitment to it. A job or career can look good on paper and sound good as described by its practitioners, but until you try doing it, you really do not know if you will be enthusiastic about it.

An all-or-nothing mentality often keeps people from using experience as a reality test. They believe mistakenly that if they try out a new kind of work they are making a commitment to it. On the contrary, you can experiment as much as you please with new fields of work, particularly if you do it on a volunteer or part-time basis. It can be as simple as helping a friend with his/her work, or volunteering to work on a political campaign, or helping out at a florist shop at night to see if you like the work routine.

The value of doing volunteer work is a well-kept secret. Often you cannot get a paying job in order to reality-test a field of work. Does it make sense to work for free? In many cases, yes, because the experience may be more important than the loss of income. If you need badly to test a career before committing yourself to it, then be willing to make whatever temporary financial concessions are necessary.

Unpaid work is a useful bridge between careers, but many people do not take it seriously. It's a secret that you can learn without earning. Take advantage of it, and understand that you are being paid in ways other than money.

You will usually arrange volunteer work on an informal basis rather than applying for a volunteer job. You would approach someone and say: "I'd like to get some experience working here, and am willing to offer my time and energy without pay. Could we talk about working something out?" As in life, almost anything is negotiable. You are offering your energetic services in exchange for getting new learning and insights that will help you develop your career future.

3. Evaluate Each Reality-Test Yourself

Be your own judge of what each reality test means to your career decision. Sometimes the people you talk with will want to offer judgments for you, such as: "Don't go into this field, it's too crowded . . . too discouraging . . . too demanding," etc. Or, their opinions may be overly positive: "It's a great field. You can't miss . . . plenty of opportunity."

Practitioners are no better forecasters about their own fields than the labor market experts are, though perhaps they are no worse. Your decision should depend not upon what they believe the future of the field to be (though this is good information to have), but upon whether you are sufficiently attracted to it and believe you have the ability to perform reasonably well. In other words, after adding up all your reality tests, if you still feel good about the field and think you might be a pretty good fit, then give it a shot.

> EXAMPLE ► Al was a social worker who wanted to switch to being a carpenter. In his first reality-test experience, he tried building a doghouse and made a mess of it. Others laughed and said that was proof he should stick to social work, but Al decided he would keep after it until he got it right. Al tried another doghouse, did a better job, moved up to building outdoor decking, did a few chairs, built a staircase, and eventually learned cabinet making from an experienced craftsman. He knew he had done bad work initially, but held on to his belief that he could become competent. His initial failures were temporary. When people began paying him well for a few side jobs, Al decided it was time to change careers.

4. You Don't Have to Be Better Than Everyone Else

"If I can't be the best, I don't wanna do it." Nonsense! If you are good enough to earn a living at it, and people respect you for it, then you'll be all right in that kind of work. We compare ourselves to others too much. Give yourself credit for jobs well done.

5. It May Not Be the Right Time but You Can Try It Later

Sometimes you do your reality testing when conditions are not quite right. Your family is having problems that require your attention . . . or your confidence is not quite where it should be . . . you have some physical ailment that is slowing you down. Perhaps you should come back at a later time and reality-test again, when other problems have faded. I am not trying to give you excuses for giving up (it *is* important to persist, and to overcome frustrations if you feel you're on the right track), but am simply acknowledging that timing can be important, and you can repeat reality tests later, whenever you would like.

6. Make a Career Move About One Week Before You Are Completely Ready

Why? Because you will seldom feel completely ready, that everything is right and the stars are all in their right places. If you feel you're within one week of having All Systems Go, then go ahead and do it. You have probably done enough reality testing and are simply sitting around gathering up your courage. Yes, there is a risk, and you're not sure what's going to happen, but do it anyway. If you find out you were wrong, you will still be right, because the experience of trying a new field will teach you something about yourself you did not know, and you will use that experience to move on to something else. But, let's not talk about failure. You've researched this thing to death by now. Do it. It's going to work.

► How Reality Testing ◄ Helps the Career Search

Businesspeople use the phrase *caveat emptor* ("let the buyer beware"). In "buying" new work, there is even more to worry about than the quality of the merchandise—the personalities of the coworkers, their life-styles, the demands of superiors, and numerous other factors. Shoes, refrigerators, and automobiles can be tested in a relatively simple manner before they are bought. *Consumer Reports* has no laboratories for work environments.

Every form of reality testing gives you an opportunity to look at a field of work before deciding whether you want to enter it. Your stereotypes do not give you accurate pictures. Does every police officer's day culminate in the capture of a million-dollar cocaine shipment? Reality testing enables you to see firsthand what the good and bad aspects of a given career will be.

Reality testing often paves the way for actual job offers because it gives people a chance to see what you can do. In such situations, your exposure to the employer accumulates and you develop close relationships with the people who may one day employ you. Two examples illustrate this point.

EXAMPLE ► Mo was a young man who had a lot of sensitivity to the drug- and alcohol-abuse problems of college-age and other people who are captives of adolescent life-styles. He spent most of his time during college and summers between terms getting to know drug users and the ways they think, the attitudes they hold toward their lives. During college, he spearheaded the creation of a study group and informal counseling service that would reach out to his friends and provide information, counsel, crisis support, and a place to ventilate feelings. He obtained a federal grant for the purpose and grew closely acquainted with community leaders in his efforts to build town support. When Mo graduated with major fields of study in philosophy and English, he wanted to continue this work. He sought the environs of a large metropolitan area and discovered that a suburb heavily populated by adolescents wanted to begin a community-based counseling and referral service for drug and alcohol abusers. Many trained scholars of pharmacology, psychology, mental health, and other disciplines applied, but Mo was hired to direct the center because he had experienced the problems of drug abuse and the difficulties of extending this service to adolescents. The selection committee felt that the youth population would trust Mo more easily and would respond to his experience.

EXAMPLE ► Sara worked in an office of local government but longed to play a role in encouraging the growth of performing arts in her city. She attended theater, concerts, dance programs, music recitals, and every artistic event that appeared within a hundred miles. One day she heard from a neighbor that a few people in town were trying to create a summer arts program for high school students. She decided this was her opportunity to learn about arts administration firsthand, so she volunteered to help in every phase of the project. She raised funds, wrote publicity brochures, interviewed prospective students, surveyed the schools, talked with potential faculty, and helped develop budgets. The summer program eventually came into being, and two months later Sara was hired by the executive director to return with her to a nearby town and become assistant arts administrator for the county.

Reality testing becomes most important for you when you practice the more intense levels, such as volunteer work and part-time work. The employer who may one day seek a new assistant or other staff member, and wonders how to decipher from résumés and other standardized credentials the quality of candidates' abilities, will likely be glad to short-circuit the selection process and hire the familiar volunteer or part-timer—you.

► How to Obtain This Skill ◄

How do you become a skillful reality tester? First, be curious. Cultivate a higher level of curiosity than you have ever had before. Snoop around as though you were a detective. It's great fun to pay attention to details ordinary mortals would not notice, pick up a few pieces of information that are hidden from public view, and push your limits of visual observation.

Second, practice taking the person-on-the-street role. This you can do in many ways: you might want to buy a new suit, seek information from a government agency, or inquire about child-abuse services from your local courthouse.

Third, play dumb. Except when you are asking someone to hire you, it ordinarily helps to approach a work site as though you know nothing. Take little for granted; ask questions about even the things you think you understand. People will be more willing to explain what you see if you approach them as though you are the novice and they are the advice givers, which is the truth. Let every informant tell you his or her own version of why things look that way, so you can collect and merge these data and opinions into a consensus view.

Finally, be willing to risk. Every instance of reality testing means doing or seeing something new to you. If your tolerance for change and variety hovers near the zero line, take some small risks first. Be prepared to try a new environment, knowing you can return to the old fireplace any time you choose.

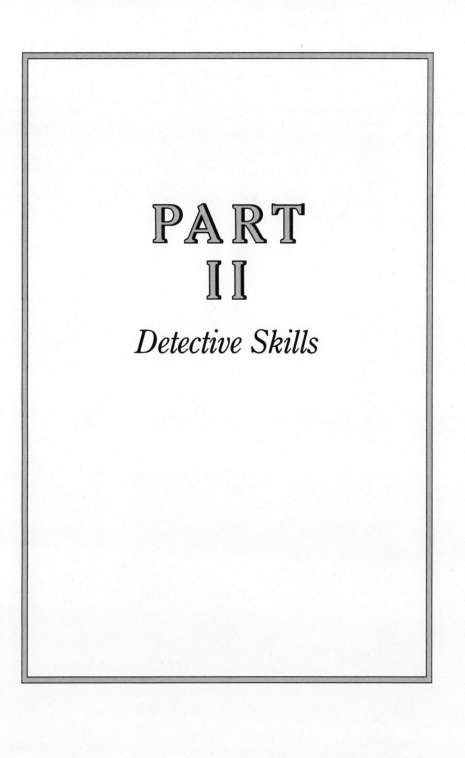

PART
II
Detective Skills

The image of the sleuth or detective is my favorite for characterizing the career search because it merges the elements of excitement and anticipation with judiciousness, the awareness that your quest for information will always bend to intellect and persistence. Just as a good detective knows the puzzle can be solved, the necessary information is at hand, and what may be invisible to the eye is deducible by the inquiring mind, so the work detective can say with assurance: "The work I want is out there; all I must do is find it."

The best work is awarded to those who are most diligent at finding it, at putting themselves in the *right place at the right time*. Since most job contacts have an element of luck in them, it follows that a good detective takes advantage of every ounce of luck available. An employer will have no particular compulsion to conduct a cross-country search for the best candidate. He or she will assume you are the best that could be found, because the others simply have not appeared.

Detective skills are a combination of gathering information from other people and using printed materials effectively. In this section you will learn about publications that help you to map the labor markets you want to enter, and you will learn how to develop a personal referral network to gain access to these markets. I will also tell you about the information interview as a way of gathering facts and insights you will need, and caution you how to avoid misusing this valuable tool. Library research rounds out your collection of detective skills, as you embark upon the pleasant task of finding many job opportunities that others will miss, because they sit at home waiting to hear about openings by chance alone.

▶ The Work Detective Has It ◀
Easier

When you consider that the crime detective and the work detective function according to similar principles, you realize that as a work detective you enjoy the advantages of the trade without the disadvantages of having criminals, paranoids, and competing sleuths attempting to hide information from you. Everything you are looking for is open to public view. Furthermore, it is offered by people who want to help you, if you will only ask them. If I want to learn more about what a carpenter does, I don't have to sneak around corners and bribe people to give me hot information. I can approach my targets directly and ask for the assistance they are willing to give.

A friend of mine wondered where in the world she would learn about the banking field and get the contacts she so desperately needed. Meanwhile, she sat beside a bank teller on the bus to work, tripped over a bank vice-president on her way into the building, had lunch with a friend who lived next door to a big money man in the financial district, and went bowling that night with a city manager who was about to close a deal with his local bank for downtown redevelopment. The best sources are walking past you, if you have the presence of mind to tap them on the shoulder.

Don't look for the proverbial needle in the haystack by yourself. It does not make sense to conduct all your detective work alone. You are not paid to be a full-time sleuth. You certainly don't have the time or patience to track down every detail on your own. What then? Let others do most of your work for you. Find the people who know the most about what you want to know and give them the privilege of showing you their storehouse of information. It has been said that the smart manager proves it by surrounding him- or herself with people who are even smarter.

▶ How to Get Started with ◀
Detective Work

As you set forth in search of people or information about your intended career, the questions to ask yourself routinely are: Who would know? Who would know anyone else who knows? Where would they meet? Do they have any formal association or affiliation group?

Any good detective looks in the places that have the greatest promise. Don't wait on park benches for the clues to sit in your lap. Let's say you want to make contacts in the field of recreation.

- *Who would know?* Town recreation boards, youth groups, anyone engaged in athletics, and people who teach recreation at the state university.
- *Who would know anyone else who knows?* People who participate in recreation a lot, such as children, older people, church leaders; and people whose business it is to know what is happening in recreation—retailers of recreational equipment, keepers of parks, and so forth.
- *Where would these people meet?* Try the obvious first, places where people engage in the recreation itself; then try the less obvious, places where people meet to plan recreation activities—church groups, youth groups, town councils.
- *Would they have an association?* Of course. Don't any groups that share common interests, problems, and needs for enrichment find a way to get together? Ask any active recreational specialist where colleagues meet when they want to share new ideas or have a good time together.

You can make useful connections through seemingly unlikely sources. Butchers know bankers, and street cleaners have made the acquaintance of government officials. I know a college professor who knows mideastern high potentates. It is within your grasp to start a chain from potentates to that special camel dealer you've been wanting to meet all these years.

EXAMPLE ► Steve always wanted to meet an alligator wrestler. He really half-suspected there were no such people. He tried the local zoo and they laughed at him. Undaunted, he slipped into the town's luggage shop on a lark and asked where the alligator suitcases came from. "I just get them from my wholesaler, Mac," replied the store owner. Thus began a trail from the owner to the wholesaler to the manufacturer to the alligator trappers in the bayous of Louisiana. A few letters and a phone call later, Steve was invited to an open market for trappers and traders. He declined the offer of a summer job, but made contact with a Louisiana guide for the day he plans to make a firsthand visit.

Seeing It from the Employer's Perspective

Consider who is really the helpless one in this job-search process. It is the poor employer, even more than you. The employer must discover you from among thousands of potential applicants. The employer has precious few resources to find you easily and literally no systematic method for even detecting your existence. You at least have the advantage of knowing what you want and being able to find the employer, who is listed in the telephone book or some other convenient directory. By contrast, you are nearly invisible to the employer who seeks you.

The Employer Doesn't Even Know You Exist   Directories are little more than organized frustration for the employer who wonders: "Who would want this job? What is this person doing now that is relevant to our situation? How do I find this person without having to interview everyone at the national convention?" It is far easier for you to know that the employer exists. Numerous reference books, stock market reports, annual reports, newspaper stories, and other research materials tell you whether an employer should be included on your target list.

The Employer Is Usually Under Great Time Pressure   When an employer has a job vacancy, it must be filled in a specified period of time. How many hires are made because the employer simply got tired of the hiring procedures and took whoever was handy at the time?

The Employer Must Depend on the Least Reliable Data   Anyone who has ever stared at a pile of a hundred résumés, trying to decide which of them reveals the right person to hire, will understand that a stack of résumés can be characterized as a parade of wooden soldiers. Any relationship between résumé data and what the person is capable of doing is often purely coincidental. Following the résumé-screening process is the thirty-minute canned interview, in which the interviewer asks questions hoping to elicit the essential qualities an individual has cultivated during twenty-one or more years of living. Small wonder that a blind interview, based on a résumé that has been carefully manufactured to present a selective truth, often results in a process resembling a Martian talking to a person from the moon.

The moral of this story is: *if you don't find the employer, the employer will not find you.* Hence, the employer will be forced to hire the cluck instead of you, and you will become some other employer's cluck because you too have managed to find the wrong job for your particular talents.

It is much easier for you to find the right employer among thousands than for the employer to discover you among millions.

7

Prospect List

The first step in any active work search is to identify a list of prospective employers. This chapter will tell you how to use published employer directories to develop a long list of names and places where you may find jobs, and why this is an effective approach to job hunting.

▶ Why Any Job, Anywhere, ◀ Is Potentially Available to You

"Where are the jobs?" is a dominant question among job seekers. The quest for openings is like a treasure hunt, but a frustrating one since, as many authors have said, much of the job market is hidden and therefore difficult to uncover. Yet we persist in trying to keep track of this ever-shifting thing called the labor market. An army of Geiger counters called "employment agencies" attests to people's desire to have someone keep sweeping the landscape, looking for the openings. It also attests to the individuals' belief that they cannot find the openings themselves.

Employment agencies, job banks, and other such enterprises are hitting certain pockets of employment, but missing large numbers of others. The job market moves too fast and is too diverse to be tracked with any thoroughness. A little like catching raindrops—the more you try, the more you become aware of the larger task before you.

You may read a job announcement or see a job listed in the local employment bureau. Meanwhile others are coming open that you, the publications, and the bureau don't know about. In many cases the employers are trying hard *not* to make the opening widely known. Employers would prefer to broadcast their vacancies only to the people best known to them (informal sources), in order to get applicants they know the most about. Hence, the hidden job market.

So, what are you to do about all this? You still want to know where the jobs are, and feel that somebody ought to be able to tell you. You don't want to waste your time looking down blind alleys or canvassing everyone you see, or calling at random in the Yellow Pages.

Don't despair. You can do an effective job of using detective skills to uncover potential jobs through the principles of Targeting.

▶ Targeting Jobs, and the ◀ Elegant Logic That Lies Behind It

Targeting is two things:

a) *Targeting Content* Identifying the specific kinds of work that you want to do and concentrating your energies on these areas of the labor market.
b) *Targeting Geographically* Identifying the specific towns, cities, or regional areas where you would like to live and find employment.

The basic principle of Targeting (and of Detective Skills) is that any job can be uncovered, no matter how "hidden" the job market may be. The accessibility of occupations can be explained in a three-step logic that opens up the entire world of work to you. Never mind "Where are the job openings?" Pay attention only to "Where are the organizations that employ people?" and "Where can I find them?"

▶ Elegant Principle 1: If a job can be imagined, there are people who are doing it.

Fortunately, there is enough diversity of employment in our economy that, no matter how specific, detailed, or far-out your desired job may be, there are (with rare exceptions) already people doing it. Never mind whether they are leaving these jobs, or whether you can compete successfully for them. Because the labor market is continually in a state of turnover, one or more of the people who occupy these jobs may leave sooner or later. Furthermore, there are strategies you can use to qualify or prepare yourself for such openings. For now, be happy in knowing that the jobs you want already exist—somewhere. And, since they exist, you can get access to them.

In those unusual cases where no one is doing the kinds of work you would like to do, consider two possibilities: (1) There are people who are doing work that is similar; (2) There are organizations that have a need for that kind of work, and may create jobs in the future to take advantage of it.

▸ **Elegant Principle 2: Since there are people already doing the kind(s) of work that you want, you can find them.**

I'm still saying nothing about whether there are jobs open. The point here is that, through simple use of detective skills, you can locate and walk right up to meet people who are doing the jobs that you might like to have one day. For the most part, people in their jobs do not hide, nor could they hide if they wanted to. There are a few exceptions to that, but mostly people at work are aboveground, not covered by burlap bags, and generally accessible. Sometimes it takes a little travel money and time and persistence to find them, but they are there. And since your target people exist and can be found, they may have some information about when and where future job vacancies are likely to exist. Or, even if they don't, they can give you some clues about how people move in this field and how you might find a way in. So, your second task is to *get there*, find the people who're doing your target jobs. Once you have found them, you're two-thirds of the way through successful Targeting.

▸ **Elegant Principle 3: Since any job can be imagined, and people can be found who are doing it, you have some opportunity to get experience that will qualify you for doing that kind of work.**

Having found the people who are doing your target jobs, looked them in the eye, and made their acquaintance, you are already ahead of many others who are still trying to figure out "Where are the jobs?" Now, let's assume there are no openings, the field is competitive (as most job categories are, to one extent or another), and you're wondering why you're wasting all this time.

Don't back off now, just when you're at the front gate. Direct contact with target people usually gives you some opportunity to ask: "How might I gain experience in this kind of work, so that I can make myself qualified when openings become available?" Good job hunters are thinking a step ahead. Seven major categories of experience are detailed on pages 212–215. Does the target person know where you might get part-time work, an internship, volunteer experience, or perhaps enter a training program? Well, maybe not, but it's all right for you to ask, and sometimes they can recommend avenues for you. "How did you get into this field?" or "How did the most recent people hired here get into this field?" are good questions to ask.

It does not pay to complain about there being no jobs. There are plenty of jobs, you're just not in them. The name of this game is early access. Get there before someone else does. Identify what you want, find the people who are doing it, and figure out a way to hook on with them. People are better than paper. Paper methods—job listings, job banks, classified ads—leave you on the outside unable to look in. People methods give you access to the possibility of any job in the world. When you arrive on their doorstep it may be just the day they decided to move on.

Easy for me to say. To take advantage of targeting, it sounds as though you would have to quit your present job, or drop out of school, and roam the countryside looking for target people, all the while going into debt and wishing there were a way to give up this search and let someone else do it for you. Is targeting nice in theory but impossible in practice? Certainly there are difficulties in the logistics of getting in touch with targets, and problems in making yourself available for the experiences they may recommend. You must work within the limitations of your time, energy, and money.

But remember this: If you want something enough, you ought to be willing to investigate it. The people who can help you best are the people who are doing the work you want. Any other method of trying to identify where the jobs are is going to be much less efficient and more frustrating, because you will be working with secondhand information.

In addition to the many jobs available through the hidden job market, new jobs are created to meet existing needs. A job may be created as a result of your initiative. Stranger things have happened. Your presence, your ability to describe your skills and experiences, and the employer's needs could come together in a chemical reaction that results in their offering you a job.

EXAMPLE ► Ron went to Washington looking for a job as a junior lobbyist. Armed with his English degree from Dickinson College, he checked with one agency after another. He got nowhere for several weeks. Since he had done some theater in college, he decided he might as well try the National Endowment for the Arts. The dance department had no jobs but needed someone to deliver sets and other materials to the public schools within a fifty-mile area, and help them set up their programs. They were having a hard time finding someone who would not mind driving a truck, loading and unloading it, and working odd hours. When Ron said he would do it, through the magic of government, they created a new job and started Ron in his career of public service. Today, six years later, he is a key administrator and lobbyist with the National Endowment for the Arts.

► Maps of the Labor Market ◄

The job marketplace seems like too vast a territory to be covered. People and their jobs are everywhere at once, and there is no central clearinghouse or grand map that shows you who is doing what exactly where. While the principles of targeting are sound, how can you get a handle on finding thousands of individuals and jobs? Hidden job possibilities are out there, but how can you efficiently tap this large keg of opportunities?

1. Keep an Open Mind Assume that ANY employer in your targeted field *might possibly* have an opportunity for you. This optimistic assumption will yield you more results in the long haul than saying: "Oh, they probably don't have anything." Because of continual turnover, and the reality that new jobs are created every day, job possibilities may exist where there appear to be none. The day you show up may be the day that Marv Ziltz decided to move to Sheboygan, or Annie Corbisher got it together to start her own beach-blanket business and now can leave the company for good.

2. Use Directories While there is no single map that tells where all jobs are and who is leaving them, there are a large number of published directories that you can use to "map" your target areas of work. In fact, these maps are so useful and available that you can find hundreds of organizations which employ people whose jobs you would like to have— simply by making an easy trip to your local library.

Why settle for a few job vacancy listings (from job banks or employment agencies) when you can scan the entire landscape that you want and select many different places to contact? The directories listed here are widely available, in either public libraries, the reference sections of college and university libraries, or the career planning and placement centers of your local colleges and universities. You can use these "maps" at your leisure and identify many potential employment targets.

A Sampling of Available Directories
Dun and Bradstreet's Million Dollar Directory
1987 Artist's Market
Literary Marketplace: The Directory of American Book Publishing
The Insurance Job Finder

The Banking Job Finder
The United States Government Manual
Education Jobs Handbook
The Official Guide to Airline Careers
The Energy Job Finder
Physical Sciences Jobs Handbook
Conservation Directory
Life Sciences Jobs Handbook
Computer Careers: Where the Jobs Are and How to Get Them
Peterson's Engineering, Science, and Computer Jobs, 1988
Social and Behavioral Sciences Jobs Handbook
Good Works: A Guide to Careers in Social Change
Directory of Counseling Services
The Top 200 Corporations
Directory of Career Training and Development Programs
Everybody's Business: An Almanac
The Job Hunter's Guide to the Sunbelt
Directory of Washington Internships
Directory of Washington Representatives
Careers in International Affairs
Directory of American Firms in Foreign Countries
Global Employment Guide
College Placement Annual

EXAMPLE ► If you were targeting social change careers, you would consult *Good Works* and *Careers in International Affairs*, because both have extensive listings and descriptions of organizations that employ people for such work. Representative social change employers include the American Friends Service Committee, the Peace Corps, Amnesty International, and Common Cause.

EXAMPLE ► If you were targeting medium- to large-sized businesses in a particular geographic area, you would consult *Dun and Bradstreet's Million Dollar Directory*.

EXAMPLE ► If you were targeting agencies of the federal government's executive branch, you would consult *The United States Government Manual*, which lists and describes in detail every federal agency, its branch and regional office locations, and names of people to contact.

Without these maps, you are lost. There are no tour guides you can hire to lead you through the swamps. There are no other ways to find employers conveniently listed and organized for you, by geography and types of work. Make it easy on yourself. Consult a map at your local library or career library, and travel on.

3. Build a List   Make a target list of fifty or more organizations from your favorite directories. The ones listed above have at least 10,000 different employers in them. Surely you can find at least fifty to put on your shopping list.

4. Find Key People Show this list to all the people you know, and ask each of them:

a) Do you know anyone who works at these organizations?
b) Do you know any people who work at similar organizations?
c) May I call or visit these people and say that you referred me?

Even if your contacts cannot help you, go ahead and call your targets anyway. People you know will help, but they should not be used as a substitute for good old personal initiative, when it is needed.

5. Meet Face-to-Face Call to make an appointment with any of the people you are referred to, regardless of their level of importance in the organization. If you're contacting them on your own, and do not know names of key people, call and ask: "Who is head of that department?" or "Who works for him/her?" Then do your best to meet with one or more of these people.

Presto! You have discovered maps of the labor market. These directories give you a way to organize your detective work, and a strategy for tapping into the hidden job market. If you show your target list of fifty employers to twenty-five people on your list of people to contact, you should have at least ten solid referrals to people who work where you want to work. Through the power of chain referrals, you're on your way to greater and greater penetration of the labor market. You can develop many additional sources on your own, apart from your list of contacts, through direct application. Overall, using maps yields the most potential opportunities, because you are covering the entire landscape, rather than the small number of possibilities that may exist in a job bank or an employment agency hopper.

Maps Are Never Complete

Don't count on the maps to tell you everything. They will inevitably miss many of your prospective employers, even though they list more for you, and more easily, than any other method you have available. Be aware of these limitations:

• Directories cannot keep pace with changes of organizations, new ones being created, or others going out of existence. If you have a current directory of a given field, it will probably cover 70 to 90 percent of the existing large and medium-sized organizations. That is a lot better than you can do on your own.

- Small organizations are often missed by national directories such as those listed here. Don't overlook the small ones in your job search. Many of them will be known to your contacts, and some will be listed in local directories. Smaller organizations are "sleepers." They do not have glamorous names, but some of them will grow into leadership roles and therefore offer more exciting potential for growth than the larger, better known companies, whose growth may be leveling off. It has been well documented that small firms create more new jobs:

Between 1974 and 1984, while the Fortune 500 gang was eliminating 1.5 million jobs—that's all the people in Phoenix, Arizona, or Cincinnati, Ohio—the little businesses were creating jobs enough to keep the economy from going to hell in a handbasket. Nowadays small companies (defined by a maximum of 500 employees) account for three out of five new jobs created in the private sector. If you're thinking these jobs are mostly small-change employment, you are wrong. Nearly half are in professional, technical, or managerial positions.[1]

The American economy is breaking into pieces. More and smaller businesses now do what fewer and larger ones did before. . . . In 1985, almost 700,000 new companies were formed, compared with . . . only 200,000 as recently as 1965. . . . The Fortune 500 companies alone employed 2.2 million fewer people at the end of 1985 than they did at the beginning of 1980.[2]

Compared to only ten or twelve years ago, a person today is much more likely to find employment in a small establishment rather than a major corporation.[3]

- Certain fields of work do not have any directories at all. In such cases, try the Chamber of Commerce or United Way of your town or city, because these organizations have overall directories of profit and nonprofit organizations, respectively.
- If all else fails, try the *Encyclopedia of Associations*. Every field of work is represented by one or more professional associations. Look them up using the Key Word Index in the *Encyclopedia*. Then write or call the association and ask if they know of a directory that will help you. If not, they usually have a directory of members and can tell you where to find one in your local area. They also usually have journals that tell about the field, and about national and regional meetings, and they will usually send you free or inexpensive literature describing careers in that field.

EXAMPLE ► By looking up the American Psychological Association in the *Encyclopedia*, you would learn that they produce several journals, hold many regional meetings, and have headquarters in Washington, D.C., where you could write for further information. Your letter could request *Careers in Psychology* and other related career materials. APA would also tell you about their member directory, and if any directories exist for mental health centers, mental hospitals, and community guidance clinics.

Often a contact with a professional association will put you on the trail of the map that you need, since there are many more employer directories than those listed here. It is best to call the association and ask to speak with the executive director, his/her assistant, or the head of the resource library, if the association has a large staff (the *Encyclopedia* tells you the size of the staff).

The names of employers that you get from these maps are enough to give you a big head start in developing your shopping list of prospective employers. The maps are readily accessible. Such a list will help to organize your job search and convince you that there *are* many jobs out there. Now your task is to find them.

► Prospect-List-Identification ◄ Exercise

Here is a step-by-step breakdown of a good strategy for making a prospect list. Go through each as it applies to your own situation.

1. Write a goal statement that defines the skills you want to use and the broad categories of employers where you would like to use them.

    EXAMPLE ► Use managerial skills with financial organization

2. Choose a geographical area that you prefer—a town, city, or small region.

    EXAMPLE ► Boston, Massachusetts

3. Choose one of the four major employment sectors—private industry, government, education, or nonprofit—in which you'd like to work.

    EXAMPLE ► Private industry

4. Select one employer type in the sector you'd most like to work for.

    EXAMPLE ► Stockbrokerage house

5. Choose three skills you would most like to use in your work.

   EXAMPLE ► Writing, organizing people, speaking to groups

6. Name three other types of employers (organizations) that could offer you work in the field of your choice.

   EXAMPLE ► Insurance companies, banks, mutual funds

7. Choose a size of organization you would prefer, in terms of number of employees in a single location.

   EXAMPLE ► No more than five hundred employees

8. If you have gotten this far, you have done much to identify the kinds of target employers for whom you are searching and can use the employer directories in your target geographical area to make a prospect list of manageable size. Choose the names of three employer directories that seem most likely to contain organizations for your prospect list.

   EXAMPLE ► Look through the *Financial Market Place, Thomas' Register of Manufacturers*, and *Moody's Industrials* for information on stockbrokerage houses, insurance companies, banks, and mutual funds in Boston.

Personal Referral Network

Dear Howard:

How will I ever get out of the miserable job I'm in? I've been hidden in this rathole for years and don't get any chance to meet people who have the good connections. I'm a forgotten soul, sinking into the swamp of mediocrity and nonrecognition. How does a rinky-dink like me get to meet the big guys? I think I might have a shot at something a little better if only I could plug in to the right sockets.

Signed,
Faulty Wiring

Dear Wired for Sound:

Do you walk with both feet on the ground? Do you live somewhere on the planet Earth? Can you fall over a stranger at the bus stop? Are there at least three people in the world who love you or at least tolerate you enough to refer you to their friends?

If you can squeak a hesitant yes to these questions, there is hope for you yet. "Contacts" do not hide in smoke-filled rooms; nor do they travel, as a rule, in bulletproof cars or walk around shielded by entourages of henchmen or hangers-on. Contacts ride buses like the rest of us, eat in cafeterias, go to ball parks, and sidle up to pizza stands. They don't wear red carnations. Contacts are you and me, Uncle Harry, and the guy who fouls you when you reach for the basketball at the local YMCA.

Your best connections are the ones you trip over every day, the people who cross your path on a natural, routine basis. They

119

may not have the keys to the executive washroom, but they inevitably know people who do and can introduce you in casual contexts—the next company softball game, the tavern after a day's work, or the motorcycle trail where everyone is the same dirt digger with gravel in the ears and sand in the windpipe.

If you have lived with people, you have contacts. Don't bury yourself with the false assumption that your friends could not possibly know anyone worth knowing. Uncle Harry may look like a toad, but he plays handball with the bank president and cuts cards twice a week with members of the city council.

Signed,
Howard

► The "I'm a Nobody, I Don't ◄ Know Anyone Important" Blues

"You need to know people in high places to get ahead." "Only people with connections get anywhere." How many varieties of this tale of woe have you heard or said to yourself lately? I do not claim that all people have equal footing as they begin the work search; some folks *do* have contacts that are more influential than others. However, this complaint is still a weak excuse for not doing anything about your situation, for not mobilizing yourself and taking advantage of the contacts you do possess.

No matter how lowly you believe your station in life to be, or how private a person you think yourself, you still have valuable contacts. This chapter discusses the wealth of possible contacts within your comfortable grasp. No, contacts will not necessarily obtain a job for you; nonetheless, they provide a vital link between you and the people you are trying to meet.

People more often find their work through direct referral by other people—usually friends or acquaintances—than in any other way. Crystal and Bolles, in *Where Do I Go from Here with My Life?*, call this *organizing your luck:*

> There is always an element of "luck," "the fortuitous crossing of paths," or "serendipity" that is beyond your control. But the question is: "How can you best organize your luck, so the factors that *are* within your control are working for you?" The answer is by choosing a target area and running it to death.[1]

Like the guy who hangs around the firehouse or the emergency room of the local hospital just on the chance something might happen, you *can* develop special antennae for work opportunities and the people who know about them. Many people who call themselves lucky are ones who have unconsciously refined their ability to learn about things as quickly as they happen and have developed the habit of putting themselves in touch with the right ears. If questioned, these talented people may not be aware of how they do it.

> EXAMPLE ► Jane asked the local automobile dealer to tell her about antique cars, where they are located, how they are acquired, and all that. She was just curious, you understand. The dealer invited Jane and her grandmother to an automobile show where antique cars were on display, and there Jane met another dealer who was looking for a young person to get into the business. Thus did Jane have the "lucky" break of meeting her future business partner in the trade that is her heart's desire.

Every planned contact can lead to unexpected ones. Expect the unexpected breaks and ask for them if they are not immediately proffered. Every time you make contact with a person who is in direct line with your career interest, you set up the possibility that he or she will lead you to more people of similar persuasion.

► Intermediate Contacts ◄

"But I don't know anyone in that field at all," you protest. "That's like trying to meet the Prince of Wales." The intermediate contact, the person who knows both you and the Prince of Wales, is the person for whom you are looking.

The skill of expanding a personal referral network is the skill of connecting people, the skill of stringing together enough intermediate contacts so that you can reach anyone. Anyone. Acquiring employment is a *social* process. People are connected to one another by a nearly infinite number of pathways. Many of these pathways are available to you, but you must activate the circuits to make them work to your advantage.

An illuminating research study known as the "Small-World Problem"[2] reveals the extraordinary power of having and using your own personal contacts. Milgram estimated that any person of adult age has accumulated between 500 and 1,000 personal contacts, and he reasoned that each link between two individuals generates a total pool of contacts numbering between 25,000 (500 × 500) and 1,000,000 (1,000 × 1,000). Three links in a referral chain permit an astronomical number of contact possibilities. Therefore, he reasoned, anyone ought to be able to reach anyone else in a populated country simply by putting a few links of the referral chain into operation. He tested this empirically by asking a sample of people in Massachusetts to use their personal contacts to reach a randomly selected group in Nebraska whom they did not know at all. Results showed that the Massachusetts people reached the town in Nebraska typically within two links ("I know a plumber here who has a brother in Nebraska who has a friend in the target town"). The implications of this research for job seekers are little short of staggering. It means that you have the power to reach almost anyone if you simply use your existing contacts.

There is no such thing as a person who cannot be contacted, reached, tapped, exploited, or otherwise made a friend. Everyone has a friend who also has a friend. Somewhere in that chain of friends you are standing with your arms at your sides and your eyes closed. Now if you carefully open your eyes, reach out to the two friends waiting on either side, and grasp their hands firmly, you will feel the electricity of a personal contact network begin to course through your body. It will be stimulating, but not shocking. You will feel alive with the circuit of energy that comes from plugging in to people networks. However, be aware that any time you drop your hands and close your eyes again, you have broken the connection. The life of the circuit depends on your ability to keep the switches open. I don't know how to help people who are asleep at the switch.

People like to make their contacts known to you. It takes a lot of restraint *not* to tell another person about your contacts. Try it sometime. Most people's natural egotism takes over. "Why, of course, I know Dradnatz. Been a good friend of mine for years." Once you subtract a constant for puffery, you have a good measure of a person's contact potential. By telling you the people I know, I accomplish two things: (1) I reaffirm my membership in the human race and show that I have some history of having kept my relationships over a period of time—no small matter; and (2) I can be helpful to you in a way that requires little effort, yet does you some definite good.

To take the fullest advantage of natural contact networks:

- Never underestimate the value of any person you know. The milkman, the druggist, the country butcher, or the sandwich-board man (now there's a person who meets and greets a lot of people) can all be helpful to you. You-never-know-who-you're-talking-with incidents happen every day. The street-sign painter on your block this summer may be the son of the local bank president.
- Keep your mouth open at all times. Get in the habit of asking anyone and everyone what they do, whom they know, where they have been lately. Curiosity opens the most unexpected doors. I once asked a woman at the dry cleaner's where she got the Maine sticker on her car and discovered she had taught at a camp

in that state where I had been trying to establish a contact for several months.

- Keep your ears open at all times. Listen more closely than you usually do to what people say about themselves, where they have been, who they have met along the way. Be curious about everyone's travels and meanderings.

► How to Acquire a Personal ◄ Referral Network

There are three basic rules for acquiring contacts:

The Best Time to Look for Contacts Is When You Are Not Looking for Contacts   When you are in a desperate hurry to find the right contact, you will probably turn this person off with your impatience. You will also probably fail to relax enough to ask the best questions, wait patiently for the answers, and allow the person the freedom to reflect. You will be focused less on the person and more on your own private anxieties, and this will transform him into a functionary for you, which he will not like at all.

The less pressure you feel to ask the person for direct job information, the more likely you are to develop a comfortable rapport, talk easily about your mutual enthusiasms, and give the other the space in which to offer personal referrals without feeling compelled to do so. I can only conclude that you should be looking for personal referrals *at all times*, especially when you are under no pressure to change your work, when you are satisfied with what you are doing.

You Never Really Know Who You Are Talking To   Take, for instance, the man who went to a magazine office one day to get some back issues, fell into conversation with the receptionist, asked her a few questions about her work, got interested a little in her as a person, and, lo and behold, discovered she was the niece of the magazine publisher, just working there for the summer. She introduced him to her uncle, who led him to the newspaper editor he had been wanting to meet. There is nothing at all mysterious about the skill of generating personal referrals. To some extent, you may have been doing it naturally all your life. Now make it more conscious and systematic, and you will have your hand gripped tightly around the throttle.

Always, Always Ask for the Names of Other Contacts   You can then say: "So-and-so suggested I call you." These linkages between colleagues, friends, or associates in the same line of work are your magical door openers. If you fail to take advantage of these connections, your work search will bog down.

▶ Don't Get Ahead of Yourself ◀

When you set about meeting people who have the power to hire you, it is important that you keep the brakes on and resist the temptation to rush headlong into asking someone to hire you on the spot. Proceed slowly. Give the person reasons to be interested in you. Give the personal referral and information-seeking process a chance to work in your favor. Don't pervert it by asking for too much too quickly.

Don't play the hidden agenda game. Don't ask to see people on the pretense of wanting information and advice, when you are sneakily trying to edge close and ask for a job. This tactic insults the other person and may haunt you for the remainder of your job search. Let the interview be a pleasant and nonthreatening one. If the person volunteers information about job leads, that is so much gravy for you, but not something you asked for.

▶ People Who Should Become ◀
Your Close Friends

Regardless of where you are searching for better work or what kind of work you desire, when you arrive in your chosen location, there are certain categories of people who are always in a favored position to be helpful to you. They are special people because they have more knowledge of the citizenry than almost anyone else in town. They are also people you would be likely to ignore if you had not read this book because they are part of the human landscape of any town, but not officially designated as job information experts. They would not think of themselves as such, but they are, nevertheless.

Policemen Probably no individual sees more of what occurs in a town or makes it his business to know more occupations and what they are doing than the policeman. He knows where the bank presidents are, where the dope pushers hang out, and where the politicians can be found when the legislature is not in session. He has to know these things because he depends on these people for information when he needs it. People make it their business to know him, so he has a continuing flow of information.

Bartenders and Beauticians These folks may well see a steadier stream of people on an individual basis than anyone else. For this reason, they know not only who does what kinds of work, but how they feel about it, the organizations they work for, and probably who's going where, how it all happens, and when the openings will occur. No one ever accused a bartender, beautician, or barber of being 100 percent accurate about his or her information, but you are less concerned with total accuracy than with getting leads and gathering data.

Cab and Bus Drivers These people are the traveling bartenders and beauticians. They too have the gift of gab; they get a rider's ear because they are anonymous and catch him breathless between engagements, ready to spill the latest crisis. Unlike the bartenders, they may not know the names or even the faces, but they know a lot about who's doing what to whom and where you should go to learn more.

Other People Supplying Personal Services This category includes manicurists, masseurs, masseuses, house cleaners, and a variety of others with whom you come in personal contact. Many of these people acquire a great deal of information from the people they routinely see, their regular customers or occasional contacts. They usually enjoy sharing this information. It is part of the reward of *their* work. Make them happy; encourage them to talk at will.

Retailers Anyone who operates a retail establishment of any kind—grocery, clothing shop, toy store, sporting goods store—sees a lot of customers and tries to know them as well as possible. He also does his best to find out which customers occupy positions of prominence because it may affect his sales.

Secretaries/Receptionists These people are gatekeepers; they have the keys to the executive chambers and the knowledge of everyone's comings and goings. They have to know the people they serve in order to survive the daily blizzard of inquiries. They are your experts in discovering where the target people can be found, who is grumpy to talk with at what time of day, and how the information you need can be obtained without violating anyone's privacy, sanity, or company regulations. They can lead you to your destiny or frustrate you at every turn, depending on how well or how poorly you have persuaded them that you are worth helping.

Librarians These almost forgotten people would probably escape your attention in any work search where you are walking streets, taking buses, and focusing on office buildings. However, librarians know more than most of us about almost everything because they are surrounded by so many resources. Even if they don't have the exact sources directly at hand, librarians are some of the few people who see it (usually) as their professional *obligation* to help you find what you want. Librarians are detectives by another name.

► How to Avoid ◄
Problems with Networks

Like any good idea, the personal referral network—often called networking or making contacts—has been overused, overdone, overbaked, and its users often complain it is underproductive. "I have loads of contacts but they don't seem to lead anywhere." "I network all the time, but I am just not meeting the right people."

Contacts are necessary to any effective job search, but you cannot build an entire strategy around them. People will not hire you just because you know them or happen to have wangled an interview with them. The overburdening of the PRN is evident in these problems:

- People try to make networking a substitute for competence.
- Networking has the potential of becoming a king-sized nuisance, and the people who overuse it are quickly labeled pests.
- We have taken innocent human interchange and raised it to the level of a high art, thereby destroying its spontaneity and making it more difficult for everyone. People who become contacts now wonder: "Who is this person talking to me and for what reasons?"

Networking functions best when it is part of a daily routine, not when it is used all at once and must carry the burden of a hurry-up job search. Too much reliance upon contacts can become offensive to those who are being tapped. A personal referral network should occur naturally, not by brute force.

The principles of networking are still valid. But those who are new to networking should use them in moderation, and those who are experienced should know better than to try squeezing more from contacts than they are willing to provide.

Some job hunters seem to follow the motto "Take the contact and run" in their rush to keep moving toward their goals. They get referrals but they do not produce results. Why not? Because often they have "turned off" the contact by their methods.

The key here is credibility. If I do not know enough about you, or you don't stop long enough to tell me, or you ask me for more than is appropriate for a relative stranger, I will give you a referral with little enthusiasm, or give you a contact of little value, or give you nothing at all. Why would I act this way? Because I do not want to lose credibility among *my* contacts. I have more at stake with these contacts than you do. I want to refer only those people who will present themselves well.

▶ Types of Contacts ◀ and How to Use Them

Much of the difficulty in personal referral networks comes from misunderstanding what a contact can and cannot do for you. Contacts are assumed to be all things to all people, but they are not. Different kinds of contacts serve different purposes, and you must take care not to overreach your expectations.

The power of contacts has been romanticized and griped over for a long time: "You gotta have 'pull' to get ahead." "It's not what you know, but who you know." Notwithstanding the large share of contact power held by wealthy, highly placed people (they don't need to read this book), *you* can get your fair share of contact power and more if you use your contacts wisely and observe the differences among them. Contacts are available to anyone.

1. Friends and Relations

These are people who know and love you. Well, some of them at least like you and are willing to try helping you however they can. You may believe that *your* friends and relatives don't know anyone, but they do. One or the other knows bankers, venture capitalists, horse traders, musicians, computer experts, well-known politicians, and even an occasional movie star. Either they know them through their own work, or socially, or through community organizations. A list of these kinds of contacts appears below.

What they *can* do: (a) Give you names of people who work in organizations that interest you; (b) Comment about your personal characteristics, tell someone you're an okay person, worth talking to.

What they *cannot* do: (a) Serve as references, because they cannot comment on the quality of your work; (b) Lead you to every field of work or industry, because their contacts may not be that broad.

2. References

These are people for whom you have worked in the past. Usually these "bosses" are in a position to know some folks in their profession, and if you impressed them, they'll try to help you make a good move. Focus on those who liked your work best, and give less attention to the others. If it has been a while since you worked for someone, give him/her a summary (in writing and in person) of what you have been doing, your accomplishments, and your ambitions.

What they *can* do: (a) Identify possible new employers for you, especially if you are staying in the same field of work, but are making a change for legitimate reasons; (b) Comment about the quality of your work, work habits, and key skills.

There are no serious limitations on what a good reference can do to support your application. Be careful not to overuse them. Concentrate your references on the jobs you want most.

3. People in the World of Work

These are individuals with whom you have talked about their work. You introduced yourself, or perhaps you were referred by a friend or another type of contact. These people are complete strangers to you when you first meet them, but if you do a good job as an interviewer, they can be helpful to you.

What they *can* do for you: (a) Give you information and insight about the fields of work they represent; (b) Refer you to others in their field, but they may not know the key people that you would like to see.

What they *cannot* do: (a) Give a reference for you, because they do not know about your work record; (b) Tell you where the jobs are in their field, because often they do not know. Occasionally they will hear about an opportunity, but there are more than they know about. Don't be bothered by this. You'll find out about openings on your own.

4. People You Have Worked With

This category includes your coworkers from previous jobs. They know many people in various industries where you might like to be. Often these contacts are the best, because they know you the best. Many are both friends and colleagues. They know your good and your bad points, but that enables them to make referrals that carry authenticity. If a person in this category sends you to someone else, you can expect a positive reception.

What they *can* do for you: (a) Comment about the quality of your work, your key skills, etc.; (b) Refer you to people in their field and others, sometimes including the decision makers.

What they *cannot* do for you: Give you access to everyone you want. Every professional has some contacts, but there are many more whom they don't know at all. Don't lean too heavily on your coworkers to get the proverbial foot in the door. Some of these connections you will have to generate yourself.

5. People You Meet Socially

These are people you meet when you're out having fun. Sometimes you seek them as contacts by design and other times it just happens unexpectedly. Many good contacts are made through parties or other social occasions, but do not be too quick to assume that this is where most of your networking opportunities are. Some people just don't socialize, and others are resistant to being networked when they are away from work. Take what comes and don't present yourself as hustling or trying hard to meet people who can help you, because the results will be counterproductive.

What they *can* do for you: (a) Give you names of people to talk with; (b) Refer you as a person they find "likable" and "worth talking to"; (c) Occasionally give brief on-the-spot information interviews.

What they *cannot* do for you: (a) Comment about the quality of your work; (b) Sometimes they cannot do what they say they can. Name-dropping at parties is common. Sometimes you will get a referral and find out the person who gave it hardly knows the contact at all.

The main message is this: Do not expect or demand too much from any individual. A contact is a favor granted. There are usually limits to what a person can or will do for you. Be grateful for what you do get, try to get referrals when you can, and then move deftly on.

► The World Runs on ◄
Personal Referral Networks

Remember that over 80 percent of the people in the nation work for companies that employ sixty or fewer people. These small employers depend upon networking, on referrals, and on front-door traffic.
—Kirby Stanat,
in *Careers Without Reschooling*[3]

Referrals are important for the employer as well as for you. Both small and large employers take advantage of them. It may sometimes seem unfair that people get jobs through contacts, but it is not. Many of the best hiring decisions will always be made this way, because employers prefer sources of information they can trust. Thus, you owe it to yourself to use the power of personal referral. If you have good contacts, use them. If you lack contacts, use the principles in this chapter to build networks in fields where you need them.

► Exercises for Developing a ◄
Personal Referral Network

► Exercise One

1. Stop the first five people you encounter today in your usual routine. Don't be concerned about who they are or whether they are relevant to your intended work.
2. Ask each person: "Do you know anyone who does the kind of work I am looking for and would this person be willing to meet with me informally to answer a few of my questions?"
3. How many of these people were able to give you a referral to another person of some relevance to you, without having to think very hard or refer to any written lists?

► Exercise Two

Choose the name of an employing organization at random from the Yellow Pages. How many people in your neighborhood must you query before you discover someone who knows a person who works there? It may be as few as one, two, or three in a small town. Even in a large city, if you cheat by crossing town to the right neighborhood, you will be pleasantly surprised at the results.

► Exercise Three

Review any checklist of one hundred or more occupations and ask yourself: "In how many of these categories do I know at least one person who does it?" If you have lived and worked in your own city for a while, chances are you can tick off at least half of the list. I tried it for myself and managed 89 of a list of 125 occupations.

► Exercise Four

Choose any two occupational titles at random and imagine how many different other occupations would have connections between these two.

> EXAMPLE ► Plumber—insurance broker. Connecting occupations: home assessor, contractor, city manager, and others.

▶ **Exercise Five**

Identify the occupation of your next-door neighbor and imagine how you could use his or her working acquaintances to help you link up with a particular kind of employer.

> EXAMPLE ▶ If your neighbor is an oil company representative and you desire to meet a publisher, use the neighbor to contact the city manager, who will help you contact the Board of Education, which can lead you to textbook salespeople, who then lead easily to the publishers themselves.

9

Information Interviewing

There is something elegantly simple about the information interview. You *talk* to people and, as long as you do it properly, good things tend to happen. Why has it been necessary to tell people that they need to talk with each other? In other spheres of life, checking with other people is natural. You wouldn't buy a car without asking around, getting opinions, and building a mental file of information, would you? Even your decision whether to see a movie often depends on what others say about it. So, why do we have to be coached to track down information about jobs and careers that we are thinking of making our own?

The answer is that people have treated the job world as if it were an impenetrable fortress, where you have to find crowbars to break in and see what is going on there. The emergence of personnel hiring procedures has contributed to this perception. Personnel offices exist as much to keep people out as to let people in.

While the information interview may not free you entirely from the shackles of personnel hiring systems, it certainly gives you a superior method for getting information about fields of work and jobs that you cannot obtain from books or formal job descriptions. For example, you can seek answers to questions such as:

What kinds of educational and experience backgrounds do the other workers in this department have?
What is the pace of work here—frenetic, relaxed, off and on, high volume?
What are the ways in which this field is changing?

Information interviewing exists to answer the questions that *cannot* be answered by anything in print that describes the field, the industry,

132

the organization, or the job that interests you. Sure, you could get some of those questions answered in formal interviews. But why wait until then? You may find out things about the job that dissuade you from applying, and therefore save yourself a lot of trouble. Or, you may learn things that fire you up and make you a much more enthusiastic job candidate.

Many have known about and used the information interview for a long time—rich folks and their clubby interconnections, people in small towns or small companies where insights about the jobs travel like brush fires, and people in tightly organized professions where practitioners often visit each others' offices or talk on the phone and share information, opinions, and the latest revelations.

But you may not have any of these advantages. Either your field of work is too big to know many people in it, or your city is too large to have natural connections, or you're changing from one career to another, or you are a long distance from the job markets that you want.

In these cases, the formal methods of information gathering (job announcements, company literature) are weak, so you must rediscover your talking muscles and put them to use. Once you have exhausted everything available in print (which often is not very much), you must move to the telephone and the in-person contact. In most any job search, they're the best games in town.

Information interviewing has had a meteoric rise in the recent literature and practice of job hunting. It is a household phrase for everyone engaged in the job search, and is regarded as an indispensable tool, one that works for high-level jobs as well as lower ones, for organizations of all sizes, for professional jobs as well as others. Popularized by Richard Bolles's *What Color Is Your Parachute?* and other books (the first edition of this book, Richard Irish's *Go Hire Yourself an Employer*, and Tom Jackson's *The Hidden Job Market*), this concept is now used by millions of job seekers.

Though the validity of information interviewing has been amply demonstrated, its rapid elevation to stardom may have been too fast for its own good.

- Job seekers expect that doors will fly open and job openings will materialize soon after they utter the magic words: "I want to ask for your advice about entering your field of work."
- Many job hunters use the method amateurishly. They exaggerate the extent to which a person will enjoy talking about his/her work, bumble in without much preparation, and often overstay their welcome, thus negating any positive impression they might have created otherwise.
- Job hunters often overdo it, operating on the theory that a hundred information interviews are ten times better than ten of them. Just

like mailing a carload of résumés and waiting for the job offers to pile in, they push for safety in numbers and thereby treat each individual interview hurriedly and perhaps carelessly.

- Even people who are not job hunting at all make the mistake of calling hard-working professionals out of the blue, interrupting their workdays, and launching into a series of difficult questions ("What are the main trends in your field?" "What do you think is the best approach for a person with my background?" "How do I deal with the credential problem in your field?") that put the respondents on the spot and ensure that all they will do is try to get off the phone as fast as possible.
- Worst of all, job searchers often crudely attempt to use the information interview to set up job interviews, even though they have been cautioned to resist that temptation.

While many people avoid these errors and use the information interview process well, large numbers of others do not. Furthermore, the sheer number of *Parachute* readers and other career changers has created a flood of information seekers in the offices of working people. Predictably, employers and professionals have caught on to this trend and have dug in their heels, learning ways to resist the advances of newly coached "information interviewers." Their work time is valuable and they are making more careful judgments about whom to see and which information seekers to turn away.

The concept of information interviewing is still quite sound: (1) You should seek as much information as you can, because you need it to actively *choose* the job or career that suits you best; (2) People may help you greatly, in ways that printed materials and secondhand informants cannot.

You cannot afford to conduct your job search without information interviewing. But, you had better do it right, or the potential gains will turn to losses. If you are well organized, do research in advance, ask answerable questions, moderate your expectations, and show sensitivity to the person and the situation, you will probably get good advice and perhaps some referrals to others. If you misuse your opportunity, you'll get very little and may even produce irritation.

Three keys to successful information interviews seem to be:

1. *Information* (a) Reading in advance about the field, the organization, and even the person, so that you can ask informed questions; and (b) Having a clear idea of the information that you most need to know.
2. *Introduction* If possible, get yourself introduced to the target person by someone you know, or at least be able to say "_____ suggested that I call to ask if you might meet with me."

3. *Integrity* Make the purposes of your interview very plain on the phone, respect the limits of what a person can do for you, and then don't fudge at all about your stated objectives.

A detailed list of cautions is given on pages 139–141 with explanations about how to use the information interview most productively.

► Levels of the Information ◄ Interview

Information interviews can have different purposes. You should be aware of them, use them all, and state your purpose clearly when you request a meeting with someone. The purpose of your interview will vary according to the amount of information you already have. You will probably do Level 1 interviews before you move on to Level 2, etc. However, it is not necessary to reach Level 5 in order to begin having job interviews. You may reach Level 2, 3, or 4 and feel you are ready. Use these various levels as they suit your particular situation.

► Level 1: Background Research on a Field of Work

This type of information interview is used when you know very little about a field or an industry and are deciding if you want to get serious about pursuing this kind of work. Use it to learn about work responsibilities, life-styles, work conditions, and so on; to learn as much as possible while accumulating acquaintances from people in that field. Interviews for this purpose should be started many months before you intend actively to pursue a change of employment. You will have many of these interviews across a long period of time.

Certain behaviors are permissible in this type of interview that are ordinarily not desirable in a formal job interview. You may make an appointment on the spot, without the benefit of a previous phone call or contact, if you desire this approach and if the respondent is willing to see you. You may also bring a notepad with you and take notes occasionally, being careful not to let note taking detract from the attention you give the other person.

Typically, you should ask for about fifteen minutes of the person's time. You may well end up with more time than this, if you ask interesting questions and succeed in getting the other person to talk about him- or herself (not hard to accomplish), but you should not make a point of asking for a long meeting.

When you make your initial approach, smile warmly at the receptionist, secretary, or target person. People like friendliness, especially from strangers; it makes the day a little brighter. A good initial approach to the secretary is to say something like, "I need to know more about the organization and its purposes." Act as though you know why you are there, because you do. Do not be timid about your request. If you are confident you know what you want, others will feel comfortable with you; if you are unsure of yourself, they will not be sure why they should want to see you (see Chapter 13: Assertiveness). Let the other person talk as much as possible. Don't try to control the conversation any more than you must in order to ask the questions you desire. Be genuinely interested. Remember that you are talking to a human being who has strong feelings about that work; you must *really want* to hear those feelings. If you are just going through the motions in order to get to someone higher up, the person you are interviewing will sense your insincerity.

When you complete a meeting, always ask the interviewee to refer you to someone else in the field of work, if you are still interested in it.

▶ **Level 2: Researching a Type of Organization**

The purpose of this method is to investigate a specific type of employer within a field of work. For example, you may want to know about organizations offering services for the mentally retarded, now that a Level 1 interview helped you to become interested in social science. Level 2 interviews are extremely useful. You should do much of your information interviewing at this level, because you can focus on the type of employer you want, without zeroing in on a potential job.

The character of the Level 2 interview is similar to that of Level 1. You are exploring, becoming familiar with the type of organization, and asking the questions which will help you decide where you want to focus your job search energies:

Does your organization prefer to stay medium sized? If so, why?
How do you locate the students who want internships?
How is your store competing with the larger clothing chains?
Is funding for the agency holding up these days? Where are you seeking supplemental support?
Does an editor's job usually involve acquiring new books as well as editing them?

▶ **Level 3: Finding out Where the Jobs Might Be**

Let's face it. By talking to people, we're hoping to tap the hidden job market, find out about those positions which are not advertised but are becoming available. It is necessary to look for these possibilities because the hidden job market is a continuing fact of life. Many jobs are publicized only on a limited basis or not at all. So, why don't you just come right out and ask about them?

Well, you can, but you should be careful about it, and probably leave this question aside until you have gathered other types of information. You should not make this your only objective for any information interview. People do not want to be job exchange bureaus. They may know about job possibilities, but sometimes they will resent being asked by a person who is largely a stranger to them. Remember, in any meeting you are building a relationship and forming an impression. If I am the person you're talking to, and I happen to know about some job openings, I may not want to tell you about them unless I have enough confidence in you that I want to refer you. The openings I know about are probably connected with friends of mine. I don't want to waste their time (and perhaps hurt my credibility in the process) by sending them people of uncertain quality. So, you have to earn your referral from me, and not ask for it prematurely.

What should you do about all this? First, hope that the person brings it up him/herself. If the person likes you, and is impressed by how you have conducted the interview, he/she may want to be helpful to you, and would have every reason to tell you about places where jobs may be. Often people will be thinking about these openings when they are talking with you. Even if they don't know about real live openings, they may suggest places where they judge there are possibilities. Let them do the suggesting. Don't push it.

Second, if you can't restrain yourself—and sometimes your instincts will tell you it is all right to ask—wait until the end of your interview and say: "I am very interested in this field, and think I may look for jobs in it. Could you suggest any places where I might apply?" Once again, don't push this very hard. A simple prompt may be enough to get a lead or two, if the person knows of any and wants to give them to you.

If you do not find much at Level 3 for the time being, don't be too disappointed. If you do your information interviewing wisely and systematically, eventually the odds will turn in your favor. There are enough hidden jobs out there that you will find some before too long. The better you handle yourself in each information interview, the more likely you will hear of an opening that fits your interests and abilities.

► **Level 4: Exploring a Particular Organization**

Usually, once you have done many Level 2 interviews, you will be focusing on a certain department within an organization, because you know the kind of work you want, and you want to talk with people who do it. At this level, you usually know there exists a job opening or a strong likelihood of one.

You have some interest in applying to this organization, but you would like to know more about it. You're not sure what the job responsibilities are and need some insights about how the department functions. Be sure to indicate that you are considering applying for the job, so that you are honest about your purposes. You might ask questions such as:

How does this job fit with the purposes of your department?
What do you hope the person in this job will accomplish?
Which people in your department and organization does this job relate to most often?

You can have a Level 4 interview with any member of the department, not just the person who makes the final decisions. Regardless of whom you talk with, remember that any conversation you have at this level, no matter how informal, will contribute to the impression you make as a prospective job candidate. If an employer agrees to see you for a Level 4 interview, he/she probably considers it an informal job interview, even though neither of you may refer to it as such.

Level 4 information interviews are often arranged through your friends, professional colleagues, or people who know you well. Typically, it might go this way: You ask around if anyone knows someone who works in the target organization/department. Hopefully, you find a friend who says: "Call ——— over there and ask her if she'd be willing to talk with you. I have known her for years and I think she can give you a few ideas about that department. I'll call her too and let her know she'll be hearing from you."

In the absence of such contacts, it is more difficult to get Level 4 interviews. But, if you need more information before you go to the trouble of submitting formal applications, go ahead and request them on your own. One good Level 4 interview can save you a lot of time and make you a better job candidate.

► **Level 5: Talking with Decision Makers**

This level of information interview has been widely recommended as a means for getting the closest possible look at a job, prior to a job interview. At Level 5, you seek a meeting with the person who has the power to hire and ask him/her questions about the job, all the while presenting yourself in a way that he/she will remember you when you apply. It can be valuable to have such Level 5 interviews, and often it is possible to arrange them. However, employers are increasingly resistant to them, because they cannot accommodate the large numbers of information interviewers, and because often they would prefer to do their evaluating during the selection process. Sometimes they even regard such requests as an intrusion, so you have to be careful whom you approach and how at Level 5. Here are the main cautions:

1. If you are considering applying for the job, be sure to say so.
2. Once again, working through friends is the preferred method. You're more likely to get a Level 5 interview if you call and say: "———— suggested I contact you . . ."
3. If you don't have any connection to the decision maker, just tell him/her: "I have done a lot of research on your department and the specific job, but I still have some questions I have not been able to answer and thought you could help me." Be prepared to explain what research you have done, if you are asked.

Most people who make hiring decisions are aware that a Level 5 interview closely resembles a job interview, even though you do not call it by that name. When you ask to meet with them informally, if they accept, they will regard it as a chance to get acquainted with you. That's fine, but you should proceed with your agenda for an information interview. Of course, if you are asked questions about yourself, be ready to answer them. If the decision maker decides to make it an informal job interview, that is his/her choice, and you must be ready to flow with it.

An interview at this level may be a way to stand out from the pack. If you can get in to see the decision maker—and otherwise you would have been just a name on a piece of paper—then anything you accomplish here might give you an edge over the other applicants. So, in a competitive situation, it is worth the effort. In many cases, the decision maker will appreciate your self-initiating and will judge that as a measure of your motivation. Level 5 interviews don't always happen, but you should definitely try to arrange them.

► Guidelines for Using the ◄ Information Interview to Your Best Advantage

We are not dealing with a new concept anymore, one that other job seekers will be unaware of. The word is out, and everyone is using this method to get an edge. Hence, you must extract the best results from the information interview and take care to avoid its pitfalls. You can stay well ahead of the competition if you use it wisely, because so many people abuse the concept and make bad impressions when they are trying to gain an advantage.

Here are some key guidelines for before, during, and after the information interview, which will enable you to develop a valuable pool of information and obtain a lot of personal support along the way:

1. *Do not be overly assertive.* Tact and diplomacy go a long way. You are asking for a person's valuable work time. Don't regard getting in as the main goal. You may get in the door through manipulating a secretary or catching a person at a weak moment, but if you are too insistent about it, the person you interview will undoubtedly remember to forget you.

2. *Be interested in the person you're talking with.* There is a tendency among information interviewers to regard the person they're talking with as "one more name and face to connect with, so I can move on toward my goal." People you interview may feel you are using them to get to someone else. While we all understand this is the way the world works, each individual still wants to be valued for him/herself, not just be another connection in a string of electric lights leading to your job interview. Genuineness goes a long way in this game, and rushing through an interview to get a connection or a key fact will not make a good impression for you. Don't follow the example of one job seeker I know who said to a person at a conference cocktail party: "It's been nice getting a few names from you but excuse me, I've got to keep networking now."

3. *Be open about everything you are doing.* Don't mislead anyone about what you are up to. If you want to know who the decision maker is in a particular department, because you plan to call there, then say so. If you have already applied for a particular job, but are still seeking information about it (which is legitimate), then tell the person you are a candidate. If you withhold some information or lie about something, it will probably come back to haunt you. Any hint of sneakiness in the job search process will undo much of the progress you are making, because an employer will regard you as untrustworthy.

4. *Be willing to talk with someone else, when you cannot see the person you asked for.* Often you will ask to interview a person who is not available. In most cases, there are other people in that department or organization who can be helpful to you. If you do not know their names, say: "I would like to know more about the ——— functions in this department. Is anyone available who could talk with me?" Any interview that you have is valuable. Especially at Levels 1 and 2, it is not crucial that you talk with particular people, to get general information about a field or an organization. Even at Levels 3, 4, and 5, if the target

person cannot be seen (as is often the case), then talk with anyone who can give you some time. Pleasant surprises happen this way. You meet someone who works closely with the target person, and you may accomplish as much as if you had met with your original target.

5. *Tell the person how he/she has helped you.* Anyone you interview may want to keep track of how your job search is going. We're all curious to see how the story turns out. As you proceed in your search, call back the people you interviewed and tell them how it is going, and what they told you that was especially useful. You can also offer such feedback during the information interview itself: "What you have told me about the company structure, and the way you handle multiple orders, is very revealing. It helped me to see that . . ." People like to know that their words have been heard and have had an effect. Don't assume they know this. Tell them. Often this can be accomplished with a personal and detailed thank-you note, but you can also telephone a person to express your thanks or even stop by to see them if the organization is a more informal one.

6. *Use the telephone when they cannot see you in person.* A telephone interview is not a waste of time. A few questions on the phone can save you and them a lot of time. Once again, it helps to have a referral: "——— recommended that I call you." Be sensitive to the person's telephone availability: "Is this a good time to ask you just two questions, or would you rather I call later?"

7. *Sample widely.* Every time you interview individuals about their work, you run the risk that what they tell you will be biased, colored by the particular lenses through which they see the situation. Therefore, you must sample as widely as possible among people who work in your field of interest. Take special care to include some of each of the following:

Happy workers—people who are pleased with what they are doing

Unhappy workers—people who are dissatisfied with the nature of the work itself

People who have different frames of reference toward their work, perhaps because of their previous work history

The career bureaucrat in government work, for instance, has a different perspective and set of attitudes about the job than does an academic person who works in government for a year or two on a temporary assignment.

10

Library Research

A great deal of the information about your intended employers is in readily available printed form—annual reports, newsletters, company magazines, articles in the commercial press, and brochures describing products and services available.

Job seeking can be a war of paper airplanes. Your paper credentials—résumés and the like—are pitted against the employer's paper job requirements. Read what the organizations have to say about themselves and turn their words to your advantage. You can demonstrate your devotion and good intentions with substantive knowledge instead of repeating a tired litany: "I wanna work here; I wanna work here."

You have probably been cultivating research and library skills for several years of your life and could produce information and references at will for a topic to be discussed in a formal classroom situation. It would be a sad quirk of human development if you should suddenly abandon these research skills when perhaps you need them most.

Once you have identified an organization or place where you would like to work (prospect list) and have identified people who can tell you more about that organization (personal referral network), you are ready to gather as much information as possible about the people and institution where you hope to be employed. You are ready for in-depth research of a few target employers. While I have stressed that personal research is usually the most powerful, you should also get data through the use of printed materials.

In its simplest terms, making use of printed materials involves locating any form of published material that can expand your pool of career information. Such information can be as broad as that which describes an entire occupational field that interests you (for instance, architecture), or it can concentrate on the particular company, organization, or department you seek. Published information can also help you illuminate the background of a given individual with whom you would like to work.

The knowledge you get from printed materials enables you to do a crucial thing: to act like a professional. When you are seeking entry to a profession, it helps to adopt the attitude that you already *are* in that profession; to regard yourself not as an outsider, but as a person who has decided this field is the right one. Your research is the first step in establishing your right to be regarded as a respected member of the group. Though you may not yet have the credentials, degrees, or other imprimatur for that profession, you can behave as though you *will* be so accredited one day; it's just a matter of time. Your attitude will influence others' behavior toward you and the seriousness with which they respond to your requests. Therefore, the research skill is important because it is an opportunity to demonstrate that you are so serious about your future work that you will devote time to becoming better informed.

► Make Good Use of Libraries ◄

Libraries are invaluable resources. The bigger ones have vast collections of materials helpful to job hunting, including industrial reference books, employment directories, annual reports, pamphlets, and catalogues of every kind. In addition, libraries contain another wonderfully useful source of limitless information: librarians.

When asking a reference librarian for information about your topic or prospective employer, be careful to be neither too specific nor too general in your request.

> If you were to go to a grocery store, and ask specifically for oranges, you might get the answer, "Sorry, we don't have any." And you would leave empty-handed. But if you were to ask for breakfast fruit, the same clerk might suggest grapes, prunes or apricots, any of which would serve your purpose. . . . At the same time, if you were to make your request so general as to ask for "food," the storekeeper would hardly know where to start looking unless you carefully explained what you wanted it for and why.[1]

If you ask the reference librarian, "What kinds of information do you have on scientific research?" your question is so general as to make an answer difficult. On the other hand, "What information do you have about research laboratories for organic tree sprays?" is too specific. A manageable question lies between the two extremes: "Can you give me information about chemistry laboratories involved in scientific research and development?"

The research librarian will tell you that one of the best resources you can use is *Subject Collections: A Guide to Special Book Collections in Libraries*.[2] *Subject Collections* tells you whether your local library, or the metropolitan or university library in the neighboring town, has special information that relates to your work search. If, for example, you are seeking employment with a food-processing company, and the library has a collection of books on cooking, you might profit from a visit to that collection.

Library research affords you an opportunity to acquire a historical perspective on your subject, because you can review what the organization has done for a long time, perhaps see trends, and possibly sense what it will do in the future.

► How to Research an ◄ Occupational Field

Any one or more of these sources is handy for researching an occupational field:

Professional Organizations See the *Encyclopedia of Associations* for whichever group pertains to your interest. Write to this group and ask for printed literature. It will be pleased to honor your request because it exists for the purpose of promoting its profession to you and others.

Local Societies Many areas of work have their local societies as well as their national groups. Ask anyone in town who does this kind of work where the local group keeps its library materials.

There may be many small or large professional societies in your area, all of which are communications agencies for the membership they represent. You can visit many of them and learn how to reach their members by simply making a polite request.[3]

Book References *Books in Print* is available in any library or bookstore. It lists all the books written lately, organized by subject, author, and title. You can find in it a listing of books on the occupational topic you seek to research.

Periodical References The *Reader's Guide to Periodical Literature,* the *New York Times Index,* and the *Wall Street Journal Index* are three standard reference works available in any library. They allow you to research magazine and newspaper articles pertaining to your subject area. If you are focusing on pharmaceutical companies, for example, use *Reader's Guide* or the *New York Times Index* to tell you all the articles that have been written lately about drugs, drug abuse, pharmacology, and so on.

Join the Professional Group Perhaps the best way to act like a professional is to join the professional society itself, so that you can attend conferences, correspond with members, receive journals, and be eligible for in-service training workshops.

If you seek employment in private industry, cultivate the habit of reading one or more of these publications: the *Wall Street Journal, U.S. News and World Report, Fortune* magazine, *Business Week,* and *Money* magazine. All these journals and others are directly involved in telling you about *change,* the shifts of human behavior and attitude that have implications for the marketplace. If you come across an article entitled "Population Shifts to the Sunbelt Region," for instance, you can conclude that more jobs will be available in the southeastern and southwestern states. "Physical Fitness Activity Upsurge" may indicate that leisure industries that market fitness equipment can expect to prosper. "Water Problems in the Nation's Rivers" implies that scientists will be needed to improve water testing and control indiscriminate use.

► How to Research a ◄ Specific Organization

To research a specific employer, these sources of published information are most readily available:

Annual Reports The first source you should seek is the annual report of the company or organization, because it offers a summary of all the operations for the year, products involved, highlight events, and names of key personnel, plus budgetary data you may want to see.

Organization Chart This chart shows all the departments and how they report and relate to each other. If it does not appear in the annual report or any of the other company publications, call the public relations office of the company and ask if one is available. If not, ask one of your personal referrals to see whether he or she can get you a copy.

Stock Reports This is a more unbiased source of information and is available at any stockbroker's office for an organization that is publicly owned. Several research services provide the brokers with data that can help you analyze the company's potential for growth, stability, and other relevant factors.

Library References   The *Reader's Guide*, the *New York Times Index*, and the *Wall Street Journal Index* can help you locate quickly and easily stories that have been written about an individual company, government agency, or other employer, provided the employer is prominent enough to rate news space.

House Organs   While you are asking for annual reports and the like, request a copy of the organization's in-house newspaper or magazine, which gives inside stories about company operations that are more up to date than what appears in an annual report.

Public Relations Office   Ask this office for any other printed materials that can help you. The staff will know about company reports you cannot identify by name, company magazines they would like to send you, and so on.

Local Newspapers   Get in the habit of reading the local paper each day to see whether your prospective employer is mentioned. Perhaps an exposé of company graft, maybe a citation by the mayor will appear.

Historical Society   If you are dying to know more about how this organization got started and the library fails you, try whatever historical group there is in town. Such groups sometimes keep documents no one else cares about.

► How to Find Out About ◄ Specific People

To obtain vital background data on individuals who are employed at your target organizations, especially those who will eventually make the hiring decisions, research these people in any of the following publications: *Who's Who in America; Who's Who in the East, Who's Who in the West,* and so on; *American Men and Women of Science; Directory of American Scholars;* and the professional directories of national professional organizations. The directory of the American Psychological Association, for instance, provides a one-paragraph work history and statement of special interest pertaining to every member of the APA.

► Research Is Easy ◄

Why is this skill easy to acquire? Every source mentioned in the previous section—the local library, the stockbroker's office, the public relations office of the company—is easy to find and is staffed by people who usually have a high degree of interest in fulfilling your request. All can be reached by telephone or in person, without a complicated series of maneuvers. In most cases, the data for which you are asking is absolutely free. Most of these places are happy to give their information away because they often feel it promotes their selfish interests to the public, which is none other than you. And you will find that this is an infectious method because the more you know about a target employer, the more your appetite will be whetted for additional data.

PART
III
Communication Skills

Dear Howard:

Most interviewers are so professional at what they do that I am simply overpowered by their command of the process. Because of this, I feel my answers are ones they have heard a thousand times before. Furthermore, they seem so in control that I am happier to let them take over and ask me what they want to ask me. Far be it from me to disturb their professional style with my amateurish inquiries.

Signed,
Awed by Power

Dear Awed Man Out:

Pity the poor interviewers: (1) they know little about you and are hoping to discover what you are like in thirty minutes or less, including your chief strengths, personal qualities, what you'd be like to work with; (2) they know that many interviewees enter the room determined to be passive, and they're thus gloomily preparing themselves for saying the same things they've said a hundred times before; (3) they try to raise their level of excitement and anticipation to what *you* are feeling as you enter the room, but know they cannot simulate it; (4) they can remember only snatches of what's on your résumé; (5) they want *desperately* to hear you say something the others have not said; (6) they struggle to think what they will say next when you look at them blankly and sit very still.

And you are in awe of this? Under the professional veneer of interviewers are individuals who really wish you would accept some responsibility for the two-way exchange so they will not have to use Ouija boards or divining rods to figure out what is inside you.

Interviewers are nervous too, in their own smooth ways. Take them off the hook. Give them a chance to depart from their prepared agendas. Live a little.

Signed,
Howard

► The Interview ◄

The formal job interview is usually handled with great care. It is treated as though it were a sacred event, with high ritual. Many believe it has mystical qualities, that the interviewee must tune in to the special wavelengths of interviewers, adopt certain magical techniques, or adopt a new personality.

In truth, this view of the employment interview as a formal presentation is heavily distorted and surely oversold by those of us who teach others how to conduct the work search. The more you are led to believe that an interview demands acting talent, intense rehearsals, and decoding the interviewer's remarks to trigger the "right" reponses, the more deeply in trouble you will find yourself when you engage in conversation with a prospective employer.

We must demystify this thing we call the interview process. Your success in an interview is a direct result of conversational habits you practice in your routine daily interactions with friends and others in your immediate life space. An interview is nothing more than a conversation between two people who desire information from each other. It has a special focus, but there are certain habits of conversational interchange common to *any* successful interview. I will assume that you know enough about the work by the time you reach the interview to affirm that you have something to offer the employer. Your problem is to *make this known* during the course of your meeting.

► You Conduct Interviews ◄
Every Day

Every time you speak or listen to what someone else is saying, you are most likely engaged in an interview. A job interview is simply a special, artificially contrived example of an ordinary two-way exchange. It is little more than two people trying to know each other better and consider a set of activities they might do jointly. You can bring your interviewing skills into play almost any time because these skills generalize to meetings with prospective employers. Practice interviewing in everyday situations like these: asking the gas station attendant how to get to the theater across town; trying to discover why your children strewed toilet paper all through the house one hour before the in-laws were due to arrive from the West; questioning your tax accountant about how to plan your next year's expenditures; resolving a quarrel with your companion, lover, or friend; explaining to your professor why you've chosen such an arcane topic; or negotiating with your family about a summer vacation trip.

▶ Interview Styles That ◀ Don't Work

There is no particular interview style that works best. In fact, any attempt you make to change your personality for the sake of impressing an interviewer is sure to fail because you will have made the fatal error of trying to be someone else. Here are a few examples of the personalities some people believe to be effective, and the reason why they ultimately self-destruct.

The Chatterer   Never a moment of silence with you. Any lull in the conversation is cheerfully rescued by your witty, inquisitive, anecdotal, charming talk. You believe an interview should race along at top speed, so that the interviewer is overwhelmed by your ability to converse with facility. This approach will fail because the interviewer will feel over-powered, perhaps even insulted, by your need to display conversational talents.

The Counterpuncher   You don't commit or expose yourself or otherwise blunder into conversational error by leading with your jaw. You wait for the interviewer to let you know what is wanted, then give a short, careful response. You show only as much of yourself as you have to because you are terrified you will make a mistake. This careful bobbing and weaving will offend the interviewer because you are so difficult to engage in two-way interchange. Your efforts to be cautious will turn sour because the interviewer wants, above all, to know you in some genuine way.

The Data Blabbermouth   You provide as much evidence as possible that you are knowledgeable, bludgeon the interviewer with facts and figures you have gathered about the organization, drop names, and try to impress with the breadth and depth of your knowledge, even if it's not asked for. While I have emphasized elsewhere in this book that gathering research data is vital preparation for the interview, you will discover that a small display of your knowledge can quickly become overkill that offends because it distracts the interviewer from the more general purposes of your meeting. Information is good to have, but the interview is also a personal exchange.

The Inoffensive Diplomat You were well mannered as a child and carry into adulthood the belief that diplomacy succeeds where insensitive blundering fails. You take care to do whatever the interviewer wishes you to do and let the interviewer control the process. Your task is never to offend and to show that you have the talent for treating people with maximum gentility. This motif distorts the entire purpose of the interview and ultimately makes you appear an obsequious fool because you avoid any answer to a question that has the faintest trace of risk, and you are unwilling to take enough control to ask questions or say things you feel must be said.

The Tiger You take charge at every turn and show your willingness to assume responsibility and be a self-starter by asking leading questions, proposing your own agenda for the interview, and volunteering information you believe the interviewer wants. You reason that the interviewer really likes these qualities and is waiting for you to demonstrate them. This attack posture will ultimately turn on you because you will have taken away the interviewer's power to assume control and obtain certain information regarded as vital. Assertiveness is prized as a quality in job applicants but, taken to an extreme, becomes a display for its own sake rather than a skill that facilitates further discussion.

► Questions Most Typically ◄ Asked in Job Interviews

The content of any job interview has certain commonalities, universal questions every interviewer seeks to have answered, regardless of the type of work being considered. Interviewers typically ask a wide variety of questions. A list of the most common questions follows:

- What career goals have you established for yourself in the next ten years?
- What do you really want to do in life?
- Why should I hire you?
- What qualifications do you have that make you think you'll succeed here?

- What two or three accomplishments have given you the most satisfaction?
- If you were hiring a person for this position, what qualities would you seek?
- Why did you decide to seek a position with this company?
- What two or three things are most important to you in your job?
- Why do you think you'd like to live in this community?
- What have you learned from your mistakes?
- How do you plan to achieve your goals?
- What kind of person are you?
- In what ways will you make a contribution to our organization?
- How do you feel a friend of yours would describe you?
- What are your prominent work habits?
- Why did you choose to enter this career?
- What questions do you have for me?
- In what ways would you change this organization?
- Where else would you like to work, if you couldn't be employed here?
- What motivates you the most?
- Do you work well under pressure?
- What kinds of work situations irritate you?
- What is one significant problem you have overcome and how did you do it?
- What is your chief ambition?
- How much responsibility do you like?

11

Listening

Then there was the story about the host at a party who greeted his guest at the door. The guest wished to discern how closely the host would listen to her, so she said: "I'm sorry to be so late, but I just murdered my husband, and it took me a while to stuff him into the trunk of the car." The host, ever conscious of his role as gracious innkeeper, replied: "Well, it's great to see you; I just hope your husband can make it next time."

Total listening is the fine art of holding your own self in suspended animation while you tune in to all the signals you are receiving from the other person. Listening, in its purest state, is the ability to restrain all your inner thoughts, to keep from rehearsing what you are going to say next, to stifle all connections you may feel between what the other person is saying and your own experience, and finally, to reject the notion that "I've heard that before."

A great listener would wait in stunned silence after the other person had finished talking in order to collect his or her thoughts for a response, not having done this while absorbed in listening. An effective listener would not only absorb all that is being said, but would also be able to report to the other person such a clear understanding of the content and feeling of the speaker's message that the speaker could recognize his or her own messages, stated perhaps even more clearly than they were originally given.

A good listener would make the speaker feel that everything said or about to be said is of great interest, that the next part will be even more worth hearing than what's already been said, and that nothing less than the whole story will be acceptable.

Does this sound like any conversation you have ever had? Has anyone ever listened to your words in a state so enraptured? Of course not. We settle for a lot less than perfection from the people who listen to us because we are happy that anyone listens at all.

All of which explains why an effective listener has a great advantage in a work search. Effective listening is the key to trust in a talking relationship.

Other people are more interested in themselves than in you. This is a cardinal rule, and you must remember it. People who feel you have come to deliver a soliloquy, give a prepared talk, or otherwise monopolize a conversation quickly lose interest in you. What you have to say has little power unless others are interested in hearing it. Their willingness to listen is a direct function of your willingness to show interest in them.

Given half a chance, many interviewers would prefer to talk about themselves, their own problems, anxieties, and ambitions, rather than listen to you. Of course, they are probably expected to listen to you as well, but your ability to allow for their needs in your conversation will influence their attitude toward you.

Furthermore, your ability to hear what they are saying gives you important clues about which of your skills or attributes is most likely to attract their attention. You will not have time to talk about everything you have ever done or are capable of doing; hence, it pays to be selective. Without knowing what the employer wants, you can only guess which parts of your experience or which items on your skill list are most relevant.

Here is an example of a young man who used his listening skills to explore a prospective career and prepare himself for entry into it.

EXAMPLE ► Dan hung around Mr. Karlson's camera shop every Saturday asking questions about the shop, what the customers buy, how Mr. K deals with the clients. In return for his curiosity he heard numerous stories about irascible customers, arguments that had ensued, return of photographic materials, and so forth. Dan even had a chance to witness an occasional spat firsthand. One fine day it occurred to Dan that he could probably handle the irate customers better than Mr. K, if he was given the chance. He proposed a part-time job in which he would field customer complaints. Today he is happily engaged as a partner in the operation of the store.

► Fake Listening ◄

I think you will agree that it is hard to talk about the art of listening because listening—like walking, eating, sleeping—is a thing we do all the time and believe we must be pretty good at by virtue of all the practice we have had. We resist with great passion the very idea that we might have to be taught such a thing. Any fool ought to know how to listen!

The problem is that we have learned pretty well how to *appear* to be listening, how to convince (we think) other people that we are in touch with them and taking it all in. We use certain cues to let others believe we are in touch—looking them in the eye, offering head nods of understanding, uttering uh-huh at appropriate intervals, delivering a knowing smile at just the right time, all this punctuated by "I know just how you feel."

But how many people really see you when they look at you? How often does a series of head nods occur *before* you have completed your thought or even before the sentence has begun? How many yeses, smiles, and other surface gestures are delivered with little connection to what you are saying outside and feeling inside? Is the person *with* you or just creating that appearance by catching enough snatches of conversation to keep the spark of interaction alive long enough to get a chance to talk next?

We have learned the skill of facilitating a conversation smoothly, at the expense of hearing a person fully. We become so preoccupied with keeping the train moving ("What will I do if the other person stops talking and I have nothing to say at that moment?") that we have trouble giving significant attention to what there is to see and hear during the ride. We figure that a conversation ends successfully if both parties were allowed to say something, there was a lot of smiling all around, and neither person made any grave errors or insulted the other too badly. We have learned to settle for less because we do not expect more.

► What Is Real Listening? ◄

You should not confuse listening to a person with listening to a train whistle, a phonograph record, or even a screeching cat. These simpler acts of listening require no particular interpretation, raise no concern about hidden motivations, and place no requirement on you to prepare a response. It is too easy to imagine that listening to a person is equally simple, just preparation of your sense receptors for some sounds that will be immediately understood.

Theodore Reik has referred to listening to human beings as "listening with the third ear."[1] This means that we can hear more than what the words are saying. What is this *more*? Don't people say what they mean?

EXAMPLE ► Marcia talked to her husband many times about her work. She complained of the long hours, the constant squabbling with legislators (she was a lobbyist), the intricate nature of written legislation, the necessity of making deals with everyone in sight. Her husband heard all this, but watched her feelings as she talked. He said to her: "Yes, there are a lot of frustrations about this work, but you seem to get a kick out of the whole struggle." Marcia nodded her agreement after some thought and thanked her husband for listening.

The husband had listened closely with the third ear to what his wife was saying and had "heard" her feeling for the work.

At first glance the term "listening" implies a passive act of taking in the content of the [person's] communication, but actually it involves a very active process of responding to total messages. It includes not only listening with the ears to his/her words and with the eyes to his/her body language, but a total kind of perceptiveness. . . . It means also that we are silent much of the time. . . . When the [listener] can answer in considerable detail the question, "What is going on in this person right now in his/her life space?" s/he is listening with all his/her perceptual capacity.[2]

► Levels of Listening ◄
Behavior

Seldom is effective listening as simple as the previous example suggests. The example illustrates how accurate a listener can be when tuning in to the other person on all wavelengths. Listening begins with wanting to hear what another person has to tell you.

In terms of the previous example, let's take a look inside the husband's mind to see what he was attending to as his wife spoke about her work.

- *Identity*. This is my wife talking; I'm interested in listening to her because her work is important and I want to help her reflect on what it is doing to and for her.
- *Voice*. Her voice is sometimes tense as she talks, though almost always excited as well. She talks hurriedly, trying to get everything in, but always volunteers more than I ask for, gets carried away, voice goes to a high pitch. Her voice is strong and confident as she talks about this.
- *Body*. She is physically animated as she talks, yet does not seem unusually tense. Her body expresses involvement with the topic, and willingness to continue because she faces me, leans forward, and talks in a relaxed way.
- *Words*. She is describing problems, struggles, conflicts, but they usually seem to resolve themselves in ways that give her satisfaction. If I connect all the words over several conversations, I get the picture that she has this job under control and needs to ventilate its frustrations.

- *Feelings.* Some feelings escape her words, but are there in her attitude toward what she is saying. In keeping with her voice, she feels excited by what she is talking about, shows this in her general state of body excitement, and seldom seems discouraged or beaten by the conflicts she is describing.
- *Values.* I suspect she feels very deeply about what she is doing, that the involvement in this political process would keep her motivated despite a steady stream of frustrations. She renews herself for this work without prodding from me or anyone else; must be something inside that keeps her going.

I have been focusing on listening as psychological attending thus far. Such mental attentiveness must always be accompanied by physical attending that enhances the overall message: "I am in touch with you, am tuning in to what you are saying." Gerard Egan, in *The Skilled Helper*,[3] writes that effective physical attending includes the following characteristics: (1) facing the other person squarely, (2) maintaining good eye contact without staring unnecessarily, (3) using a posture that is open to the other person, (4) leaning toward the other person as a sign of involvement, (5) being physically relaxed during the conversation.

▶ Nonverbal Communication ◀

Much of what you are seeking in effective listening will come to you through nonverbal channels. Here are a few cues that suggest what you can look for:

- Is he giving cues that he wants to end the conversation?
- Does she watch me closely?
- Is his body posture relaxed and facing me?
- Are her hands wringing while I talk?
- Is he giving cues that he wants to end the conversation?
- Doe she watch me closely?

Nonverbal signals can be the individual's unconscious effort to tell you what cannot be put into words or is difficult to describe in rational terms (because, perhaps, it does not feel reasonable). Such signals far more frequently refer to feelings than to ideas and as such tell you more about the person's inner experience than what is being put into words. Eyes, hands, feet, and other body parts are all mirrors of the soul; words are sounds we sometimes use to fog that mirror so that you are not sure what you are seeing.

Though your concentration in any conversation should be focused on the person talking, you must also be alert for cues within yourself, both when you are listening and when you are talking. Listening to yourself with the third ear means attending to your own nonverbal cues:

- Why do I feel relaxed with her?
- Am I getting sleepy?
- He raises my energy level.
- She makes me edgy when I listen to her.
- My voice is less confident.
- I avoid looking at him.

► How to Become an ◄ Effective Listener

Your total effectiveness as a listener depends on what you see, what you say, and how well you integrate the two. The key elements of effective listening are described below. Before you focus on them, however, you should recognize that your personal *attitude* must be the foundation upon which your listening behavior rests. The attitude with which you must begin any communication is that you care to hear everything the other person is saying, knowing that he will say more to you than words, and that you must concentrate to hear his messages at all levels. You are not interested in simply facilitating conversation, but in absorbing as much meaning from the speaker as you possibly can.

Distinguish Content from Feeling You must learn to distinguish between what the other person tells you has happened and how he feels about it, the emotions he attaches to the events. As noted before, much of the feeling that lies underneath the events is carried by the speaker's nonverbal behavior. Does he fidget when talking about that job? Do her eyes widen with joy when describing a project she did last week?

Listen to the Voice In *The Voice of Neurosis*, Paul J. Moses claims that the voice is a highly reliable index of a person's emotional state.[4] The voice is much more difficult to control than the words it is uttering, and you should look closely for clues regarding the person's inner emotional state. Hitches in speech, tiny stutters, voice cracking, the high pitch of tension, the rich sound of excitement and confidence—all these tell you feelings you'll want to know.

Notice Body Movements Though we cannot claim hand, facial, and body gestures can be read for total accuracy, you should recognize that these communicators are powerful and that people tell you many things from their gestures that their words do not reveal. A shrug of the shoulder, a wink, a posture of utter dejection, or a wild gesticulation of excitement—such gestures constitute a universal language and must not be taken lightly, especially in view of how effectively people use words to mask their inner attitudes.

Give Encouragement The easiest signals you can give to indicate you are a willing listener are those that urge the speaker to continue. These can be nonverbal signals or brief spoken cues, such as "tell me more about that" or "go ahead." Without these simple cues, the person speaking will take the more cautious view that perhaps you really don't want to hear more. With them, you can trigger the speaker to continue.

Allow Silence Little empty spaces between bursts of talking are the all-purpose oil that lubricates any conversation. Your careful silence following the other person's talk tells him you are not sure he is finished, that you want to be sure he's completed the thought. Since most of us think and speak in fragments anyway (we do not speak in paragraphs), silence from the listener allows us to piece these fragments together. Silence tells the speaker you were actually listening, not mentally rehearsing yourself to speak once his lips have stopped moving.

Use "I" Statements You should be amazed to discover how often people use *we*, *they*, or *people* instead of "I" to describe how they feel about a particular situation, person, or event. Any such pawning off of your ideas or feelings on other sources distorts the personal quality of the interchange because it suggests you don't want to own what you are saying. It leaves the other person wondering what belongs to you rather than others.

> EXAMPLE ► You: They say that working in advertising involves a lot of pressure.
> INTERVIEWER (*to herself*): Does he mean he doesn't like pressure?

Paraphrase While silence and verbal encouragements facilitate the flow of the person's conversation, they do nothing to demonstrate that you have actually heard what the person told you. You must use your own words to give evidence of what your facial expression, body posture, eye contact, and other nonverbal clues have said—that you were really listening. A paraphrasing response attempts to capture the person's basic message in a much smaller number of words. ("You mean that you really like dealing with the customers.") A simple paraphrasing response usually expresses feeling as well as content in its attempt to hear the person as fully as possible.

Check for Meaning The most powerful form of listening behavior you can employ is asking whether your summary of what you have heard is correct. It is your way of saying: "I want to be really sure I am with you, so I will check my perception to see if I am on the right track." This response, which can also be called "clarifying" in nature, is more complicated than the paraphrase in that it seeks not simply to repeat, but to capture an essence that may not be explicitly verbalized.

> EXAMPLE ► It sounds to me as though you would like to move away from the profession you are in. Is that right?
> I wonder whether you feel torn in several directions by your various interests. Is that true in what you're saying?

Listening is a skill you have countless opportunities to practice, in terms of both the listening you do in the presence of others and the quality of listening people exhibit when you are talking. There are as many opportunities for practice as you are willing to seek. Furthermore, you have direct feedback available to you in terms of how well the individual responds to you. You can practice your skills and observe the results without resorting to anything more elaborate than a simple dinner conversation.

Finally, you will find many opportunities to sharpen your listening skills because most people prefer to be listened to, will regard your attention as a compliment, and will probably reward you with more conversation.

► Listening Exercises ◄

Select a person you know, but one who has been relatively difficult to talk with. Don't take the extreme of choosing a recluse, but simply find someone you regard as a challenge for your listening skills. Engage this person in conversation on an informal, nonthreatening topic (sports events, how the car is running, pets) and use the following guidelines:

1. Give small verbal encouragements each time the person says something.

   EXAMPLE ► How did you like that game?
   What makes your car run that way?

2. Allow three to five seconds of silence each time the speaker finishes talking.
3. Paraphrase or clarify (check for meaning) in *one sentence only* what you believe the person told you at pauses in the conversation you are pretty certain finish a thought.
4. Look for contradictions between content and feeling (often ex-

pressed in nonverbal cues) and let the other person know you
have noticed this when appropriate.

5. Don't practice the above skills to such excess that it all sounds
   phony. Intersperse your listening skills with natural comments
   of your own.

Choose another person of similar shyness and direct the conversation
in the following ways:

1. Interrupt at various times.
2. Change the subject whenever he or she is done speaking, rather
   than adding any comments of your own.
3. Don't clarify anything that has been said. Assume you heard
   correctly and move on to a different topic.

Compare the two conversations. How long was the first person willing
to continue talking? The second person? What nonverbal expressions of
pleasure, boredom, frustration, or other emotions did you receive from
each of the other persons? How willing was each person to speak with
you again on later occasions?

12

Questioning

Your right to gather information is represented largely by your right to ask questions during an interview. In this chapter I shall discuss the skill of questioning within the context of the formal job interview; you should recognize, however, that all these principles and ideas apply equally well to any variety of information interview (see Chapter 9).

Questions take the lid off the interview. They give you a chance to free the interview from a rigidly structured format that may have been used a thousand times before. You will be thanked for this, and you shall get your reward in heaven. The unpredictable nature of questions makes them enjoyable for the interviewer; you may be even asking something new, or at least something not heard in the past few days. Try to make the interviewer happy in this way. Is your question the one that will make him or her wonder how much thinking and background research you had to do to come up with it?

► The Purpose of Questioning ◄

There are three major purposes of questioning. The first is to gather information. Most frequently your inquiries will serve this purpose, as you acquire information you need to clarify your view of what the work will be like.

EXAMPLE ► How do you train new management people?
In what ways is your product different from your competitors'?
What new programs is your department planning for next year?

The second purpose of questioning is to clarify. You will often use a clarification-seeking inquiry in conjunction with an information-seeking question. Your intention is to remove your confusion about a particular matter, clear up a misinterpretation, or illuminate an issue that is important to you. This purpose of questioning is very similar to what I called "checking for meaning" in the previous discussion of listening skill.

EXAMPLE ▶ Do you mean that the company is planning new foreign offices?

I don't understand the stock option plan. Could you explain?

I am confused about what you mean by editorial responsibilities.

Third, questioning can be used to check on the progress of the interview, and let the interviewer know that you are open to further inquiry.

EXAMPLE ▶ Did you want to know more about my managerial experience?

Would it be helpful to you to know where I learned about supervisory techniques?

What other information about my public relations background would you like to know?

The word *question* is derived from the word *quest*, "a search." Let this be a reminder that questioning should not be a search-and-destroy mission. If you use questions too boldly, too frequently, or too insistently, you risk alienating the affections of your interviewer.

Questions can be lethal weapons. They can be used to hammer people, bludgeon them or at least make them a little uncomfortable. Use questions sparingly. A few well-chosen inquiries can be a positive index of your curiosity and intelligent forethought; too many questions can create a dynamic of interrogation from which you will find it hard to extricate yourself.

Questioning skill keeps you from entering an interview flat on your back. It forces you to prepare questions in advance, to decide what is important for you to know. It pushes you to rank your information needs according to priority and decide which questions you must ask first, given the limited time available.

Questioning keeps you in the role of chooser. It reminds you that you are the person who has the most at stake in this search process and that your questions will help you decide whether you will accept an offer if it is made.

Coming prepared to ask questions forces you to concentrate more closely on the flow of the interview because you must look for suitable places in which your questions can be posed. Questioning keeps you from lapsing into a passive stance that might imply: "Go ahead and interview me." You have as much responsibility for the conduct of the interview as the interviewer does, and questioning allows you to assume this role.

Every question you ask requires an act of initiative from you. Do not make the mistake of waiting for the interviewer to ask: "Now, do you have any questions for me?" If you wait for that permission, it will probably be a cue that the interview is just about over, far too late for you to get substantive responses to your questions.

When your question relates to something the interviewer said, don't delay your inquiry; ask as soon as possible. Occasionally, you may even interrupt if necessary, if the question is vital enough to your plans. If you don't want to leap in at once, intervene with: "May I ask you a question?" Such interrupting, however, is less desirable than tagging your questions on to the flow of the conversation. Insert them naturally, as issues arise, if possible.

► Effective Questioning ◄

After perhaps one or two warm-up questions—though these are not always necessary, especially if you have had previous contact with the person—be sure to pose the questions you regard as most important early in the meeting. This lets your listener know your priorities and minimizes the possibility that you may not get to ask your crucial questions at all. Questions asked in a hurry toward the end of the interview usually get short shrift; they are answered in a cursory manner because the respondent simply does not have time to think about them.

Here are some of the ways to ask questions most effectively:

Ask Open Questions The open question is highly recommended because it encourages a respondent to answer in the broadest terms possible. It gives her the freedom to say whatever she pleases, does not restrict the boundaries of the responses. Open questions most often begin with *what, how,* or *in what ways.*

The open question is broad, the closed question is narrow. The open question allows the interviewer full scope; the closed question limits him to a specific answer. The open question invites him to widen his perceptual field; the closed question curtails it. The open question solicits his views, opinions, thoughts, and feelings; the closed question usually demands cold facts only. The open question may widen and deepen the contact, the closed question may circumscribe it.[1]

Closed questions usually call for a yes or no response. Compare the way in which a single inquiry can be posed in both open and closed ways:

Closed: Did the college decide
to expand enrollment?
Open: What future plans does
the college have for its enrollment?

Closed: Is the company going
to seek new markets?
Open: In what ways does the
company anticipate seeking
new markets?

Ask Answerable Questions   Be sure you ask a question you believe can be answered without difficulty. It makes the interviewer feel good to have the answer, and you can smile appreciatively at the information you receive. However, if you unwittingly ask a stumper, be careful to express your concern and stay clear of that area for the rest of the interview.

Be sure your questions actually have answers. Don't ask an impossible-to-answer question just because it sounds clever. The interviewer will regard you as pretentious, and you will deserve every bit of displeasure.

Ask Nonthreatening Questions   Questions that are low in emotional content and do not require deep thought can be used early in the interview to warm yourself to the task of more serious inquiry and to cue the interviewer that you will be active in the process:

EXAMPLE ► I'll bet it's been a long day for you.
How many people have you spoken with today?
When did the company acquire this property?

Express Puzzlement   A good interviewer reads the puzzlement on your face before you express it in a question: therefore, you should speak up when something is said that you didn't understand. Interviewers appreciate your giving them a chance to clarify some of the more difficult topics or issues.

Ask Well-Informed Questions   Often the best use of a question is to show you have done some homework on the organization. Ask a question that demonstrates your knowledge. Generally some questions not only yield good information but also remind the interviewer that you are well organized and self-motivated. Be careful, though, not to push the well-informed question too far. In your haste to prove yourself, you may mistakenly ask a probing question that should have been avoided. A well-informed question, for instance, might be: "How does the company plan to market its new line of ski equipment?" A probing question, on the other hand, is something like: "When did the company decide to take over the southern markets?"

Use Indirect Questions   This method allows you to ask a question without insisting that the person answer it. As Benjamin says: "The indirect question usually has no question mark at the end, and yet it is evident that a question is being posed and an answer sought."[2]

EXAMPLE ► I'd sure like to hear a little more about that project. You must really be busy with these new departments.

► Poor Questioning ◄

It is easy to fall into the trap of thinking that any question asked is a point in your favor because it displays your initiative. An interviewer can usually detect when you are asking a question simply to sound impressive; you swing rapidly to another topic and usually string one nonsensical question after another. Stick to the questions that matter. Anything else will expose your tactic as superficial window dressing.

Here are some other kinds of questions to avoid:

Use of Why   Though *why* is a perfectly legitimate word in our language, it carries an unavoidable risk when it is used in an interview questioning process. Simply put, it is threatening and should be used with greatest care.

Loaded Questions   Loaded questions imply that you have an attitude or strong feeling about the subject and know or suspect what the answer is. They are asked to elicit a particular response. They insult the interviewer's intelligence and put him or her on the defensive.

EXAMPLE ► Did the company decide to close that office because they didn't want to pay the high wages being demanded?

Double Questions   Probably one of the most common blunders, the double question reveals your desire to get a lot of information fast. You ask the interviewer to answer several things at the same time. Make it easy on your respondent, even if it means you may forget one of your precious questions entirely. Choose the most important question first and trust you'll find a chance to ask the others later.

Curiosity Questions   Don't waste time with questions about things that have piqued your curiosity but have little relevance or importance. It is easy to get sidetracked by something that "crosses your mind," especially in your anxiety to fill the time. That is precisely why you must have your important questions prepared in advance.

Machine-Gun Style   Avoid like the plague asking questions in series; the interviewer feels he or she is in the path of a dangerous weapon and must find a way to divert it. Each question should be followed by non-question interchanges. Wait for the interviewer to say something, make a comment based on the response, volunteer some new data about yourself, and then perhaps come back with another question.

Shifting the Subject   Be careful not to let your questioning move away from a topic area that interests the interviewer. It may seem that you are deliberately avoiding the topic. As noted later, abrupt shifts of topic are less desirable than questions that flow naturally from the previous response.

Intellectuality   This is probably the first cousin of the well-informed question, but it reaches too far. In your effort to display the depth of your thought and the way you can tie a contemporary question to a universal concern, you go too far, perhaps off the deep end. Avoid such pretensions, even if you *are* an intellectual, because most interviewers are not.

> EXAMPLE ▸ Could you tell me how Herzberg's theory of internal and external motivators relates to the distribution of work incentives among your professional staff?

Probing   The brother-in-law of the loaded question, this one will hurt you most dearly if you fail to see you are putting pressure on the interviewer. No interviewer wants to be called to task by a job seeker, so if you are in doubt about whether your question touches a sensitive area, drop it. If it even *sounds* probing to you, in all likelihood it will land on him or her like a bombshell.

▸ Speech ◂

Highly correlated with poor questioning are the ways in which your manner of speaking can intrude upon a free exchange of information. These are some of the key things to keep in mind.

Speak Clearly   If your natural speech pattern is too fast, slurred, garbled, or otherwise fuzzy, give it some attention. No one expects you to be number one on the diction or elocution list, but others have a right to understand what you are saying. Practice with your friends, people who will be honest with you. Play back a tape recorder if you need further evidence. You won't like the sound of that strange voice you hear, but you'll know whether it's understandable or not.

Natural Tone   Within the limits of reasonably good diction and clarity, stay with the voice that is your own. Any effort you make to assume a different persona through adopting a voice that *sounds* better will reach the listener's ear as phony, and you will be caught up in your own duplicity when you drop the new voice and return to the natural.

Modulation Some people talk too loudly; others much too softly, so that they cannot even be heard. Speech volume is important because energy devoted to adjusting ears and body to your abnormal vocal level is energy subtracted from attending to what you are saying and feeling.

Vocal Flatness Some people believe that it is "professional" to be even-toned, carefully modulated in their talk, not excited about anything because that would sound so childish. Rubbish. If you have feelings associated with what you are saying, it is vital that you express them. Of course, this can be overdone by a screaming cynic or a laughing hyena, but you get the idea. There is nothing professional about vocal flatness— it is simply boring.

► You Are Your Questions ◄

The questions you ask are a Rorschach of your career personality. By these inquiries shall ye be judged. If you ask a lot of stuff about salary, fringe benefits, vacation time, you will be spotted as a person who is clearly motivated by the external rewards and less driven by internal needs. You may not have intended this impression, but your questions will reveal it. If you talk about the company's future plans, you will be tagged as a person who thinks in terms of the big picture. Let your questions create an impression of yourself that accurately reflects your attitude. Imagine that you have only three questions to ask. Which three best reveal the self you would like the interviewer to remember? Avoid the temptation to be pretentious. Choose those questions that clearly represent your highest priorities.

13

Assertiveness

No one can make you feel inferior without your consent.
—Eleanor Roosevelt,
This Is My Story

To the job seeker, darkness seems to cover this world of work. Imagine a huge pasture in which a thousand people are wandering around at nighttime trying to find each other with lit matches and you have an idea of the perspective of both employers and people who want better work. Employers have little idea where the right candidates are, and people who want to improve their work situations have even less idea where their talents can be used. Occasionally someone comes along and shines a spotlight on this pasture for a moment, foolishly believing he has illuminated The Job Market. Two minutes later he is gone, people shift their positions, and his picture is already out of date. Such feeble efforts to throw light on the process of work patterns may be called job clearinghouses or job banks; they fail to capture a restlessly shifting scene.

Most of your self-assessment will be wasted effort, done for naught, if you fail to make connections with employers who need you. Assertiveness is the skill that permits you to make these connections. This vital skill enables you to plug in a number of lights that will illuminate your place in the world of work, allowing you to stand out in the darkness that pervades so much of the hiring process. Assertiveness allows employers to see who you are and permits you to discover what they are doing. Keep in mind that there is no central control switch in this blind-finding-the-blind process known as hiring. If you do not make the connections yourself, you leave the employer cruising the pasture with a flickering match, trying to find her way to wherever you are hiding.

► What Is Assertiveness? ◄

Assertiveness is not, contrary to popular belief, walking up to a bull elephant and asking him to whistle "Dixie" for you. Nor is it bulldozing your mother-in-law into changing the TV channel from her favorite show. These are examples of *aggressive* behavior, which can be defined as taking away the rights of another in order to satisfy your own. People frequently confuse aggressive with assertive behavior.

Assertiveness can be defined for our purposes as (1) expressing what you feel about the work you are doing and the work you would prefer to do; (2) taking those actions necessary to put you in touch with the people and situations that appeal to you; and (3) asking for their advice, insights, information, and referrals to others.

Bower and Bower, in *Asserting Yourself*, their detailed treatment of the subject, remind us:

> Some people believe that assertiveness training must turn a nice person into a constant irritant, a rebel, a complainer, and a general all-around pain. Others charge that assertiveness training teaches people to be calculating and manipulative, and helps them control others for selfish ends. Views like these are based on a misunderstanding of the goals of assertiveness.[1]

Assertiveness is the simple act of asking for what you want. It is not a matter of winning, outwitting, bludgeoning, controlling, or even manipulating your foe. The person from whom you seek assistance in your work search is not a foe at all, but a willing accomplice.

Nearly all the work-search activity in the detective and research stages can be stunted if individuals believe they have no right to do what they are doing. "Why would anyone want to talk to me?" "What makes me think others would want to help me?"

There is an old story about the man whose car has broken down on a deserted rural highway. He walks a mile to a farmer's house to ask for help. During the walk, he ruminates about the farmer's possible responses to his plight. Being of pessimistic bent, the driver creates a scenario in which he imagines that the farmer will be reluctant to help. Thus, by the time our poor beleaguered driver reaches the farmer's door and the door opens, he says: "You can keep your automobile tools to yourself. I didn't want to use them anyway!"

Many of us concoct scenarios of this kind before we approach people to ask them for help with the job search, and these anticipations prevent us from acting. Though there is never any guarantee that an individual will assist you, you always have the right to ask. There is nothing in anyone's code of professional or ethical behavior (confidential matters excluded) that says a person is prohibited from talking about his or her work or from referring you to others in similar positions. Furthermore, there is every reason to believe that people will do so willingly because people generally *like* to talk about themselves and their ambitions, frustrations, accomplishments. And they like to be helpful in ways that enable them to feel potent.

▶ Passive, Aggressive, and ◀ Assertive Behavior

Let's settle once and for all that assertive behavior is neither passive nor aggressive in intent. Passive behavior will kill your work search because there will be no search at all; you will snuff yourself out before you start. Aggressive behavior will kill your search because you will stifle your listeners, attempt to railroad them into giving you information and leads you require, no matter what their objections. Assertive behavior permits you to ask for help in a way that respects the rights of respondents to satisfy you or refuse, as they please. Since you are not asking for the keys to the safe, the secret formula for Coca-Cola, or a seat on the New York Stock Exchange, you can reasonably expect that most people will try to help you.

> EXAMPLE ▶ *Passive behavior*: I'd better not go in here; they will think I am disturbing their workday.
> *Aggressive behavior:* I'm going to find out what they do with their used nuclear fuel, or they'll have to drag me out of here, kicking and screaming.
> *Assertive behavior:* Would you mind if I asked a few questions about your job, only those you feel comfortable answering?

There is a delicate balance between asking for what you want and imposing your needs upon the rights of others. Those I call assertive boors believe they can make requests anytime as long as they preface them with "I would like," look directly at the person, and speak in a clear voice. Assertive boors fail to observe cues supplied by the respondent: that she has not yet finished speaking, that his nonverbal leave-taking behaviors indicate he has no more time to talk or listen; that she shows nonverbally some discomfort with the last question asked. And boors fail to recognize the needs of others in a group to be heard. It is always important to watch anticipatory nonverbal behavior in the people to whom you are speaking; assertive boors usually miss most of it.

Failure to observe your respondent's nonverbal cues can be disastrous for you. If you trigger in your listener a "get this person out of here" feeling, by virtue of your insensitive assertion, the feeling will undo any progress you have made, and you may not even get a decent referral to another person. Accurate observation of cues from others and respect for their time and their needs to be heard will not prevent you from saying or asking what you desire. They will facilitate the process.

► How to Be Assertive ◄ Without Muss or Fuss

How do you steal a piano? By behaving as though you have every reason to be there in the first place. You act in a way that leaves no suspicion about your purposes or your right to be engaged in what you are doing. You walk in the door, enter the appropriate room, set up your moving equipment, and remove the piano with dispatch. Although the ethical dimension is twisted in this analogy, the *attitude* is one that should pervade your assertive behavior. You have every right to explore, question, inquire, volunteer, and be assertive in other ways toward your vocational objectives. There are four rules you should follow:

State What You Want Without Hesitation

EXAMPLE ► I want to know what kinds of public relations work your firm does, how you go about completing your contacts, the methods you use, and the ways in which you are usually successful.

In speaking, face the other person with your body, so you are not turned away at an angle, and do not appear to be looking in another direction. Look at the person directly; your eye contact should be direct and steady but not so fixed that you are staring; occasional glancing away is fine. Speak with a tone of voice and diction that are clear, and speak slowly enough to be understood but not so slowly that your listener becomes impatient.

State What You Do Not Want Anticipate any misinterpretations that might stem from what you are saying.

EXAMPLE ► I am not interested in asking you to hire me, and I have no intention of trying to sell you anything.

Be as Specific as Possible

EXAMPLE ► It would help me to know how you recruit your staff, what skills you believe are most important in effective work here, and what kinds of training and experiences are most beneficial.

Adjust Your Requests as Necessary

EXAMPLE ▶ I understand you have less time than we'd originally planned for. Would it be okay to ask you just the few questions I have regarding how you get your contracts and the methods you use to fulfill them?

This last step is particularly important. A juggernaut style of assertive behavior will quickly backfire if you do not pay attention to how the other person is receiving your requests. Each request you make or question you ask must be modified by the willingness of the respondent. Assertiveness engages you in a friendly negotiation process that yields results because you have no intention of alienating the other person.

Here are some examples of how assertive language is used with a wide variety of people.

- *To a secretary:* I would like to speak personally with one of your financial analysts so I can gather some information about that job.
- *To an employer:* I would like to know more about your branch services; could you give me the name of one of your branch managers so I can ask a few questions?
- *To a public relations department:* I would like a copy of your annual report.
- *To a receptionist:* I would like to know who does the long-range planning work in this company. Could you direct me to his or her office?
- *To a referral source:* I am interested in speaking with other people who do work similar to yours. Could you recommend a good person?

▶ Shy People Can Be ◀ Assertive Too

Philip Zimbardo, in *Shyness: What It Is and What to Do About It*, reports:

> The most basic finding of our research establishes that shyness is common, widespread, and universal. More than 80 percent of those questioned reported that they were *shy at some point in their lives*, either now, in the past, or always. Of these, over 40 percent considered themselves *presently* shy.[2]

Let's assume you are shy too. You are generally afraid of people in positions of authority, feel intimidated by secretaries, fall over at the sight of a business suit, and would faint if you had to approach three strangers at the same time.

In the long run, you might resolve to read Zimbardo's book and practice the behaviors he recommends. For now, try these three simple rules:

Don't Be the Life of the Party It is never necessary for you to laugh a lot, tell jokes, or otherwise entertain your hosts. Your quiet, unobtrusive attention to their work and lives will be enough to excite their sensors and keep the conversation moving.

Bring Along a Scrap of Information An easy way to stimulate conversation is to scrounge a morsel of information about your target person, offer it, and let the conversation carry itself from there.

> EXAMPLE ► I heard your agency is planning to move into a new building.
> I saw the new store that opened up across town; it has a lot of merchandise I've seen in here before.

Use Your Observational Powers What kinds of material are displayed on the work desk? Trophies, plaques for some kind of service, diplomas, copies of new books you can ask about? What pictures are there on the wall? What do they represent to this person? How is the office decorated? Who decorated it?

► Self-Putdowns ◄

Sitting around trying to screw up the courage to ask a stranger for advice or information, how many times have you said to yourself: "She really wouldn't want to hear my silly questions." "I'm not interesting enough for anyone to talk with." "He couldn't possibly have enough time for me." "She won't understand what I am looking for." "I know he gets bothered all the time by people like me."

Though there is no guarantee that you will get what you want, you can succeed in eliminating yourself from the game if you let self-putdowns dominate your thinking. Rather than assuming the worst, *let the other people decide*. Don't you decide for them whether a conversation should take place; they have a right to make that decision without your assistance. Ask yourself: "What's the worst thing that could happen?" The most severe consequence of your rash, impatient act would be a simple no, a polite request that you come back later. As my wise grandmother used to tell me: "If that's the biggest problem you have in your life, you'll be all right." And remember, *you don't have to be interesting;* the target people are interested enough in themselves. You don't have to provide the entertainment; just be prepared to listen.

14

Self-Disclosure

Dear Howard:

I don't know how to talk about myself. I'm terribly self-conscious about saying anything complimentary about myself because I know how conceited it would sound. It seems to me that the interviewer who asks me about my strong points is just testing to see whether I will trip up and make excessive claims about my abilities. So I feel better playing it safe and not claiming any great talents that I would not be able to defend under more intense questioning.

Signed,
Modesty Becomes Me

Dear Mod:

Contrary to what you may think, interviewers are not waiting to pounce upon your self-revelations with demands that you prove yourself immediately or never darken their doors again. And, you will discover from bitter experience if you stick with your self-effacing stance, modesty gets no points when a potential job is on the line.

Rather than think you are shouting, bragging, or otherwise falsely representing your qualifications, follow these simple guidelines. First, be as *specific* as possible about your abilities. Don't say "I am a quick learner" or, worse, "I can deal with a variety of situations." Instead, tell them concretely: "I organize detailed paperwork well" or "I can do numerous computations quickly and accurately." Second, back up your statement with a specific life experience. For

178

example: "I learned how to work with numbers when I was a kid by figuring out batting averages in my head and computing all the statistics for my team" or "I learned how to organize data when I was leader of a new department in my previous job; we had to draw up budgets, select new employees, and write the job descriptions within a month." Third, don't ramble to excess in describing your strengths. Take one sentence to tell what the skill is, then one or two sentences to back it up with life experiences. Finally, don't hedge your self-statements with words that permit you to back off from what you've just said: "I really wasn't the greatest at this" or "I could've done a better job." A hedge remark does nothing to further convince the listener of your sincerity.

Signed,

Howard

One would imagine it is the easiest thing in the world to talk about yourself, to reveal lovingly and fluently the person you know best, but most of you who read this know better. The beast that lives within you tells you to keep under cover, protect against injury, show only the better side. Or it whispers: "Who would want to know anything about me, anyway?"

Perhaps you prefer to rely on paper credentials, recommendations from others, or the power of sheer happenstance to get you a job, because these devices minimize the extent to which you must reveal yourself. Once you let the beast out of its cage, the jig is up.

We live in a time when all but the most outspoken of athletes and entertainers are loath to declare they are good at anything or to stand for any particular value or point of view, lest they face ridicule from others. Better to be quiet and unassuming than to be the target of barbs or angry witticisms or, worse yet, to have to live up to something.

Shyness, reticence, self-protectiveness, and defensiveness are rampant in our lonely society:

Shyness is an insidious personal problem that is reaching such epic proportions as to be justifiably called a social disease. Trends in our society suggest it will get worse in the coming years as social forces increase our isolation, competition, and loneliness. . . .

Hawthorne may have been thinking of the shy person when he wrote: "What other dungeon is so dark as one's heart? What jailer so inexorable as one's self?"[1]

Of course, you are not self-protective with everyone. You tell your little brother how great you are or share you deeper aspirations with your friends. But when it comes to sharing yourself with a stranger in a situation in which you are being evaluated, you are understandably cautious. It matters who is doing the listening, because an interviewer is more likely to make you prove what you are saying.

You're not sure whom you can trust with revelations about yourself. Is this person going to use it against you, put what you have said in a record somewhere, perhaps embarrass you by reporting it to someone else? Do you have enough time and does the other person have enough patience to listen to the supporting evidence for what you have just said?

All these thoughts weave through your mind as you try to decide whether to reveal yourself. Given the fears and the uncertainties, it seems the prudent course of action to play safe, tell only as much as you have to. Like folding your cards before the betting gets heavy, it seems better to avoid the big blunder, the genuine faux pas, and hope your paper credentials will deliver you safely to your goal.

Set in the context of the job interview, your self-disclosure includes talking openly and fully about your chief strengths, skills, abilities to perform certain functions; the values you regard as most important in your choices of work; your private ambitions, what you hope to accomplish with your work; experiences you have had that reflect your unique work history.

All the most common questions employers and interviewers ask call for some measure of self-disclosure. These questions are designed to draw you into the open. They are not meant to engage you in a fencing match to which your response is: "Let's see how I can dodge this one."

When asked a self-disclosure question, you cannot say "I don't know" because there is no excuse for not knowing yourself. Self-protection is characterized by filtering, screening your responses, planning what you will say and what you will try to hide. As you learn self-disclosure, you will discover that it creates a state of mind in which you feel little need to filter because you are pleased to tell who you are without any need to alter the script to suit the listener.

Of course, it is unrealistic to suggest that you talk about anything and everything in a work-related conversation—or in any conversation, for that matter. Your private personal concerns are off limits if you choose to protect them, and you can be carefully selective in what you say. You can feel free to defend yourself against invasion of privacy or the risk that your words will be misinterpreted by choosing your language judiciously. However, if you are comfortable with your career aspirations and enjoy talking about them, you will not often need to use defensive tactics to screen or modify what you are saying.

If you cannot reveal who you are, then certainly no one else can do it for you. There is nothing earthshaking about that statement; it seems the most self-evident of principles. But we have become so accustomed to letting paper credentials (résumés, application forms, and so on) tell our stories that we depend more heavily upon these so-called legitimate sources of data than we do upon accounts delivered in our own words.

If you are a soft-spoken person, you need not feel this message is inappropriate for you. In revealing yourself to someone else, it is not necessary to be a bubbling personality, the life of the party, or an effervescent talker. Many people prefer understatement as a style of conversation because it makes fewer demands on them and is generally easier to take. Be yourself, but show yourself, and the other person will respond warmly to your genuineness.

Don't rely on your work history to speak for you. Paper summaries of your existence are sterile, past-oriented documents. They fail to capture the flavor of what you are doing now, what you feel ripe for at the present moment.

Increasingly, employers have little personal knowledge of the people who apply to them for work. It has been estimated that 40 million Americans change their residence every year; hence, it is increasingly rare that an employer has seen you before or even heard anything about you. This makes it doubly important that you tell him in your own words about yourself, instead of letting him make erroneous judgments from the labels and categories squeezed onto a piece of paper.

► When to Let Out the Beast ◄

Is self-disclosure a pell-mell rush to declare who you are, delivered as a soliloquy to the breathlessly waiting interviewer? Not necessarily. Your choice of a moment to speak about yourself depends on the format of the interview.

If you are the one who requested the interview, it is your responsibility to make a *brief* opening statement about yourself to explain why you are there:

> EXAMPLE ► I want to talk with you because I feel I can offer the sort of experience and abilities you need to keep this greenhouse running and expand its business.

Your opening statement declares the purpose of your meeting and gives your listener a chance to say whether he or she wants to hear more. A long opening statement, replete with your numerous skills and experiences, is not going to help you because you have little idea what the other person would like to know.

If the interviewer has called this meeting, which is more likely to be the case, you should ordinarily wait for appropriate cues that you are expected to tell about yourself.

EXAMPLE ► Tell me why you decided to apply here.
What have you done before that relates to our operation?

However, if the interviewer fails to ask you questions that allow you to talk about your chief qualities, you must volunteer the data you want heard.

EXAMPLE ► I would like to tell you why I believe I could do this job.
I have some experiences that relate closely to what you are doing. I would like to tell you about one of them.

► How to Practice ◄ Self-Disclosure

Self-disclosure questions in the job interview generally reduce to one of three varieties: (1) Why us? Why have you chosen to apply here? What interests you about our organization? (2) Why you? Why should we be especially interested in you over others? (3) Why now? What makes this the right time for you and us?

There are three parts to any self-disclosing response that characterize the best statements you can make: (1) the basic self-statement in response to one of the three types of questions noted above; (2) evidence to support that statement; (3) an evaluation that you use to summarize your view.

EXAMPLE ► I want to work here because there is more opportunity to grow with a company that is creating new product lines (self-statement).
I have read articles about your product changes and your interest in creating new customer service (evidence). I welcome the challenge of trying new markets, and feel the risk is worth the potential gains (evaluation).

Self-disclosure may seem dangerously close to bragging, but it is not. The braggart attempts to convince his hearers that he is a little bigger than life; your self-disclosures are plain revelations of what is you. To become comfortable with self-disclosure, you must practice it according to these guidelines.

Support with Evidence   Any statement about yourself should be accompanied by evidence that you can support what you say ("I did this before").

Focus on the Present   Show how your past experiences culminate in the present, in terms of what you can and want to do now. Past experiences can also be leavened with a strong dash of future imagination.

Use One-Sentence Bites   Avoid rambling at all costs. There is no value in setting endurance records for talking about yourself. Listeners appreciate concise self-statements that can be remembered easily. If they want more, they will ask for it.

> EXAMPLE ▶ I believe I am ready to take over a managerial position because my supervisory experience at the mill taught me about handling personnel problems and planning an efficient operation.
> I feel I can offer your school some competencies that you don't currently have—namely coaching for soccer and directing a performing theater troupe.

Serve Them, Not Yourself Though self-disclosure grows from your knowledge of yourself, it should be oriented toward the needs of the potential employer. Focus on what you have done that would serve her interests, not on what the employer can do for you.

> EXAMPLE ▶ Since you want someone who can take over the programming functions, let me say that my work with the radio station will enable me to do the job. I feel I can give you the popular style of programming you need.

▶ Revealing Weaknesses ◀

Though honesty is the best policy and full self-disclosure means not having to engage in a hiding contest with the interviewer, your primary objective is to show what you are capable of doing and why you can do the job, not to provide reasons why you cannot do it. Thus, there is no value in admitting your liabilities as an exercise in honesty. Think of it this way: Any interview is brief enough so you can fill it talking about your strengths, your experiences that support these strengths, and your high interest in this particular opportunity. Why save time for the liabilities? If you are pressed directly to talk about your weaknesses, remember (1) that the interviewer is probably more concerned about how smoothly you deal with the question than about the content of your reply and (2) that a weakness can usually be coupled with a strength, if you anticipate this possibility in advance.

> EXAMPLE ▶ It takes me a little longer to do a project than most people, but I make sure it is done thoroughly, without slip-ups.

▶ Other Forms of ◀ Self-Disclosure

Talking about your strengths and expressing your belief that you can do the job are not the only forms of self-disclosure. Other kinds of self-disclosure call attention to a particular feeling you have about the work being discussed, rather than to the work itself. These feelings are important to introduce, but you must use them with care lest you risk being labeled a "complainer," "overly emotional," or some such epithet. Choose your spots carefully, but say what you feel you must say. Here are some other ways self-disclosure can be used:

- *Admit conflict.* I believe we have different ideas about what the manager of this department is supposed to do.
- *Express confusion.* I do not understand how the purpose of this department differs from that of the production department.
- *Share opinion.* I believe that this agency could be directing more of its attention to older people.
- *Share values.* I feel strongly that teachers in this school should be given the chance to broaden their knowledge by teaching different courses each year.
- *Reveal anger or disappointment.* It bothers me that this job is saddled with so many tedious duties.
- *Express concern.* I am concerned that most salespeople who deal with pensions and annuities do not have knowledge of estate planning and cannot handle investment portfolios.

▶ Self-Disclosure Exercise ◀

Practice during your daily routine any three or more of the activities listed below. Note how you feel when doing each of them. Awkward? Shy? Happy? Keep a chart of how you feel from week to week to discover changes in the self-disclosure activities you are able to perform and how you feel about doing them.

1. Tell a friend about something helpful you did.
2. Describe a strong personal trait you possess.
3. Name an experience you felt excited about.
4. Reveal an experience you had previously kept secret.
5. Talk about something you do that you feel is superior to most other people's similar efforts.
6. Describe a strong attraction you have to a certain kind of work or career.
7. Talk about your fantasy ambitions for the future.
8. Describe a career you've imagined for yourself that doesn't even exist yet.

15
Writing

Dear Howard:

I am tired of all this traipsing around the streets, talking to everyone in sight, peeking in stores, sneaking around corners trying to catch somebody in the act of working. Maybe it isn't all that bad, but I need a break. Can I just sit in the comfort of my room and write to somebody for a change? I know you said people don't answer letters too fast, but I'm willing to wait.

Signed,
Pen in Hand

Dear Penrod:

Off with your shoes, feet by the fire. Up with the pen; there is method to your madness. You have a right to retreat from the madding crowd, and you can take comfort in the fact that writing still counts. In fact, good old-fashioned letter writing may achieve a breakthrough door knocking has failed to attain.

If you like writing to people, translate that urge into making pen pals of prospective employers. Forget the hogwash that says applying for work is a formal process and you shouldn't let your silly old informal self gum up the works. An employer is a human being just as you are. Treat him almost like a prospective lover. Let him know you've been thinking about him, that he's the only one for you, that it matters a lot that you get together. This approach can be stretched out of shape and distorted to be more ludicrous than beneficial, so use your good sense. Employers like to be courted like anyone else.

185

Letters to your intended employer must be written with taste and a sense of what is believable. Selling yourself is not appropriate in letter form; your objective is to establish a relationship and build a bridge to in-person meetings.

The letter is a subtle wand. It requires only a few moments of reading time, but can leave an indelible impression on the person who likes to be appreciated. Write on, Macduff.

Signed,

Howard

Words give shape and substance to your thoughts; they bring your feelings to life and create pictures where before ideas were scattered and fragmented. Writing forces you to make coherent sentences of your un-shaped flashes of insight. It puts flesh on the bones of your ideas and allows you to capture images that dart to and fro in your mind.

Can the pen be mightier than the tongue? Yes, on many occasions your written communication to an employer can be quicker and more effective than an in-person interview. During the days or weeks (if you are far away) that you wait to see an individual personally, you can pen-etrate his consciousness with a well-timed note. I will confine my dis-cussion of writing skill to the personal letter because I believe traditional forms of written communication in the work search encourage passive behavior and are ineffective if used without more active methods of inquiry.

The warlords of the working world seek to standardize your written communication in the form of business letters, the résumé, and the formal job application. These are tools you must be familiar with, but you should note that they give you limited opportunity to set yourself apart from the crowd. Thus, I shall leave discussion of formally written job-seeking ma-terials to other publications and attempt to persuade you that your ability to use writing to your advantage depends largely upon the *personal* and *informal* qualities of what you say.

We are all egotists. We wait by the mailbox for letters to arrive and remind us that someone remembers. The mailbox game never loses its excitement because it offers a pleasant surprise, an unexpected compliment, a voiceless hello that you prize because the sender took time to remember you. Don't you still sort through your office and home mail, looking hope-fully for an envelope that is personally typed or handwritten to you?

No matter how resolutely and tightly the employment world attempts to depersonalize itself, there will always be individual egos. People will be proud of what they have done and will generally appreciate another person who notices. In view of the numerous impersonal communications that are enforced in a hiring process, the *personal communications* stand out because they escape the trap of formalized language and structure.

The written medium is made to order for those of us who like to think slowly and carefully and say things in just the right way. No one asks you to defend yourself while you write; nor do they hurry you along with their own restless needs. You can talk to your target person at your own pace. Moreover, you can control the agenda by organizing your thoughts in the order that seems most likely to make an impact. The best quality of the written word is that you can take as long as necessary to get the desired result. You can make countless mistakes without reprisal and show your audience only the finished product.

A letter affords the receiver the same degree of freedom. He or she can imagine the reply a hundred times, reflect upon your words, turn them over and over, and savor them if they are complimentary. And whatever effect you achieve with your written communication, you have the pleasure of knowing that it lasts and lasts.

▶ Getting Personal ◀

The résumé, application, and other standard forms of written communication are impersonal; they lack the single most potent quality in any writing—a direct connection between one human being and another. Even personally addressed letters can lack this quality. Of the two following letters, both personally addressed, the second—more specific and personal—is far more likely to evoke a positive response and be remembered.

> EXAMPLE ▶ Dear Ms. Jones: I have been reading about your company and would like to know more about its operation. Could you send me literature describing your overseas branches?
>
> Dear Ms. Jones: I have read about the Universal Company in a recent article in *Business Week* magazine. Your work with new metal alloys in foreign markets interests me. Could you send any literature that describes these operations?

I believe a job is a very personal matter, second only to family relationships in its intimacy and demand for interpersonal cooperation. Therefore, I will focus this chapter on methods that will help you cultivate the personal touch in your writing. The more you depend on stiff, aloof, and structured forms of business writing, the more you surrender your chance to reach your correspondent and be remembered, because your letter will sound like everyone else's.

The personal quality can be established by a combination of three approaches in your writing:

1. Comment directly about the person to whom you are writing.

> EXAMPLE ▶ I have read your study of the ecology of local wildlife.

2. Comment about the organization for which the individual works, even if you don't know the particular function of the person to whom you're writing.

EXAMPLE ▸ I am aware that your agency has been studying local wildlife and would like to know more about your findings.

3. Tell something about your own background that relates to the purposes of the organization to which you are writing.

EXAMPLE ▸ I have done a study of deer in the local area.

A combination of knowledge about the individual or organization to whom you are writing and reference to your own experiences is best because it establishes a basis upon which you can meet for a mutually profitable discussion.

▸ Behind-the-Scenes Writing ◂

There are several ways you can practice your writing skills without having to take the risk of exposing your words to target employers. Any of the following kinds of writing sharpen your prose and build your confidence for future writing in the job marketplace.

Letters to Friends   Perhaps the best way to begin putting yourself into print, the informal letter provides you with the protective cover of a friendship and allows you to be free with your language, convey feelings without embarrassment, and make mistakes without consequences. If you can tell a friend why you want to get into a particular line of work, why you believe you ought to be hired, and what you value in this kind of work, then you can say the same things to the employer when that opportunity occurs. But practice first without the threat of being evaluated. As Ernst Jacobi points out:

> Writing in the form of a letter to a friend gives you several immediate advantages. It forces you to focus on one specific person, preferably one whom you respect and especially like; this immediately influences your communicative attitude. You will tend to be warm, direct, informal, and spontaneous. You will instinctively take care to stress why you are writing and why you think that what you are writing will be of interest. And you will probably avoid being pompous, stiff, and self-important. You are, after all, writing to a friend. You are not trying to impress him. You know he knows you're not stupid, and you need not be afraid of his criticism.[1]

Fantasy Letters   What would you write to a fantasy employer if you had the courage to send this person or organization a letter expressing your loftiest ambitions? Try a letter of this kind, with no intention at all of ever sending it. Assume instead that you have an imaginary reader who will accept and welcome anything you say and believe it as well. Make sure you tell the letter's receiver what you feel about the work but are embarrassed to tell a real person ("I really want to be the sort of insurance salesperson who sells a policy only when I believe the family needs it and who looks after the family's entire financial program").

A Letter to Yourself Your inner conversations flicker in and out of your consciousness hundreds of times a day. Try putting these exchanges into more coherent form by addressing yourself directly and attempting to convince yourself that your course of action in the work search is justified. Take it even a step further and imagine you are persuading yourself to hire yourself. If you are your own worst critic, this may be a useful crucible in which to test your aspirations.

► Writing Employers ◄
Informally

It is a good idea to make written contact with target employers before you formally apply with letter and résumé. Three informal categories of writing can be used to great advantage.

Thank-You Notes These subtle little devils offer you ways of getting across your interest and enthusiasm for the work without professing to be bargaining for a job. Usually the thank-you note follows an information interview. In such a note, you can tell the person how much your talk reinforced your interest in the work, perhaps set the stage for future contacts, and express personal interest in the individual, all in the context of showing gratitude for assistance.

Note from Admirer If you have done any measure of research on an individual or an organization, you are in a position to write this kind of note. For example, an aspiring advertising executive who researches a particular ad agency can identify the name of an account executive, study the ad campaigns for an account he or she handles, and write a letter of admiration for the way in which the campaign has been formulated. Such letters out of the blue are so rare in business communication that the receiver will be surprised to realize that someone actually noticed and thought enough to comment. Be careful not to overdo this kind of letter; make sure you are speaking with definite knowledge and sincerity and that you are not effusive.

Portfolio In any profession where the work you have done can be shown in writing, this form of communication is an excellent supplement to the résumé because it gives evidence of your résumé's claims and demonstrates that you had the foresight to prepare yourself. Articles, reports, memoranda, advertisements, newspaper copy, training manuals, sales reports, or anything else you have written provide proof of the work you have done. If you do not currently keep a sample book of such materials, now is the time to begin collecting and organizing them.

► Warning: Writing Can Work ◄ Against You

Like a piece of spinach stuck in your teeth while you are talking, poor writing can distort the quality of your essential message. J. Mitchell Morse cites examples of the written communications he gets from college students: "What is needed is the restorement of confident in fair taxes. The fairest are the sail tax which the rich pay more than the poor because they buy more and are not discriminating against them they feel."[2] The Public Relations Society of America reports:

> Now, bear in mind, the following excerpts are from real letters written by real applicants seeking a real job as editor. Most possessed graduate degrees, many in English! . . . "My doctoral program provided an interdisciplinary continuation of the Master's program emphasizing research, management and organization theory and practice, decision making, theory, personnel and business administration, and directed institutional communications." You can't help but like a guy who gets right to the point.
> Another Ph.D. in English wrote, "I have become proficient in quick but competent research and apprehension of complex matters." Well, at least he writes shorter sentences.[3]

If you want to use writing skills in your work search but have always been afraid of making errors like these, here are a few suggestions for you. First, write as much as possible in the same style you use in talking. Don't adopt one style for writing and a different one for talking. Use a tape recorder if necessary to hear your conversation or that of others, and do what is necessay to make complete sentences of it. Second, ask a friend or teacher to serve as editor for your writing; accustom yourself to hearing criticism and learning from it. Most people who are good editors love doing it for their friends occasionally because they like to show their proficiency. Third, practice, practice, practice on nonthreatening targets.

Write letters to your sports heroes, politicians, the television networks, and any other people or places you know are not likely to be offended by what you say or how you say it.

► Guidelines for Effective ◄ Written Communication

Ernst Jacobi, in his excellent book *Writing at Work,* urges that every piece of writing can be improved by attending to several important guidelines. Though his guidelines apply to writing that would be done after you are hired, I feel these recommendations apply equally well to the writing you do in your career search.

Make Every Word Count   Do not write for the sheer sake of writing. Words by themselves are empty shells, signifying nothing, if they are not focused toward a message. Say what you have to say economically. Don't say it again to remind your readers that they might have missed it the first time.

Adopt a Point of View   Try to leave your readers with the impression that you have reached a particular conclusion, so that they know how they and their work have affected you.

> EXAMPLE ► It is clear to me that your organization is trying to reach the youth who need help but do not use traditional helping services. This is the kind of effort I am interested in joining.

Watch the Mechanics   Anyone who has ever made a spelling error or a mistake in grammar or shown sloppy syntax will hate me for bringing up the subject, but errors of this kind distract the reader from your intended message. Hence, you are unwise to let them occur. Even typos jar some readers and leave the impression of carelessness. Proofread your writing. Enough said.

Use Strong Verbs   If you want to tell a person you were impressed with her work, try to say a little more than that you "liked" it. Say the work "stimulated" you or "encouraged" you to do additional reading. In describing your own work experience, choose such verbs as *managed, directed,* or *organized* over weaker verbs like *coordinated* or *compiled.*

Give Specifics   If you make a complimentary comment, do your best to back it up with specifics, lest the reader think you are pulling phrases from thin air.

EXAMPLE ▶ I will remember your presentation on the new laser show because it reminded me of the relationships between physics and art.

Read It Aloud It has been said that Guy de Maupassant read all his stories aloud to his cook, and if the cook couldn't understand their themes easily, he threw the stories out. Test your writing on a friend, preferably one who has no familiarity with the specific content of what you are saying. See if your writing stimulates interest.

Use Your Own Vocabulary I cannot emphasize this strongly enough. If you try to adopt words that sound lofty and impressive, your phoniness will be detected. Speak in your own familiar words, as long as they represent plain English, so that you can retain the informal, personal quality of your writing.

▶ Sample Letters ◀

The following sample letters to an employer whom the job applicant has never met show the contrast between an impersonal, business style of writing and a more personal, informal style. In both cases, the applicant has done appropriate research and feels it is possible to create enough interest to obtain a formal job interview.

First, the business style; note how dry it seems.

Dear Ms. Beaumont:

In your capacity as personnel manager of the Robinson Crusoe Company, you have many occasions to talk with people about the responsibilities of your office. In this regard I would like to request that you let me know whether I could meet with you on an appropriate occasion to discuss matters of some importance to me.

I am interested in requesting information about the nature of your operations, key personnel, organizational structures, and institutional policies. This information would assist me in expanding my knowledge of facilities similar to that which you direct.

I have collected certain background information about your organization that would provide suitable preparation for my visit with you. In my efforts to conserve your time, I have prepared a formal agenda that will not make undue demands upon you.

Could you reply to me at your earliest convenience, so that we can arrange this meeting for our mutual benefit? Thank you kindly.

Now the informal style. Note how the writer uses specific terms about his or her qualifications and language that is personal and direct.

Dear Ms. Beaumont:

I have learned from contacting your office that you are personnel manager for the Robinson Crusoe Company. I am writing to you because I have read about personnel work in the business world for the past few months and would like to meet a person who does it as a professional. I have read several books on the topic and have spoken with relatives who work for International Tool and United Ball Bearing. These relatives told me that personnel work involves a lot of activities similar to what I am doing in college. I am social chairperson for my sorority and look after the staff of the school newspaper. I like these responsibilities and would like to hear what you have to say about personnel work before considering it as a career.

Perhaps you could tell me how you got into this work and why you feel it is the right field for you. I would benefit a lot from the insight you could give me. I have prepared a small number of key questions I would like to ask you. Would you be willing to see me for thirty minutes?

I have known several people who have applied for and worked at the Robinson Crusoe Company, and they have told me how pleased they are with their jobs. One, John Meharry in the automotive department, even wrote you a note of thanks a few months ago, I believe.

I suspect it must be frustrating to be concerned about the welfare of every employee in the entire company. I am interested to hear how you deal with this responsibility and why you like it.

I will be graduating from college within the next year and a half, so your views will be a great help in shaping my own plans. Thanks very much.

Finally, here is an example of a good letter to an employer with whom you would like an interview.

Ms. Carolyn Randolph
Editor and Publisher
Outdoor Education Press

Dear Ms. Randolph:

I read about your publishing company in a recent issue of *Printer's Ink* and was very much intrigued with how your started the business with only one title (your own book) and used your advertising experience to generate contacts with authors so the business would grow. I notice that you have a particular interest in encouraging authors whose books might be turned down by the publishers who seek mass-market potential. I appreciate this sensitivity on your part to the need for helping good books to appear despite marketing constraints.

Since reading the article in *Printer's Ink*, I have read many of the books you currently list because I have considerable experience with outdoor matters and would like to become more closely involved with this kind of publishing. I noticed from the article that you market your books by direct mail and coupon advertising and do not use a sales force to enhance your efforts. I would like to propose that you experiment with the direct sales approach by considering my services. I have a particular preference for marketing your products on college campuses.

Before writing to you with this proposal, I tested my idea by phoning or contacting personally twelve different college bookstores in our local area. Each told me it would be willing to stock your books if they were more readily available. Hence, I am encouraged to believe that there is sales potential that has not been tapped.

I believe I can help your sales for several reasons: (1) my previous experience (résumé enclosed) as a graduate school representative taught me how to make contacts on large university campuses and the value of the personal approach; (2) I sold computer equipment during my college years and thus learned to be comfortable with selling skills; (3) my experience with outdoor activities includes ten years as an active supervisor of the Appalachian Trail, a term as president of the local hiking club, and occasional articles for the Sierra Club (see enclosed sample).

I believe we should get together to talk about this idea, if you feel it has some potential for you. I will call you during the week to discuss a time we might meet.

Sincerely,
Chris Jones

I have chosen to emphasize writing as a separate communication skill because I believe you can enhance your career search greatly with a personal letter on those occasions when the written form is most convenient and appropriate. A clear and personal writing style is the natural complement to an effective set of interviewing skills. Often the potent and readable letter creates invitations to interviews that would not have occurred otherwise.

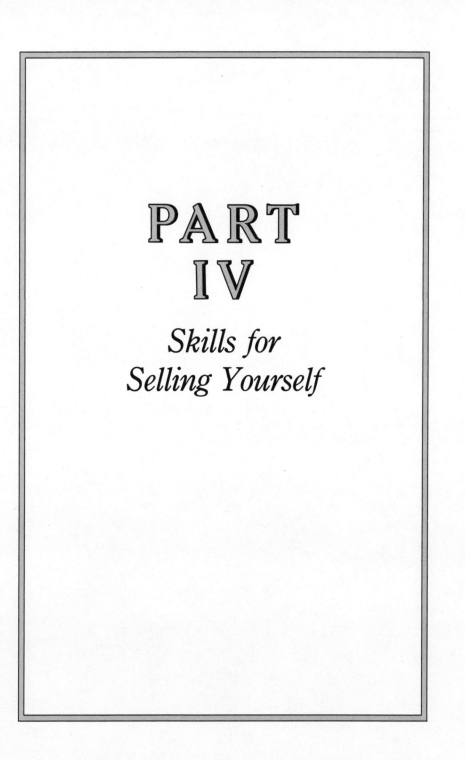

PART IV

Skills for Selling Yourself

16
Self-Marketing

If the work search were simply a matter of having certain credentials—academic degrees, certificates of experience, and the like—and a résumé detailing your work history, there would be little debate about hiring decisions. Your fate would be in the hands of the technocrats, and there would be little need for a book of this kind.

Fortunately, there is still considerable debate about the appropriate preparation for most jobs of responsibility, except those that are highly structured and technological. The flexibility regarding appropriate background for a particular job stems from the transferability of skills, our recognition that experience in one context can be applied to a different context once the person acquires a necessary base of knowledge. For example, many military officers who have managed supply operations can transfer their skills to inventory control in private corporations.

I shall use the term *self-marketing* to refer to your ability to see and use transferability in all your life activities. With a little practice, you will recognize that everything you do allows you to cultivate certain skills that can be used profitably in future employment settings. Self-marketing is the ultimate transition skill to carry you from one job to the next because it allows you to see links between what you are doing now and the work you will choose tomorrow.

Self-marketing is important because you must make the fullest possible use of your past experience when seeking a change of work; otherwise you are judged on the basis of superficial credentials and other external criteria, such as test scores, manner of dress, and prestige of previous employers. Your ability to communicate your worth is a function of your ability to recognize value in your own experience and see how it can be translated into new capabilities.

► Selling Yourself: A Simple ◄
Three-Step Process

Selling yourself. A simple phrase, but one which makes some readers cringe, and probably raises more anxiety than any other part of the job search. Selling yourself. It sounds like you're a laundry detergent, or peanuts being barked at a circus. A product to be peered at, picked over, eyed skeptically, and—despite your best efforts—at times rejected. Doesn't sound like much fun.

It also feels demeaning to be pushing yourself on people. As if you have to point and say "Here I am. Notice me" to get their attention. Somehow life would be nicer and you would feel better about yourself if they came looking for you. Saves wear and tear all around if someone spots your potential. Seems a lot more dignified than making a sales pitch to an uncertain audience. Not a bad idea. Most job seekers would probably prefer the no-search job search, discussed on pages 297–314, as an ideal to be sought.

Meanwhile we had better talk about selling yourself, because you will be in many situations where a job can depend upon how well you project your potential to an interested listener. Selling yourself may feel awkward at first, but it need not involve high-pressure tactics and can often occur in informal settings. The more you do it, the more natural it becomes. Calm down. You probably already do it a lot, but you don't call it "selling."

Don't Blow It Now—You've
Come Too Far

You have assessed your abilities, values, and interests . . . you've gone through various decision-making methods, including the career matrix (see pages 87–90 . . . you've done detective work till you're blue in the face . . . you've information interviewed . . . you've done research . . . you've built a prospect list . . . in short, you've put a lot of time and effort into this. And now do you want to fritter it all away? Just when you've got yourself at the doorstep of good opportunities, do you want to blow it?

Of course not. But that is just what will happen to you if you are gun-shy about selling yourself, unwilling to tell people who you are and what you can do. They won't know if'n you can't tell 'em. They won't divine your full potential from your résumé; they won't assume that your academic credentials mean you are the greatest; they won't stop you in the grocery store and say: "Wait a minute, that face, that hard-driving look, that can-do expression, we gotta have it!!" Even when you work hard to get into job interviews, the interviewers will not look deeply into your eyes, feel your pulsating forehead and say: "You're just what we're looking for!"

To get their attention, you have to show more than paper credentials. Selling youself in job interviews is more than giving stock answers that sound positive but mean little:

I want this job (So what else is new?)
I'm really good with people (That's better than being really good with reptiles.)
I'm a hard worker (Did you think we wanted a sloth?)
I'm a high-energy type of person (Are you a battery?)

These are useful sentiments, but they are not enough. While they may sound fine to you, the interviewer has heard them a thousand times before. He/she wants to know in more specific terms what is special about you, and how your background is suited to the job. Fortunately, this selling job is easy to accomplish, because you get to talk about the one topic in the world that you know best—yourself.

Selling yourself is your payoff for all the hard and effective work you've done in the earlier chapters of this book. You've done a great job of finding the jobs that you're a good candidate for. You've probably already spoken to people with whom you'd like to work, and will talk to many more of them. They'd like to know what you have to offer, but often will not ask the right questions to find out. Don't lose your momentum now. Give them the information they need.

An Easy Three-Step Process

If you cultivate the following three easy and enjoyable skills, you'll have the tools you need to do well in any job interview or other situation where a person is evaluating your potential for a particular job. There is nothing mysterious about these skills; they do not require complicated techniques and they are not related to the high-pressure methods that are taught to insurance salespeople and other professional sales personnel. These are simple, everyday skills that all successful job hunters use. In fact, as you read them you'll see that you have probably already practiced these skills in previous job seeking or other circumstances.

► 1. Give Them Some Reasons ◄ to Want You

The job interview is not a courtroom, where lawyers fight over the right and wrong of what you are saying. The interviewer is not your adversary. He/she is on your side. Interviewers want you to succeed, do well in the interview, because it makes their job easier. Of course, they are not always perfectly congenial or clear about what they want, but that is because of their imperfect interviewing skills. Fundamentally, they hope you are the best candidate for the job, because if you are, their job is completed.

Therefore, the interviewer wants you to cooperate in his/her search for the right person. So, the first rule to keep in mind for any interview is this: Give them a reason to want you.

As noted before, the interviewer cannot rely too heavily on your résumé (even though you still must have a good one), your academic credentials, or your other paper qualifications. These are necessary items, but often they will not distinguish you from a number of other applicants. Thus, the first question you must face in selling yourself for any interview is: "How can I stand out from the pack of other applicants?"

As an interviewer, I am looking for that something special or different about you that the other candidates may not have—a reason to be interested in you. So, your job is to help me find it. Put an idea in my head. Give me something to chew on, something that would help me to justify choosing you, something besides your degree and bland statements such as "I love the business world." Say something that attracts my attention, and draw it directly from your understanding of yourself and your understanding of the job in question. Speak to me.

EXAMPLES ► I would be good at organizing your data projects, because I have done that several times before.

I think I could do well in your economic development area because I have had experience with our university's Bureau of Business Research.

I believe my writing ability would help in that division, because there are so many reports to write for different audiences.

I could use my experience as a grants administrator for the government to help your department apply for new grants.

I am comfortable working with quantitative data and statistics, so I think that research analyst job would be a good one for me.

I have a lot of patience with difficult people, and am sure I could help out in the customer service department.

My work as a camp counselor taught me a lot about how to manage children. I could apply that to what you are looking for in the Parks and Recreation Department.

I know where to get many of the building materials you need for that construction project, and I can get them at good prices.

You would not pull any of these statements out of thin air. Each would come only after you had analyzed the job at hand, and related it to your particular background.

The first rule of selling yourself is to find some way to distinguish yourself from the competition. State something that is unique about yourself that perhaps the others cannot offer. A dimension that will enable the interviewer to remember you. A factor that may enable you to do the job better than others. In the final analysis, try to provide one or more reasons they should want you.

What if you cannot think of anything? Or you believe that nothing in your background is especially pertinent to the job? Try this list of questions to help scan your background for possible reasons to want you:

- What skills do you have that are similar to those required in the job? (writing? research? organizing? planning? supervising? teaching?)
- What type of client/customer have you worked well with before?
- What college courses have you completed that are job related?
- Do you have any knowledge of their competitors?
- Which projects or programs in that department are you familiar with?
- What personal experiences have you had that connect with this job?
- What personal qualities do you have that would be especially helpful?
- Are there people you know who would be useful contacts for this work?

You should be ready to give your "reasons to want you" whenever you have an opportunity. This first element of selling yourself is the first step toward getting you into an interview, or the first round you fire during the interview itself. Without some concrete way to distinguish yourself from the competition, you may not get much farther. If your "reason to want you" is sound and reasonably stated (you don't have to be excessive; it is not necessary to say you are the best ever at a certain task), most interviewers will want to know more about you.

EXAMPLE ► Susan wanted a job with ABC Instruments, a national computer technology firm. But she had a liberal arts degree in history, did not want a sales job, and couldn't figure out how to attract their attention. With a little research (a skill honed in history courses), Susan discovered a job as a junior management trainee that involved studying new product designs and reporting on their potential to higher management. She didn't know a lot about technological products, but decided to make her pitch as follows: "I have strong writing and research skills and, if you'll teach me the technical things, I can produce and write very clear and useful reports." It happens that ABC had been complaining about the reports developed and written by other junior management—they were not clear and the data were often incomplete. They bought Susan's "reasons to want me." She worked there for four years and then, on the basis of her contacts with local industry, was hired by the chamber of commerce to be vice-president for technological development. Her career had started modestly

202 • *Skills for Selling Yourself*

enough—with a job for which she might have been seen as "unqualified" if she had not given the employer a specific rationale for hiring her.

▶ 2. Tell Them Stories ◀
About Yourself

The second major step in selling yourself is storytelling. No, not sitting around the campfire telling tales about Indians, nor seeing how many bold and creative lies you can construct, nor entertaining the listener with narratives about the great Southwest.

The stories I want you to tell are stories about *you*. Giving them "reasons to want you" is a good start, and most necessary in attracting your listeners' attention, but it is not enough. You want to give a fuller picture of your capabilities. And the easiest way to provide this fuller picture is from stories of your past experiences.

Anyone who hears you say "I can do this . . . I can do that" will be likely to ask: "How do you know you can do that? What makes you say that you can?"

Essentially, your listener is saying: "Prove it to me." Your best support comes from the things you have done before. That is where the stories come in. If you tell me you are good at something, but you cannot tell me where you acquired the skill or how you come to have the knowledge, I will have a hard time believing you. So, tell me a story.

EXAMPLES ▶ I think I would be a good computer programmer, because it involves logical thinking. I got my logic skills from philosophy courses in college. I am also good at chess and won an analytical thinking contest during college. One time I spent three days and nights working through a math problem that no one else could do, but I did it.

I have always been able to work under the stress of deadlines, as this job calls for. I was a news editor in my hometown and was continually assigned the late-breaking stories that had to be covered, researched, and written up in a matter of hours. I also worked summers at the local plant, where packages had to be completed during peak periods, with a lot of the workers complaining, and being interrupted by telephone calls too.

Probably the best reason to consider me for this accounting job is that I was financial manager of my fraternity. When I took over, the books were in a total mess. With only the introductory accounting course under my belt at the time, I got the whole system in order, including purchasing, dues, investments, and a complicated loan arrangement with the local bank. I got the job done with almost no supervision, and enjoyed working out the problems.

I think you should hire me as manager of member services here at the racquetball/fitness center because I understand how to keep members happy. I used to work at a tennis pro shop and developed many tournaments, deals on equipment, social events, and clinics for injury prevention. I would hang around with the members a lot and find out what they were complaining about, then try to develop a program to satisfy them. One year I had them all out there doing stretching and conditioning exercises when they complained about getting tired late in their matches.

Stories are easy to listen to, especially if they are told concisely and they are convincing. Stories beat trying to "explain" in analytical terms why you are good at something ("I'm good with people. They like me . . . they come to me . . . I'm just *good* with them, you know what I mean?").

Stories explain without having to explain. They *show* you as a problem-solver; they reveal what you have done and lead the listener to believe that you can do it again.

What if you have no stories to tell? If you cannot back up the statements you make about yourself with a story or two, you may not have the skill or the attribute that you claim. But let's not get pessimistic yet. Maybe you are lacking direct experience ("I have never worked with that type of problem or customer before"), but you do have indirect experience that can be related to the new job.

EXAMPLE ▶ You want a job as a retail store buyer.
Story: I have been manager of purchasing for the community theater. In this job, I have purchased costumes, and done a lot of negotiating with the merchants. I know what it's like to cut a deal, and how important it is to develop relationships with people. I have never been in retailing, but I think I can apply my experience and do a good job.

When a story is needed, almost any story will do. If you think you may be unqualified but you want the job badly, reach back for a story that demonstrates some positive quality that you think will get their attention.

EXAMPLE ▶ Joan wanted a job as director of the women's center at the community college, where the job called for working with inner-city students, many of them older than traditional-age students. The idea of the job was to develop programs highlighting the career potential of women. Joan had never done anything like it before. However, at one time Joan ran a day-care center. She told the Women's Center interviewer: "I worked with a lot of older women when I took care of their children. I found out a lot about their ambitions to advance career-wise. I encouraged many of them to apply to school after their children grew up a bit. That makes me think I can do this job, because I know what their problems are and how to handle them." Other candidates had more experience on paper, but Joan's timely story got her the job.

The listener wants some evidence that you can back up what you have said about yourself. A story is convincing, because it is believable and provides concrete examples of skills you have used and problems you have solved. Come armed with the stories you need to demonstrate your qualifications.

▶ 3. Develop Your ◀ Social Skills

*Life is a contact sport. . . . People deal with and help
the people they like. Learning how to become likeable is
what developing social skills is all about.*
—Jack Falvey,
"Developing Party Skills"[1]

You don't have to be a party animal, but you should learn how to handle yourself smoothly and positively in mixed company. The least mentioned, but important, part of selling yourself is the fine art of being liked by those whom you want to hire you. Given a choice, employers will always try to hire the people they like best. "Likeability" impressions are formed from the informal contacts you have with interviewers and with everyone else in the work setting.

While you are giving them reasons to want you and telling stories about your past experiences, people will be forming impressions about you:

Is he easy to be with?
Does she seem to get along easily with everyone?
Is there anything about him I am uncomfortable with?
When she talks with me, do I feel she's really interested?
Do I think I could trust him if I worked with him?

The answers to questions like these may affect your chances of being hired as much as the content of what you can do for the job and the organization. Sometimes a person who is more congenial is hired over someone who has better experience and credentials, because the latter made people feel uncomfortable, or "acted like he wanted to run over us," or "seemed too task oriented, not interested in us."

Selling your personality will not always be a crucial factor, but it will be hard for you to judge how much it is being weighed in the hiring decision. Therefore, you might as well assume it is a key variable, and give the social dimension your full attention.

If you are feeling a little short on the socializing end of the job-search process, what can you do about it?

Informal Partying Going out to boogie with your friends and a few strangers is a good place to start. Even though this stuff is strictly for fun, it helps you to practice being with people. If you don't do it much, now's the time to get hopping. If not dancing, go to house parties, or picnics, or cocktail parties, or tailgate parties . . . or *something!*

Formal Partying The norms and ways of socializing at work are important. Often they will be part of a job interview, to see how you mingle with people and how well they like you when the structure of the interview is let down. Such events usually include eating and drinking, where it's easy to make mistakes.

> What you eat and, especially, drink at a party are important. Try eating something before you arrive so you aren't hungry. Practice moderation in drinking. Most business social gatherings aren't parties even though they look like it. "Parties" are for doing business standing up.[2]

Get some experience with this kind of partying. If you have no other access to it, try your family members in the working world or other contacts. Get them to invite you to cocktail parties or other such events, so you can learn how to handle yourself there.

Take a Contact out to Lunch Lunching is part of socializing, and an easy way to get comfortable with the social skills that are part of the working world. Try this with your easiest contacts first, and then invite to lunch some you know less well. Take them to unfamiliar restaurants, so you can get used to new situations. Invite a contact someplace where you will run into his/her friends, so you can get accustomed to the unexpected encounters with other people.

Give a Party Yourself This is not always within people's means, but where possible, creating your own social events is a good way to improve your ability to mingle with others and get to know them. Once again, be careful not to let eating or drinking get in the way of your interacting.

Many a job has been lost because the otherwise qualified candidate did not do well socially and was vetoed by one or more of the office staff. In such cases, the rejected person is often not told that social skills were at the root of his/her problem. How do you tell someone they turned people off, or they did not project much warmth? Instead, the candidates might be told they were simply "not as qualified as others."

The social dimension is easy enough if you're comfortable with it, you do a lot of partying, and people usually like you. But, if you back off from socializing at all, check out your social skills in one or more of the following ways:

- *Ask for feedback from interviewers.* Once hiring decisions have been made, it is all right to call an interviewer and ask: "Can you give me an idea of my strengths and weaknesses in the interview? Was there anything in my interpersonal style that you'd recommend I change?" Sometimes this kind of honest inquiry will yield helpful advice.

- *Ask your friends for feedback.* Do I interrupt when others are talking? Do I sometimes express myself hesitantly? Am I a good listener? Do I get my point across firmly? Is there anything in the way I speak that makes it hard to listen to me?
- *Be true to your own personality.* We are not asking for a personality transplant here. If you are a low-key person, then go on being that way and communicate in the style that is comfortable for you. However, pay attention to things you do that may make it more difficult for people to talk with you.

Maybe this all makes you feel self-conscious. Well, in a way it should. Socializing does not come naturally to everyone, but it is a necessary factor in anyone's job search. If you jump into the social pool more often than you are used to, and take the licks and kicks that come with unrehearsed talk, you'll be a new and improved socializer before too long.

► Why This Book Says ◄
So Little About Résumé Writing

Many job-search books make résumé writing a centerpiece of their presentations, and certainly a résumé is a necessary part of most people's job-search strategies. Résumé-writing manuals are everywhere, and people worry a lot about getting their résumés in shape. Yet this book gives it little attention, other than a brief discussion in the "Writing" chapter on pages 185–194. Why have I largely ignored a topic that is so prominent in job seekers' minds?

Your résumé must be written with clarity and focus, must be easily readable, and must do a decent job of presenting you as an appropriate candidate for the job you want. *But* it is a mistake to use your résumé as a leading player in your job search:

- Sending résumés to prospective employers has a far lower yield of positive responses than most other forms of making contact.
- The résumé offers more reasons that you can be eliminated from contention—poor layout, experience that does not fit the reader's concept of what he/she wants, stylistic factors, grammar, etc.—than it does positive reasons to keep you in the running. In other

words, résumés are often used as a "knockout" factor, a way to screen people out, because they are so impersonal.

- The résumé reader evaluates you without knowing anything else about you. Evaluations of written material have a certain amount of guesswork and arbitrariness built into them. Who is this guy? Did she really do what it says she did? Does this job mean that she was in charge or not? Why did he leave that job for this one? I don't know anything about that company; it must not be very good. Judgments such as these are made all the time, and you have no chance to counter them.
- The résumé is a passive document. It sits there like a lump and tries to sell itself, but readers can buffet it any way they want, and you can't fight back. The résumé does not smile, it does not act energetically, and it does not make any pitch for itself beyond the bare words it offers. It is a shy wallflower in the ballroom dance known as the job hunt. It can be deposited by the reader in any number of places without any resistance from you, and most of these places will be far from the employer's view.

Therefore, the résumé should not be the card you pull first off the top of your job-search deck. Whenever possible, make personal contact with a prospective employer first, before you ever show your résumé. An active personal presentation is more likely to get you serious attention than a passive résumé which arrives quietly in the mail.

Résumé preparation is covered in great detail in other books, which do a good job of helping you to write yours with care and effectiveness, for those situations where you are forced to rely upon the résumé to gain entry. I would recommend the following:

The Perfect Résumé, by Tom Jackson, Anchor Press, 1981
The Damn Good Résumé Guide, by Yana Parker, Ten Speed Press, 1983
Résumés That Work, by Tom Cowan, New American Library, 1983

I have not given you any examples of good résumés, because the more of these you have, the more you may bend your energy toward résumé writing. I would rather you view the résumé as the modest, imperfect document that it is, and pay attention to other, more crucial aspects of an effective job search.

You will make far more progress if you do information interviewing, research, positioning, interim jobs, and self-marketing long before you show your résumé. If you do these things first, (1) You will get many job interviews before people even see your résumé, (2) By the time they read your résumé, many will already have a positive impression of you.

You'll have to take my word for this, or read the chapters on personal referral network and information interviewing for an explanation of why interactions among people are more natural and productive for any job seeker than sending pieces of paper through the mail, hoping somebody who is busy with a thousand other things will give you a tumble.

17

Experience

► Identifying Your ◄
► Identifying Your ◄
Experience When You Think
You Have None

Likeability, motivation, leadership, skills, ambition, and other factors count right alongside experience. So, you must use all the tools in your kit to give yourself the best chance of competing for the jobs you want. And you have a lot more experience than you think.

Here's the situation: You've just been rejected for a job because you "did not have experience in that kind of work." You're entering an occupation for the first time and, sure, you haven't done it before. But how are you supposed to *get* that experience when no one will hire you?

Calm down. You lost that one, but let's talk about how you can get the next one. Chances are, you have some experience related to the job you want, but you did not know it. How can this be so? I'm not asking you to lie, am I? No. Almost anything you have ever done that involved significant effort can be viewed as experience that is relevant to many different jobs and careers.

Now, that's a pretty grand statement, but we'll look at some examples of how experience lies hidden in a person's previous activities. And you need to know this, because otherwise you are likely to *discount* all of the good things you have done and overlook their relevance to your future goals.

You Must Be the Translator

If the process of selling yourself were reduced to a single, central element, it would be this:

You must make connections between *what you have done in the past and what you can do in the future*.

You must help the interviewer see that you have potential for performing the present job well, by showing him/her something you have done or learned before that provides clues to your potential. When the interviewer says "You lack experience," he/she is often saying: "You have failed to show me any connection between your past successes and your future aspirations." He/she cannot jump into your memory bank and see what those connections are.

Why do employers make such a fuss about experience? Why do they so often ask for it, even though we know that many jobs can be learned as you go?

1. *They don't want you to foul up* if they hire you. "Experience" on your record gives them the delusion that you know what the job is about. So, even if you haven't done this particular job before, your task is to give them a reason to believe you can do the job without mishap.
2. *They want you to know what you are getting into.* They don't want you to be surprised by the expectations and norms of the job. So, don't act like a dumbo who is ignorant of the job. Show that you have done some research. Your knowledge of the job can be interpreted as experience.
3. *They may want to eliminate you for some other reason,* and "lack of experience" is a good excuse, a straw figure for their purposes. Look for other factors where you may have slipped. Review the hidden agenda of any job interview (pages 233–244).

Enough of this abstract talk. Let's find a few career changers with unlikely backgrounds, so you can see some of the many possible connections between past and present.

EXAMPLE 1 ► Joe is a new college graduate who wants a job as an account executive trainee for an advertising agency. However, he has taken no advertising courses, has never worked in an advertising agency, and apparently has no experience.

Relevant Experience: I painted houses to support myself in the summertime, and learned how to negotiate with people, keep them happy, and understand their needs. I also raised money for the alumni fund in college and there learned how to make group presentations, such as you do in the advertising world.

Comment: There is enough in Joe's background to believe he has potential to be an account executive. Anyone who can run his own business and ask other people for money has some business sense and people skills, and that is what ad agencies look for in new trainees.

EXAMPLE 2 ► Sarah wants to change from being a social worker to becoming a bank loan officer. She has had no business courses and no banking experience, and has been in human services work since graduating from college.

Relevant Experience: I have handled numbers in my budgetary work as a social worker and am comfortable with them. My husband and I built a new home and I did all the negotiating with contractors. I'm experienced in working with the public from my work in low-income housing.

Comment: Sarah sounds like a serious candidate. Loan officers have to be tough-minded people who are used to public contact. Sarah could make the transition, with her people skills and apparent enthusiasm about business.

EXAMPLE 3 ► Karen hopes to become a retail buyer for a department store. She has a college degree in history, and has been working as an insurance underwriter for several years. She has never worked in a department store.

Relevant Experience: My father has a stockyard business. There I learned my business sense, I dealt with tough customers and suppliers, and worked long hours. I don't imagine those garment district people could be any meaner or more ornery than cattle people. All my sorority sisters shopped at these big department stores, and I have an idea what they look for.

Comment: Sarah is not afraid to make a big leap from the cattle business to the world of high fashion. Her toughness will come in handy, and her zeal for hard work will attract attention. She merits consideration, because she portrays confidence and has people skills that will be needed.

EXAMPLE 4 ► Leo has designs on becoming a stockbroker. However, he has been a school counselor for many years and has no business experience. He was a retail clothing salesman prior to being a counselor, after graduating with a liberal arts degree.

Relevant Experience: I have developed strong interpersonal skills as a counselor, and know I can use these in a sales environment. Also, I was a good card player in college and learned how to make decisions about money under pressure. I am very social and would have a good head start in developing clientele.

Comment: Leo has obviously thought about what it takes to be a successful stockbroker and has found items in his background that present him as a good candidate. He can make the transition from being a counselor to being a broker, because his skills will carry over well.

EXAMPLE 5 ► Gloria wants to be a political lobbyist. She has been an arts administrator for three years, and prior to that was head of volunteer services for the Board of Probation and Parole. She has a master's degree in social work and no experience in politics.

Relevant Experience: I have worked with legislators in trying to get funding for my arts program, and also came to Capitol Hill frequently to hear about probation and parole legislation. I have "lobbied" on behalf of my programs with various constituencies and know what it is like to build relationships with funding sources and the public.

Comment: Gloria has been around political people for quite a while, because she has needed their support. Thus, in a very real sense, she has political experience and can apply it as a lobbyist. In addition to this knowledge, she also has the people skills needed, and radiates confidence about her future role.

► Getting the Experience ◄ You Need

If you don't have the experience you need, you can usually get some of it, one way or the other. Consider how you can obtain experience that will enhance your marketability for future employment. Here are seven types of "experience" that are available, to make you a better job candidate.

Seven Kinds of Experience

1. Part-Time Work   Some kinds of work can be done part-time, either concurrent with your present employment, while you are in school, or while you are looking for full-time work. Part-time work is often an easier way to enter a field, because the employer does not have to make as big a decision about you. Either the job is temporary, or the level of responsibility is low, or you are filling in for someone else. Part-time work is the classic foot in the door, whereby you can have a chance to show your stuff and also get to observe the setting firsthand. Many fine careers have begun with part-time employment, where you and the boss have a chance to get to know each other without any great pressure, yet you are building your credibility for future jobs.

2. Unpaid Work   This may still be one of the better-kept secrets of developing one's career. While voluntarism has had the connotation of social service work in the community and the Red Cross, hospital auxiliary, and nursing homes, unpaid work is far broader than that. You can offer yourself in many work settings, and get valuable experience. Giving your services for free creates a strong incentive for many employers. They may be willing to let you learn and make contacts in exchange for your talents. You have nothing to lose by working without pay.

Unpaid work gives you the freedom to apply wherever you want, without worrying if there is a job opening there. Thus, the governor's office, the research lab of the sports physiology program, the city council, the new products division of the local computer company, or the field station of Sea Lions Incorporated are all potentially available to you. Once again, think about the skills and experiences you have had that would be useful, and make them an offer they'll have a hard time refusing.

3. Internships These are usually available to college or university students, but they can be offered to recent graduates as well. An internship is a limited-time work/learning experience in which the organization agrees to have you work there primarily for the purpose of learning what the field is about. Internships are often unpaid. They use your services in exchange for the skills and experiences you acquire. In addition to the prearranged internships, students and graduates can often create and negotiate their own internships by simply approaching employers and proposing work/learning relationships that would be satisfactory to both parties. Employers often use internships as a way of looking closely at people whom they may want to hire for permanent jobs. Don't disappoint them. Give one or more an opportunity to look you over. You have no obligation to work there, but will be in a great position to get their attention if you decide to apply.

4. Informal Experiences There will be situations where you cannot get the experience you want through part-time work, unpaid work, internships, or in any other way. In such cases, consider doing it yourself. For example, suppose you want to be an investment analyst, but no one will let you play with their money. Try some fictional "investing" with your own portfolio of $10 million. That's experience, and if you back it up with research, you may get results that are impressive to a prospective employer.

Or, suppose you want to be a river tour guide, but the commercial groups just won't take you on. Get yourself a boat or raft or canoe, learn the river on your own, and then talk your friends into going with you for a few trips, once you know what you're doing. That's experience, and you can use it to build your skills as well as make an argument for including you on the staff of a commercial tour guide operation.

These are valid experiences even though you were not hired by someone to get them. Hiring is always a judgment call. Your informal experiences are marketable if you believe they are. In the absence of other experiences, these allow you to get your hands into many areas of work. You can't build an ocean liner in your backyard, nor can you perform brain surgery on your brother, but many occupations can be done on an informal basis. Want to sell fitness programs for a living? Work up a few and "sell" them to your friends. Want to turn your hat collection into a little business one day? Keep digging up hats, hold an auction or two, and see what develops.

5. Start Your Own Small Enterprise In the world of entrepreneurship, experience comes from doing it yourself, or working with someone else who's trying to get a business started. While most of us don't have the capital to stake a large business before breakfast, you can try a small one almost anytime. More often than not these days, small enterprises are services (career counseling? plant consultation? home cleaning? appliance repair?) and you can start one with a telephone and a business card. Experience comes from trying it, seeing if there is a market and how you respond to it. Small-business operators are also attractive to larger employers offering the same products or services, so you may be acquiring experience toward a future job without even knowing it.

6. Campus Activities If you are a college student, work-related experience is available to you in many forms. Campus political organizations, fraternity house leadership roles, campus newspaper jobs, radio station positions, membership on budgetary committees, leadership of college organizations, human service work (such as drug abuse education, or work as a counselor in the residence halls), fund-raising, and public relations work (traveling with the admissions office) are some examples of campus jobs that develop career skills. Each of these jobs is valid experience that can be part of our self-marketing strategy. If you have gone straight through school, have never had a full-time job, and are trying to set yourself apart from the crowd of other college graduates, campus jobs and activities give you the edge you're looking for.

7. Academic Coursework Many college courses have work experience components in them. Cooperative work/study programs are the most obvious example of this, but there are many others. Field placements are common in social work, journalism, pharmacy, hotel/restaurant management, and many other vocationally oriented programs. In addition, many colleges offer an independent study vehicle, which allows you to design your own course around an area of interest. Such a project (for example, investigating the political lobbying process) may give you permission to study firsthand a work setting and acquire experience. Since a large number of college and university curricula are openly regarded as career preparation, it is not surprising that many of them integrate experience into their progams.

Employers cannot measure precisely how much experience weighs in successful performance on a job, but they ask for it anyway. The biggest distinction is between *zero* experience and *some* experience. If you can show you have *some*, they're much more likely to look at you. Often they will ask for experience to see if you can translate your background into something that is related to the job. If you can see the connection, then say so. It is a measure of your motivation. Claim as much experience as you can without exaggerating. Then, while you're waiting for the right situations to develop, go out and acquire some more.

The best evidence that you are acquiring suitable experience is if you are gaining marketable skills. Here are the skills you should try to develop as you get involved in a variety of experiences.

▶ The Ten Hottest ◀ Transferable Skills

Some skills are more equal than others. I have been encouraging you to identify your most powerful talents, with the implied assumption that every skill can find a home somewhere. While you can expect all functional and adaptive skills to have definite value, you must recognize that certain skills are universally greeted with enthusiasm by almost every employer because these skills occur with some regularity in every job having responsibility and requiring decision making and good judgment. You should pay special attention to them in the work you are now doing, look for them in the nonpaid activity of your spare time, and comb your past experiences for evidence of them.

Budget Management   Get your hot little hands on any budget you can find, no matter how small, and take responsibility for it. Manage how the funds are dispensed, keep control of the budget, learn what fiscal control is all about.

Supervising   Take responsibility for the work of others in a situation in which some accountability is called for. Have direct contact with the work of others; expose yourself to the difficulty of giving orders, delegating tasks, taking guff, understanding the other person's viewpoint. Here is where listening can become a real feat of skill.

Public Relations   Accept a role in which you must meet or relate to the public. Greet visitors, answer phone complaints, give talks to community groups, sell ads to businesspeople, explain programs to prospective clients, or even collect taxes.

Coping with Deadline Pressure   Search for opportunities to demonstrate that you can produce good work when it is governed by external deadlines. Prove to yourself and anyone else that you can function on someone else's schedule, even when that time frame is notably hurried.

Negotiating/Arbitrating Discover and cultivate the fine art of dealing openly and effectively with people in ambiguous situations. Learn how to bring warring factions together, resolve differences between groups or individuals, and make demands on behalf of one constituency to those in positions of power.

Speaking Take a leadership role in any organization, so that you are forced to talk publicly, prepare remarks, get across ideas, and even motivate people without feeling terribly self-conscious. Good public speaking is little more than the art of dramatized conversation, but it must be practiced so you can discover your own personal style.

Writing Go public with your writing skills, or even the lack of them. There is nothing quite so energizing as seeing your own words in print; exhilarating if they look good to you, and a spur to improvement if they look awful. Practice putting pen to paper. Write letters to the editors of every publication you read routinely. Write a newsletter, however informal, for a club or organization to which you belong.

Organizing/Managing/Coordinating Take charge of any event that is within your grasp. It doesn't matter what you organize—a church supper, a parade in honor of your town's two hundredth birthday—as long as you have responsibility for bringing together people, resources, and events. If nothing else, the headaches of organizing events or managing projects teach you how to delegate tasks to others.

Interviewing Learn how to acquire information from other people by questioning them directly. Start by interviewing the neighbors, your friends, and other people easily available. It doesn't matter what you ask them, but imagine you are a newspaper reporter who needs the information for a story. Discover the fine art of helping a person to feel comfortable in your presence, even though you are asking difficult or even touchy questions.

Teaching/Instructing Refine your ability to explain things to other people. Since most teaching takes place not in the classroom, but in ordinary everyday exchanges between people, you should become familiar and comfortable with passing information and understanding to others. Any position of leadership or responsibility gives you many chances to teach ideas and methods to others.

If you cultivate any three or four of these skills to a high order of proficiency, you are doing quite well. If you practice most of them and feel you are improving in each, you should expect to have positions of decision making and responsibility before long. Conversely, if you anticipate any managerial or leadership job in the future, you will find it difficult to avoid using many of these skills in large measure.

► Making Your Pitch ◄

Once you have indentified any highly marketable skills you possess, you must consider how you are going to present yourself to a prospective employer. Usually one or two prominent skills are sufficient to give you a basis for introducing yourself. There are three central things to keep in mind: (1) describe your skills in concise, unambiguous terms; (2) back up your claim to the skills by referring to actual experiences in your life; and (3) make a clear connection between your skills and the needs of the employer.

EXAMPLE ► YOU: I enjoy drawing factual material together into written form. I have written grant proposals for state government, training manuals for a local service club, and newsletters for my church. I believe my ability to do this kind of writing could help your fund-raising department.
EMPLOYER: How could you help us?
YOU: I could prepare proposals for government research money, send news reports to interested citizen groups, write an annual report that would generate positive publicity.

► Physical Evidence ◄

It would seem from our talk about interviews, writing letters, and general conversation that self-marketing is largely a verbal matter, a process in which interpersonal communication must be your chief vehicle. On the contrary, you are not limited to talking about your accomplishments in the work search. In many situations, it can be even more potent to show evidence of the work you have done.

- *Portfolios*. Keep a file of articles you have written, advertisements you have written and designed, stories published about yourself, reports you have written for management.
- *Products*. Show products you have made. These might include furniture, crafts work, musical instruments, mechanical devices, or others.
- *Displays*. Keep photographs of physical displays you have arranged and designed, such as promotion for an arts program, Christmas displays, historical exhibits, and so on.

• *Programs*. Maintain a file of brochures or fliers from programs you have organized—the program of a drama you staged, the program of a conference you coordinated, or the outline of a scouting trip you planned.

► Apply for a Job You Don't ◄ Really Want

If you want to practice your self-marketing skills without the threat of being evaluated for a job you really want, get your act together and try it out with an employer who is interesting enough to attract your attention but for whom you really would not want to work. Go through the routine of talking to the individuals who would do the hiring, so that you can practice seeing the relevance of your past and present experiences to work opportunities and learning what skills are desired by employers. Once you have been through this experience a few times in nonthreatening situations, you will know how to talk about yourself effectively when you apply for a job you really want.

If you are offered a job in the process of applying for something you really do not want, you can respond in one of two ways: politely say you will think it over and then write or call indicating you've decided to stay in your present work; or look a little closer at the offer, keeping in mind that you may have unconsciously gravitated toward a field you are interested in without having thought about it in great detail.

18

Interim Jobs

If your need for reliable earning power is so pressing that you must obtain immediate employment without regard to its suitability to your primary career interests, what you need is an interim job.

An *interim job* can be defined as work that provides you with regular income at a level that permits financial survival. You accept this job as a stopgap without any intention of staying in this line of work on a permanent basis.

You recognize that such a job may have little or no relationship to your more enduring career interests, but you must keep this employment as long as necessary, until you find a position in your desired occupation. This means, of course, that you will continue to search actively for a more desirable career while you are engaged in the interim job.

Ideally speaking, every job of this kind should fulfill four criteria.

- It must ensure a large enough income on a regular basis to allow you (and your dependents) to survive without difficulty.
- It should be obtainable with relatively little or no advance preparation, and more readily available than most types of work. This affords you rapid entry.
- It must be moderate in its demands on your working time so that you have enough time remaining during the week to continue exploration for a permanent career.
- It should afford continual contact with a wide variety of people in the course of the work, so you can make contacts during work time that might be helpful in your career exploration.

As you can readily see, an interim job possessing all these characteristics is little short of a fantasy. As the list below suggests, however, it is possible to obtain certain positions that possess at least some of these desirable qualities.

► Interim Jobs Unrelated to ◄ Career Goals

If your immediate income needs are not large, there are many interim jobs you can consider that provide relatively easy entry, moderate work demands, and exposure to a wide variety of people. While you are not likely to consider many of these jobs as serious career options, you should examine them first because they make minimum demands upon you other than your devoting the requisite number of hours. They therefore provide the best conditions in which you can save energy for the continuation of your serious career exploration. The jobs listed below[1] also offer you relatively good access to large numbers of people in a variety of work situations.

- *Census taker.* Collecting information most people consider non-threatening gives you the opportunity to talk with many people about their work.
- *Opinion poll interviewer.* Same as above, with even more opportunity because polls are growing in use and acceptance.
- *Commuter train conductor.* Plenty of opportunity to talk with commuters about their jobs as they ride to and from work.
- *Retail store clerk.* Especially in a bookstore, cigar store, clothing store, or drugstore, people often have time to chat and provide insights into the work they do.
- *Cab driver.* Repeated chances to pick up valuable clues about various professions; businesspeople often chat with cab drivers.
- *Marketing research interviewer.* Obtain product preference information and, in the process, ask people about their work situation.
- *Bartender.* Perhaps the ideal opportunity to listen to people when they are relaxed.
- *Museum guard.* Chance to observe and talk to a variety of people.
- *Security guard.* If you can overcome the barrier of the uniform, there are plenty of people to talk with.
- *Golf caddy.* People who have the time and inclination to play this game usually have rather interesting professions and often depend on you for conversation.
- *Short-order cook.* People are more agreeable when they are being fed, and you would probably serve them at lunchtime, between halves of their working day.

- *Comparison shopper.* You get exposure to a lot of people by visiting a number of stores each day.
- *Receptionist.* You are the first person to meet people who visit the organization. Choose an organization inhabited by employees or customers you would like to meet.
- *Employment agency interviewer.* A good way to learn about job availability from an insider's vantage point.
- *Photographer's helper.* People like to have their pictures taken and do not mind talking with the photographer on a variety of subjects.
- *Travel agent.* Everyone travels at one time or another, often for the purpose of looking for a new job.
- *Advertising space salesperson.* Sell space in newspapers, on radio, in trade magazines, on TV to a wide range of organizations.
- *Mail carrier.* A vital service and an opportunity to visit homes, businesses, stores, government offices, churches, hospitals.
- *Handyman.* Offer a maintenance or repair service for homeowners and you will have a chance to visit with many people about their jobs.
- *Temporary office worker.* An all-purpose interim job available in metropolitan areas; the all-time champ for giving you an opportunity to sample a variety of work situations because you work for a few days or weeks for various employers in different settings.

► Career-Related Interim Jobs ◄

Perhaps you cannot afford to fool around with nonserious jobs, either because they pay too little for your income needs or because they are not challenging enough on a day-to-day basis. Furthermore, you hope to find an interim job that has some inherent connection to your intended career.

If you pursue such a job on an interim basis, please keep in mind that it should still retain two essential qualities: it must give you exposure to potential contacts, and it should not be so demanding that you have to suspend future exploration.

Sales Sales jobs probably represent a decent example of interim jobs in this category. Many sales positions in real estate, investments, insurance, and other fields can be entered with relative ease and give you sufficient freedom to make numerous outside contacts. Often a salesperson can choose to produce only the amount of income required for living purposes. Of course, there are sales jobs that have stringent quotas, and the interim job seeker should avoid these.

Consultant A consultant markets his or her knowledge of a given industry, occupation, profession, or geographical territory to people who pay for such service. For example, a former member of the chemical industry might consult with plastics or rubber products manufacturers. Or a former educator in the social sciences could sell advice to industrial corporations that are developing educational programs for their employees.

Student A temporary return to formal education often provides numerous professional contacts and an opportunity to be a research assistant while waiting for a career opening to occur. An increasing proportion of the enrollment in higher learning consists of people who are either currently employed or have recently been at work; hence, the person who returns to the classroom finds numerous contacts and sources of career information there.

Apprentice A somewhat different example might involve a person who wants to become a carpenter, but must wait for an apprenticeship or suitable position. In this case, an acceptable interim job might be with a lumberyard, in order to become familiar with wood products and the people who use them.

► The Interim Job Can Be ◄ Much More Than a Stopgap

The interim job is not the one you want, but it may be the one you need right now. Take a load off your back. Don't expect to find the job you want straight out of the chute, because often it will not happen, and sometimes you don't even want it to happen. The interim job gives you some breathing room, some room to maneuver and rest your big guns until the target job is available and you're ready to go for it. It allows you to say: "I'll get there, but let's stop this wagon and look around at the scenery for a while."

You take the interim job in order to earn immediate income and keep yourself occupied, but it can serve other purposes as well:

- It gives you more time to explore target jobs.
- You can work to improve the skills you need to go after the target job.
- If your recent work record had something go wrong, the interim job can give you a positive work experience to call on, a good reference to use for the next position.
- It can even give you time for personal projects that you have been wanting to do, since the interim job may require less intense involvement than a target job.

The Texas Two-Step

The two-step approach to job hunting means looking for one job to set up another, especially when the desired job is blocked for the time being. Dancing across the job landscape, you may find that two steps are better than one. In some cases, an interim job can be used as a bridge toward your target job. Being in the right place at the right time is often a matter of *putting* yourself in the right places—

- allowing others to see the work you can do;
- working for people who know people in your target organizations;
- being there to hear about emerging opportunities.

The interim job can allow you to position yourself:

EXAMPLES ► Rudy wants to be comptroller for the Private Industry Council, so he signs on as accountant for one of the projects funded by the P.I.C., gets to know their staff, makes his talents known, and is Rudy-on-the-spot when the assistant comptroller resigns a year later.

Angela has her sights set on being head trainer for the Women's Athletics Department. She takes a part-time job as staff writer, research assistant and general flunky for the department, gets to know the staff, and volunteers to be there at ball games to help with equipment. One thing leads to another, and guess who hears about an opening for assistant athletic trainer when it occurs?

You're a good candidate for an interim job if:

- You are changing locations, moving to a place you've not lived before, and are still building your contacts.
- You are an entry-level college graduate.
- You are retooling yourself, either through school programs or other skill building, and are not ready for the Big Leap yet.
- You know that you need a change, a new challenge, but you aren't sure what it is yet, or have not been able to find it.
- Your present situation is intolerable, and you need to earn income in some other way, but you're still shaping the new career direction.

► An Interim Job ◄
Is Not a Comedown

After years of successful and responsible work as a ———, you may be embarrassed to say you're now doing work that has less of everything. Or after years of expensive and ambitious schooling, you don't want to admit that you've taken a low-level job. It looks to all the world as though you have settled for less.

But what do they know? The truth is you have made a smart move. By taking the interim job, you're giving your career more time to develop at its own speed, and your body more time to do detective work instead of accepting defective work. You're moving to the place you want instead of moaning and dying on the vine back there in East Overburn. You're moving into scoring position.

Instead of waiting to be discovered, you're making a daring chess move, one step closer to your goal. Seeing the job market as a board game, you look for an opening that will position you to create an even bigger opening in the future. Sound clever? Well, it is.

EXAMPLE ► Ann took a job as a desk clerk at Hotels International when she could not get hired as an assistant manager. The pay was awful, the clientele overbearing, and the sight of her friends registering at the hotel was almost more than she could stand. But a manager noticed her efforts on behalf of important guests, and she became first in line for the management training program. During the interim, Ann had also taken computer skills courses and public speaking courses to sharpen her qualifications for the opportunity she knew would develop eventually. Without the interim job she would have been a less qualified candidate.

Interim jobs thus serve both short-term economic needs and long-term career development needs. For people who are making any significant change of career direction, or shift of location, or movement from school to the marketplace, an interim job is a good strategy, not simply for its immediate benefits, but also for the positioning and personal growth that it makes possible. Instead of rushing headlong toward your new goal, and perhaps stumbling along the way, taking an interim job may be a sensible and productive first step that becomes a bridge to your longer-range objective.

19

Selling Yourself Long-Distance

You are fifty to three thousand miles from where you wish your eventual employment to be and are wondering what exactly to do about this stark reality. Of course, it is very difficult to conduct a work search at a distance. Scattering résumés across the landscape yields little, and you must wonder what else is worth doing. You cannot expect to receive job offers by mail. There is, however, a considerable amount of preparation you *can* do that will greatly assist your efforts after you make the move.

You may wonder whether it makes any sense to do long-distance work searching. Keep in mind these three things: First, very few people do any preparation at all before they set foot in their target areas. Thus, any advance work you do will put you that much ahead of your competition. Second, every day you are in your target area, you will be hungry and anxious to find work, so you will be sorely tempted to skip much of the recommended detective work and research. Hence, it pays to do as much as possible before you go there. Third, getting an interview by mail and telephone is a challenge. If you succeed in arranging even three interviews this way, you have set the tone for what is likely to be a very successful campaign when you arrive in Target City.

This chapter assumes you have chosen a target geographical area, preferably a town or city, and that you have a goal statement that describes the kind of employment you are seeking.

EXAMPLES ▸ I want to work with flowers or plants in Boise, Idaho.
I am seeking administrative work in a college or university in the Boston area.

If you fail to target geographically and frame at least a tentative working statement, you will be unable to focus your long-distance attention on specific employers.

► Advantages of ◄
Long-Distance Activity

The methods you can use involve three varieties of contact: letter, telephone, and in-person. Each of these has a built-in advantage accruing to the person who operates at a distance.

The advantage letter writing gives you is that people are flattered to receive personal attention by mail. When you receive a letter from someone who is aware of your work and has taken the time to study and think about it, you assume the person is impressed by what you and your organization are doing.

Using the telephone is advantageous because people are generally programmed to be responsive on the phone; it is easier than responding in writing. To increase your probability of getting a good response, use the name of the organization for which you work ("I am calling from XYZ Company") and be specific about your request ("I need some information about your work with low-income housing").

The advantage in-person contact affords you is that since you are going to move to the new town anyway, all contacts you make in the local area can be regarded as practice. You can make mistakes, acquire information without fear of facing an unexpected job interview, and ask people to be sounding boards for your ideas.

Let's turn now to the ways writing, telephoning, and in-person contact come into play.

Writing

Write letters requesting background information about work available in the area. Direct these letters to the chamber of commerce, United Way, or other groups that exist to provide this information.

EXAMPLE ► (Letter to United Way): I would appreciate your letting me know how I might obtain a listing of social service agencies in your area which relate to senior citizens.

Write letters requesting information from a target employer.

EXAMPLE ► I would like to know about the programs and services of the Community Health Clinic and would be pleased to pay for any publications you may have available.

Write letters to individuals who work at your target employers. You will have gathered these names either from previous literature or from inquiries by telephone. Write to a person whose job title intrigues you, even if you know nothing about the work.

EXAMPLE ► Dear Ms. McShain: I am writing to you because you are director of programming for the Community Health Clinic and perhaps you can tell me a bit about the kinds of programs you offer in a typical year.

Write follow-up letters to everyone who responds to you. Be sure to research whatever information they have provided in their replies—key articles, books, other information. Include in your reply an example of your work, if possible. Ask for permission to make an appointment when you arrive in the target area. You can enclose a résumé, but emphasize that you are not asking for job help, but are simply including the résumé as a convenient summary of your background. You don't want to lose these people as contacts by demanding foolishly that they do your job hunting for you.

EXAMPLE ► I read your report on the year's programs and was intrigued by the variety of field trips you take within a limited budget. Could I arrange to visit you, when I arrive in Minneapolis, to ask a few more questions?

Telephoning

Request printed materials you may have mentioned in your initial letter to the organization. A phone call will probably hasten the arrival of these materials by several days. Ask for the public relations office, the public information office, or some similar department title.

EXAMPLE ► Would you send me a copy of your annual report and any other publications or brochures describing your activities?

Request the names of key officials mentioned in the annual report, company newsletter, or similar publication. Ask for the personnel or public relations department if the operator is confused about where to refer you.

EXAMPLE ► Could you tell me the name of the vice-president for finance?

Speak with a target person, preferably after you have received a reply to your initial letter. Request one or more of the following: (1) an appointment to see him or her when you arrive in Target City; (2) suggestions about additional reading you might do to better understand the individual's profession; (3) recommendations of names of other people in the profession whom you could write to or see when you arrive there.

EXAMPLE ► Thanks for the letter you sent me about investments work in the insurance industry. I read the book you recommended—can you suggest similar titles? Would it be possible to meet with you when I arrive in Hartford? Before I arrive, are there other investment analysts there you would suggest I write to?

In Person

Your present town or city is like your target city in the following respects: It has many of the same kinds of organizations you're interested in; it has many employers where your skills are needed and values can be satisfied; the process you use to reach employers in your present town is the same as what you would use in your target city. You should (1) obtain printed materials—newsletters, magazines, annual reports, and so on; (2) visit these employers in order to practice your information interviewing; (3) practice the process of getting referrals from one employer to another, perhaps even a referral to someone in your target area, and ask about branch offices in other cities or towns—maybe the headquarters of the organization is located in the place where you are going.

► "But I Don't Have ◄ Any Contacts"

The importance of having contacts cannot be overestimated. When you don't live where you want to get a job, you need people in the new area to serve as guides for you. Even if they do not know where jobs are, they can help tell you who the employers are in that town, how small or large they are, and give you names of people to seek for advice and orientation.

So what makes you think you do not have any contacts? Sure you're all alone and far away, but remember the Small-World phenomenon (pages 121–122). With a little effort, working through people as links to other people, *you can reach (just about) Anyone, Anywhere.* That includes the mayor of the city, or the local TV star, or the woman who runs that fancy-sounding boutique, or the publisher of *Power Tools Unlimited*, that magazine you just heard about.

What makes me think so? A contact is simply a person who will talk with you for five minutes even though he/she does not know you, either because you called him up, walked into her office, or got referred by a friend. You don't expect the contact to get you a job or throw a party for you, just move you along toward a new source of information and get you a little closer to target employers. Now that's a modest enough expectation, isn't it?

If you still think you have no contacts, try this. Ask anyone in your present town or city:

Who do you know in —— (target city)?
May I call —— and say that you suggested I call?

That person will probably be in a different line of work from what you want. No problem. You're just trying to get the chain started. Ask the first contact:

Can you tell me something about what it's like to work in ———— (city, town)?

I'm looking for work in ———— (field of work). Can you suggest any organizations I should know about or people I could talk to?

If you don't know anyone in that field, who can you suggest that might be close to that field in some way?

By keeping your demands minimal (you just need a name or two, or a suggestion about where to call next), you can keep the chain going, and before too long, you will find someone who knows someone who works in your target area. At the same time, you can also do the Direct Approach. Call one of your target organizations directly and say: "I'm moving to the area and am looking into work in the ———— field, and would like to know something about what your organization does. Could you tell me your main programs and services?"

There are no rules against this, and if you are good on the telephone, you can speed up the contact process that way. If you want to play it a little safer, call one of your lesser Targets, get some information, perhaps a lead to someone better, saving that name for when you visit the town in person.

Often the direct approach won't be necessary. If you question your local friends and contacts diligently, you are very likely to find several people who know someone in the town you're aiming for. Commercial air travel and geographical mobility have been common for long enough that people know people all over the map of the United States, and the cross-connections increase every day. Your job is to tap into them.

► The Loneliness of the ◄ Long-Distance Job Searcher

Life on another planet is no fun. You're here, thinking about how to get there. Your friends and everyone else are now seeing you as pulling away or already gone. You're excited, they're not. You're looking, they're not. It can make you feel awkward, and not very much a part of either place. What to do?

• Cultivate colleagues there. Start a correspondence with any contacts you've met on the phone who sound particularly interesting, or whose work you'd like to know more about. This probably should not be someone in a target organization. Someone else who may become a friend, a person there in a different field with whom you might share some mutual interests.

- Build bridges to people here. Make a special effort to cement a relationship with people in the local area with whom you intend to maintain a connection. Take them to lunch, show interest in their career problems, try to get information that will help them.
- Have a timetable for getting out, a target date for moving there. Try to squeeze in a trip to the new locale before you move there, so you can reinforce your telephone contacts with in-person visits.

Loneliness is not fatal, and not even a long-term ailment. If you stretch the ropes between here and there right now, these will become lifelines, and they will still be in place when you are there. So, when you're there, part of you will still be here. Got that straight? These "ropes" are people who help you get there and follow your progress after you have moved.

► When You Should Move to ◄ Target City

You probably should not move permanently to the target area for your work search until you have accomplished the following. First, you need to have accumulated a list of at least fifty prospective employers, using employer directories, telephone books, and other resources. You need this many to convince yourself that there *are* more than a handful of possibilities there.

Second, you should have reviewed enough printed material from the specific employers, the commercial press, and professional organizations so that you are reasonably prepared for a job interview if one should occur the day you arrive. A detailed review of this kind should focus on the top five employers on your prospect list.

Finally, it's not a good idea to move permanently until you have at least five specific places of possible employment in the target area where some individual is personally aware of you as a result of your correspondence, a direct referral from a person in your present area, telephone communication, or any combination of these. Contacts of this kind will ensure that you can begin your search on a personal basis as soon as you arrive. These five should probably be the same as the five organizations you have researched thoroughly prior to your arrival.

▶ When and Where to ◀
Begin Your Long-Distance
Search

As you must suspect by now, long-distance activity cannot wait until two weeks before you intend to move. You should probably begin six months before you intend to move. This means you will be researching, writing, phoning, and canvassing long before you have resigned your present position.

All the following sources are good places to begin your efforts:

- *Newspaper subscriptions.* Lay out the funds for out-of-town newspapers to be delivered to your doorstep or post office box on a regular basis. This will acquaint you with the newest developments that may have work potential for you. Such items as "New Plant Opens Up" or "Government Contract Renewed" tip you off about employers you didn't detect in the phone books.
- *Regional magazines.* Currently many regions of the country produce magazines that focus on topics and people of local interest. In the East, for example, you can find *New York*, the *Washingtonian*, *Philadelphia Magazine*, *Pittsburgh*, the *Bostonian*, and others. These publications will keep you abreast of regional currents of change that may suggest employment opportunities.
- *Polk's city directories.* If the phone book for your target city is not available, try the local library and ask for Polk's. It gives you the same information as a regular telephone book, and it locates the people and employers for you by section of town.

Anticipation is important, but it takes time. The more time you allow yourself between long-distance activity and the eventual change of location, the less anxiety you will feel and the more chance there is that "lucky" connections will happen.

▶ When Your Target Is ◀
Narrow, Broaden Your
Possibilities

When you have your sights set on working in a particular location, often you are limited to that particular town, city, or area. Either your spouse has just gotten a new job there, or the family has decided this is the right place to live, or you decided to move back home near your parents, or some other reason. Thus, you must take the work that is available in that location. You may not get the job that you had before, and may feel some keen disappointment about that. However, it is possible to take an optimistic view about what this might mean.

Because your geographical scope is now limited, you can open yourself up to a broader range of types of work. Now may be just the time to be creative about how your previous work experience can be applied. It was harder to do before when you had a regular job, but now circumstances allow you to consider other possibilities.

Suppose you are a high school counselor. Consider how your skills might be applied to a broad range of social service work, or the human resource departments in private industry, or educational agencies in the government. Suppose you are a nurse with administrative responsibilities. Consider how your background might be applied to health insurance companies, health maintenance organizations, or even to the health and fitness programs of local businesses.

Inevitably you will feel some loss of identity if you leave one field and try to enter others. However, this may be a temporary loss if you find a new kind of work that you would not have thought of before. A new job can make you stronger overall, because several kinds of work experience will make you more marketable. I'm not saying this just to make you feel good while you suffer a difficult transition. People who have the gumption to change their work usually come out ahead in the long run because they learn more, adjust better to change, and tell more interesting stories.

Interviewing

Interviewers are merely professional gamblers who have been provided a thirty-minute tip sheet analysis to help them decide on which candidate to place the bet.
—John L. Lafevre,
"A Peek Inside the Recruiter's Briefcase"[1]

The job interview is almost always the centerpiece of the job-search process, your chance to show your stuff, the place where your motivations and the employer's needs come together. So let's find out what goes on inside those cubicle walls and inside the interviewer's heart and mind.

Is the interviewer just a heartless villain dedicated to dismembering your well-laid preparation and ripping away your careful facade to uncover the real you lurking somewhere under the surface? Or is he/she a friendly confidant who will give you every opportunity to show your best side and try mightily to discover your most glorious abilities and potential? The interviewer can be both of these extremes at times, but mostly he or she is like an earnest and congenial detective who is trying to solve the mystery of who you are by looking for clues in your responses to questions.

There is a hidden agenda consisting of nine items in every job interview, regardless of the nature of the job or the type of industry. I will outline how you can respond most favorably to each of these themes. Nine sounds like a lot of factors, like a ton of things to worry about. Will your mind be filled with so many do's and don't's that you can't relax? It's less complicated than you think. When the interviewer asks a question and you answer it, you're often covering several factors at the same time. Being aware of these themes helps cue you about how the interviewer will evaluate you. You won't score perfectly on each point (nobody does), but your awareness will help you understand "Why did he/she ask me that?"

Why be afraid of this little devil, the interview? The other candidates have as much anxiety as you do, and probably more if they have not read this book. The nine qualities below give you nine different ways to shine. Of course, you will make mistakes, some of them so clumsy that you will laugh at them later.

You've had bad interviews before and you'll have them again. So what? There's no great Interviewing Scoreboard in the Sky that says: "Ding Him Forever Because of Previous Interview Sins." In this game you get plenty of times at bat, and eventually you will become confident and handle the interview process well.

Some of these nine items are openly stated in the interview, and others are not. Certain aspects are difficult to address openly, such as "likeability." But you can be sure this is a factor in selection, even though it is judged only indirectly. Others may be stated clearly if the interviewer chooses, such as "Tell me about your leadership experiences." However, just because an interviewer does not name a factor does not mean he/she is ignoring it. "Leadership," "communication skills," and others can be inferred from your general responses to questions, so keep all of these themes in mind. If you are not sure whether a particular aspect has been covered, you may want to bring it up yourself: "I'd like to tell you why I am motivated to pursue this job."

What kinds of jobs are included in this discussion of interview themes? Almost any job requiring a significant amount of responsibility will be applicable here, including jobs for new college graduates, jobs for experienced executives, or jobs for career changers. Job interviews have a common character because, regardless of the content, you have one person trying to judge the capabilities and compatibility of another.

► How Are These Nine Factors ◄ Combined?

Who knows? If there were a formula for combining job selection factors that predicted successful job candidates with any degree of accuracy, we'd all know it by now. But, fortunately for the sake of individual judgment, there is no such formula. All that we know is that every item on this hidden agenda is important, since each taps some dimension of your job potential.

However these nine factors are combined, the result is wholistic and subjective in the mind of the interviewer. He/she may even use an interview scorecard, but the final decision will still be an intuitive combining of all themes. Therefore, you should treat all nine elements as being of equal importance and give your attention to each of them.

► 1. Personal Impression ◄

What the Interviewer Is Looking For

"I wonder if this person will be an effective representative of our organization. Will he look professional, serious, dress attractively? Will he socialize well, make clients feel at home, make the customer/student/ visitor want to be involved with us? Does this person display confidence, warmth, interest? If I were coming here for the first time, would I be impressed by him?"

What You Should Do

First of all, dress appropriately for the interview. Do enough research to know what is suitable for that work environment, and then dress about 10 percent better than the norm. Enough has been written about dressing for success that I need not rehash it here. Neatness, grooming, and a professional look are the keys. Have more experienced people check you out, if you are not sure whether your appearance will make the grade.

Personal sociability is important in almost every job. Generate friendliness, warmth, and enthusiasm as much as you can, without portraying someone other than yourself. First impressions do matter. Your ability to move into new situations and meet new people comfortably contribute to how you are first received. If this is a difficult area for you, practice placing yourself into new social situations, at offices, parties, and elsewhere.

Take a look at some of your nonverbal factors, such as vocal quality (do you speak clearly, firmly, not too fast or slowly?), body posture when sitting or standing, hand gestures, eye contact (a strong indication of your assertiveness and ability to relate confidently), or facial expressions. If you are unsure about any of these, get some advice from a career counselor and practice any skills in which you are weak.

► 2. Competence ◄

What the Interviewer Is Looking For

"Can this person do the job we have here? Has she had related experiences? Can I detect skills in her background that will help in this job? What does the résumé say? Can I believe what's on it? How do I know she can do those things? What can I ask that will cue me about her abilities?

Maybe she can do the job minimally, but how good is she? Can she tell me things that will reveal her capabilities?"

What You Should Say

An interviewer will already have some idea of your competence if you have submitted your résumé, but you should assume that he/she wants to know more, or have some verification of what the résumé says. You should become a "talking résumé." The best thing you can do is tell stories (see pages 202–204) about your past experiences, which reveal your abilities to perform the job. Don't make the interviewer work hard to find out what you can do. Anticipate what the job calls for (with the help of your research), and make connections between your skills (as derived from past experiences) and the skills the job requires. Don't be modest. Give some idea of why you believe you can do the job *well*. Interviewers like confidence as long as you don't overdo it. We're not talking about bragging here, but simple declarative statements such as: "I am a good supervisor, and the reason I know that is my work last summer at the ———, where I oversaw the entire operation of ———."

In many cases, the interviewer is looking for multiple competencies, your ability to perform many tasks well. Anticipate as many different competencies as you can and be prepared to talk about them.

> EXAMPLE ► I can organize data projects, supervise staff, and do research in the technical libraries. I can also do public speaking when needed, and I like to write reports for management in clear language. I know this job calls for a lot of different skills, and I have had some experience with all of them.

Sometimes you will be referring to your previous experience in the same type of job, but often you will be applying for a different type of work, and will have to make connections or "translations" between one job and another, between your past experiences and the responsibilities of the new occupation: "In my job as a data processing manager I took care of the budget and managed the department's resources, so I believe I can do those things well in this job as a purchasing agent."

In general, the more clearly you relate your past experiences and present motivation to the job you want, the more an interviewer can believe that you have the capacity to do the job well.

► 3. Likeability ◄

What the Interviewer Is Looking For

"Would I like to work with this person? Is he enjoyable to be around? Will he get along with the others here in the office? If I ask him to work with a wide variety of people, will he handle that okay? Does he listen well? Will he relate smoothly to the higher-ups? Does he have some fun about him, or is he all work and no play? Is there anything in his personal life that might affect his attitude or moods on the job?"

What You Should Say and Do

How do you go about being likeable? Well, there is no easy answer to that, but we'd better pay attention to it, because this is a powerful yet always unspoken factor in hiring decisions. Unless there is a strong argument to the contrary, people tend to hire people they like and find congenial. They do so for a variety of reasons:

- It is more enjoyable to work with likeable people
- Relationships in the office will be better
- Likeable people tend to get more cooperation, and thus more work is usually accomplished
- Such people tend to have greater potential for advancement

Likeability is hard to program into your interview behavior, but there are things you can do to stay on the right side of this key factor.

a) *Be genuinely interested in everyone you meet*, from bosses through staff people, secretaries, receptionists, and anyone else. Word gets around fast in the office and everyone has a say about "what's this person like?"

b) *Be a good listener.* Easy to say, but hard to do when you are focusing on what you are going to say next. Pay attention to the questions you are asked, the statements your interviewers make, the feelings they show between the lines, and even their attitudes toward each other. Maybe what they are saying is even irrelevant to the job. Listen anyway. Listening, more than anything else, begins to cement the relationship with a person. Let them know you are listening by rephrasing or summarizing what you heard them say.

c) *Be as at ease with people as you possibly can be, given the circumstances.* They are not going to bite your head off, and you will not fall into a deep hole somewhere, never to be heard from again, if you don't get this job. Try to imagine you are at a party and you are getting acquainted with some folks you think you're going to like.

d) *Be loose.* Take what comes. Interviews can have unexpected little wrinkles in them, like phone interruptions, mistaken arrangements (so what if they lost your plane ticket, or gave you the wrong directions to the office), encounters with people you were not prepared to meet, spilled coffee, and maybe even a fire drill. The questions interviewers ask can be oddball and perhaps even designed to rattle you. Maintain an upbeat attitude no matter what answer you give. "Poise and Maturity" below discusses stressful questions in greater detail.

e) *Don't be manipulative.* Don't try to endear yourself to anyone by making an obvious play for their approval, such as excessive comments about the pictures on their walls or the trophies in their offices. These ploys are recommended in other books, but most interviewers will view your comments as transparent and thus discount them. Worse yet, such attempts to curry favor may work against you.

f) *Avoid negative talk.* Don't be critical of former employers or indulge in stories about people you don't like. Even though your criticism may be legitimate, it casts a negative light on you. Sometimes an interviewer will even bait you, because he/she knows that your former boss is a difficult person. Don't be tempted to tell war stories, because the interviewer may assume you will be just as critical of his/her operation if you are hired. Don't be negative with anyone.

Interviewers may show you where you stand on likeability by their smiles or other nonverbal responses, but they will seldom tell you directly. You need not press hard with your likeable behaviors. Just avoid the traps implied above, and remember that congeniality counts.

▶ 4. Motivation/Enthusiasm/ ◀ Commitment

What the Interviewer Is Looking For

"I wonder how badly she wants this job. Is she fired up about it? Does she project this enthusiasm to me? How hard a worker is she likely to be, based on the intensity she is showing me? Is she really interested in this field, or is she just looking for a job? If we hire her, will she be with us long enough to make a real contribution? I wonder how I can find out what she really wants from her career. How do I know if this job is her first choice?"

What You Should Say

Depth of motivation often makes the difference between an ordinary employee and a great one. How can you demonstrate it? If they ask whether you want the job and you say yes, that doesn't quite settle the matter.

a) Show your enthusiasm verbally and nonverbally. Don't be stiff. Let them know you like the job and would be very energized by it.
b) Relate this job to your previous experiences. This is another place where story telling comes in handy: "I have done projects like this before, and have really thrown myself into them. For example . . ."
c) Talk about your ambitions, your desire for future growth in this field of work. Give some general idea of how you hope to progress with this company, and why such advancement appeals to you.
d) Tell exactly what you like about the company, the department, the job, the products/services this company sells, etc.

Motivation can be done to excess, of course. Jumping up and down screaming "It's me! This job is me!" would be a little over the line. But I know I can count on you to be tasteful.

A good interviewer will ask you about your motivation and potential commitment, so be prepared to answer. Interviewers usually try to see how this job will fit into your career history; this is one way of gauging how motivated you might be. If you are changing careers, you will have to give the interviewer some insight into why you are moving in this direction and how it fits with your larger career goals and ambitions.

Interviewers usually believe that the most motivated applicant will do the best job, even if he/she has a little less relevant experience or needs a little more training. Thus, even if you have the qualifications on paper and you have answered questions satisfactorily in the interview, *don't be cocky or complacent.* More than one job offer has been lost by candidates who said: "I thought I had it made."

▶ 5. Leadership ◀

What the Interviewer Is Looking For

"Does this person have potential for taking responsibility in our organization? What makes me think so? Do I see evidence that he has been a leader in other settings? Does he seem to want to move ahead and be in charge of things? Would he be a good example for the rest of our staff?"

What You Should Say

Leadership is one of private industry's favorite words. It also gets high marks from nonprofit employers. In fact, everyone likes leadership and tries to get as much of it as they can.

First let's agree that "leadership" refers not only to being head of an organization, or club, or committee, or team; it also refers to taking responsibility for a project, even when you are not the appointed leader of a group. Leadership is a broad concept that denotes seeing a goal and bringing together the people and resources to achieve that goal. Often leadership will involve supervising or managing other people, but that is not always so. Leadership can mean building a boat by yourself in your backyard, or lobbying the city council to do something on behalf of the homeless.

Interviewers would like to see some evidence that you are a take-charge guy, or a woman who makes things happen. They believe that such qualities will pay off for the company, because you will exert the same leadership skills on the job. Thus, you should call attention to any significant responsibilities you have had, even if the results were not completely successful. Failures can be as important as successes: "We almost got the board of trustees to agree to have a basketball team at my college. I organized the effort, lobbied the board, called the referendum, and met with the president. . . ." Tell interviewers about your leadership roles, even if they do not ask. Identify skills in your leadership positions that will help you on this job. Leadership usually is a good sign that you know how to get along with people and manage them. The interviewer is looking to the future as well as the present. The entry-level job may not have leadership in it, but the interviewer envisions bigger things for you. Show that your thinking is ambitious and that your previous leadership experience was no accident.

Talk about your accomplishments. If, during your reign as leader of the scout troop, the group organized more trips and earned more merit badges than in previous years, say so. If your leadership of the high school guidance department led to an increase in the number of students attending college and an expansion of the facilities, report that on your résumé and during the interview. Leadership activity can occur on the job, in community affairs, and in college organizations.

▶ 6. Communication Skills ◀

What the Interviewer Is Looking For

"What evidence do I have that this person writes clearly and effectively? Would she represent our organization positively as a public speaker? Is she a powerful communicator? Will she communicate well to other staff members? Could she write a speech for our president if she had to, and could she deliver it if necessary? How much writing and public speaking has she done before?"

What You Should Say and Do

Writing and speaking skills are highly valued in a wide variety of jobs, particularly for jobs that lead to greater reponsibility. Organizational leaders are always required to communicate effectively, in writing and in person. Therefore, you should go out of your way to provide evidence of these skills. Offer examples of your writing style—perhaps management reports, publicity materials, or newsletters that you have produced. Take care that your résumé and cover letters are well written; these are obvious examples of your writing talent. Any problems or sloppiness in these materials will be interpreted by the interviewer as a sign that you cannot write well.

Every time you open your mouth you give evidence of your speaking ability. If you have done public speaking, say so, but don't overemphasize this, lest it sound like bragging. The interview itself is a prime example of your speaking skill. Speak concisely yet with sufficient detail, don't mispronounce words, and work on your vocal quality if you speak too softly, too rapidly, or in some ineffective way.

Don't try to blow the interviewer away with your speaking style, but make sure that you answer questions with conviction and speak with a tone of confidence. If this is a problem area for you, it can be corrected or improved through speech classes, Toastmasters clubs, and practice in your daily life.

► 7. Poise and Maturity ◄

What the Interviewer
Is Looking For

"Can this person handle himself under pressure? Does he have the depth and maturity to deal with questions that are almost impossible to answer? How would he project himself as a representative of our organization under trying circumstances? Could he handle difficult customers? Will he come apart when things get crazy around here or people challenge his ideas? How would he do in a heated argument? Is he calm under fire?"

What You Should Say

This is the area where the interviewer turns to stressful questions and lovely thoughts of how to rattle your cage. Interviewers do not always do this, but they will create some stress if they feel the job requires your ability to deal with pressure and they need to know how you conduct yourself. Sometimes your prior experience will reveal your ability to work under pressure, but if the interviewer is not sure, he/she may create some tension or uncertainty on the spot to see what you do with it. The interviewer may ask questions such as:

What would you do about our sales problems if you were the president of our company?

What is the biggest mistake you've ever made, and why did you let it happen?

Tell me why you think our company is so hot when you really know very little about it.

Who's the worst boss you've ever worked for and why?

Above all, remember that *how* you answer the question—your calmness, your reasonableness, your ability to remain positive and congenial—is as important as the content of your answer. Grace under pressure is a virtue, and the interviewer wants to see that you have it. You can admit to a bit of uncertainty before answering (a pause to give yourself time), but do so with poise, because that is what people in leadership roles are called on to do frequently.

The interviewer may try to argue with you and get you to admit you are wrong, perhaps even badger you about a point of view. This is a test of your diplomacy and ability to engage someone on a difficult issue, maintain their respect, and still get your points across. "Winning" the argument is not as important as having a constructive, peaceful discussion, even if the interviewer is trying to rile you.

Stressful questions are not standard parts of an interview, but you should be ready for them. Sometimes stressful moments will occur, even though they are not planned. An interviewer may misinterpret something you say, forcing you to clarify yourself in a tactful way. Or the interviewer may make a joke about something you said and you don't think it's funny. These incidents call upon your poise and maturity, your ability to manage the conversation with style and self-control.

Poise and maturity is another item on the agenda that is seldom stated (No interviewer asks, "Are you mature enough for this job?") but often noted. It contributes greatly to your overall impression, so don't let little glitches in the interview process get you upset. If you stumble around, have to say "I don't know," or get caught in a misstatement, what's important is that you handle the mishap with dignity and calmness.

► 8. Outside Interests ◄

What the Interviewer Is Looking For

"Is this person one-dimensional, or does she pursue things away from the job? Does she show any flair or originality in her outside interests?

Do I see signs that she can get intensely involved in something, that she is productive, works hard toward goals? Maybe I can understand more fully who she is by considering the other things she does. Do these show any strong convictions? How about an ability to organize herself? Would people who work here be interested to know what this woman does off the job? Is there any evidence of achievement in her outside involvements?"

What You Should Say

Whether you are a passionate handball player, a rock collector, have a collection of quilts you have sewn, or you make wine from your own vineyards, it is generally good to talk about your personal interests, especially if you are asked. Don't push these interests into the conversation where they don't belong, but be alert for opportunities to point out skills you have developed or knowledge you have acquired in your hobbies that may be related to the job you want.

> EXAMPLE ► I take geological field trips on my own, and have made maps of the area. This has developed my drawing skill, and I have learned a lot about the Surveyor's Office. I think this background will help me as a junior planner here at the Office of City Planning.

Even if your interests are not directly related to the job, your involvement in them can be a positive sign of enthusiasm and your ability to organize your energies. Interviewers often like to know more about you and may ask: "What do you do in your spare time that you really get fired up about?" The interviewer is trying to determine if you have a spirit of dedication and intensity that may carry over to your involvement with the job. People who organize themselves for maximum efforts in their personal interests usually can display this kind of self-management and commitment in their careers.

While some interviewers might want you to say that you have no outside interests, because you are fully dedicated to your career, this is an unusual point of view. It is more common for an interviewer to prefer a balanced individual who works hard but also gets involved in personal activities. Interviewers recognize that most workers do not meet all of their needs from paid employment, and assume that a diverse individual will probably be a happier employee.

If you have not had any recent strong interests, either because you were involved in school or had family obligations, it is fine to talk about interests that you intend to pursue in the future. Even a little exposure to an outside activity should give you enough to talk about, if you are asked.

► 9. Your Relationships ◄

What the Interviewer Is Looking For

"I know I'm not supposed to ask these things, but I'd like to know if his relationships are okay, because I don't want to hire someone who has marital, roommate, family, or other problems of this kind. Of course, that is none of my business, but I know that relationship trouble almost always shows up on the job and subtracts from a person's productivity. So, if I can hire someone who is on sound footing at home, he will undoubtedly do more for the organization. Maybe I can get him to talk about this stuff without my asking him directly."

What You Should Say

Yes, it is none of their business. But they may try to find out anyway. Right or wrong, fair or unfair, the interviewer usually believes that relationship stability is a good indication of your stability and effectiveness on the job.

Of course, the interviewer is not going to come right out and ask you: "How are things at home?" But he/she may encourage you to talk about your relationships, even if only in subtle and indirect ways:

What led you and your wife to move here?
How does your husband like his work?
Do you have any brothers and sisters? What kinds of work are they in?

It is reasonable to answer questions like these. Any general or implied reference you can make to solid and stable relationships will probably work to your benefit.

In these days of two-career couples, a lot of job dissension comes from conflicts between spouses' respective careers. Interviewers often try to find out whether your spouse has a job too or if that is a problem.

Relationships are off-limits for interviews, in the strict legal sense, but it makes sense to talk about them if you are asked. It is more trouble to refuse to answer any question about your spouse or family member. Sometimes the interviewer will ask out of plain and simple curiosity— "What kind of work does your wife do?" In some cases your spouse's work will be seen as an asset to you, if it is in a field that is related to the job you are seeking. You don't want to trade on your spouse's career, but it doesn't hurt to indicate what it is. The fact that you know a lot about your mate's work is another sign of a positive relationship.

► Follow-Up ◄

In job hunting, it isn't necessarily over when it's over. While you con-centrate your attention on a job interview, and breathe a sigh of relief when you're out of there, there is still more to be done. You can make some of your best progress after the interviews have been completed.

Job hunting is an ongoing process, not just one brief appearance on the interviewer's stage. Interviewers can call you back for encores, and they can be helpful links to the rest of the job market, so consider the things you can do to enhance your prospects:

If You're Still in Contention
for the Job

Write a letter to the interviewer Graciously thank him/her for the meeting, say what you learned from the interview, and reaffirm your interest in the job. This is an opportunity to state more emphatically why you want the position and why you think you are well qualified. They say in theater "Always leave 'em laughing." Translated to job hunting, you might say "Let the last word they have from me be a good one." You can also be a bit more personal in this letter, since you have met the employer and can recall key things he/she might have said.

Ask one or more of your key references to call for you You don't always have to wait for the interviewer to call your references. If there is one who you believe will say especially good things about you, ask him/her to call the interviewer. Tell the reference what you know about the job and why you believe it is the right one for you.

Send any materials the interviewer asked you for If there are examples of your work, reference letters, or other materials he/she men-tioned during the interview, send them right away and accompany them with a thank-you note.

Call to ask how the selection process is going "I'd like to know the status of my application, and reaffirm that I am still very interested in this job" is a good way to say it. How soon after the interview should you call? If the interviewer has not told you when to call, anywhere between one and two weeks is good. How often should you call? Take your cues from the interviewer's timetable. If you're unsure, ask when it would be all right to call again.

If you have received an offer of another job, but you would prefer this one, it's good to call right away and tell them when you need to make a decision. Then you will negotiate regarding the selection timetable and you will have to decide whether or not to take a "bird in the hand."

Follow-up gives you several ways to demonstrate that you—like your job search—are well organized. If an employer has several forms of positive contact from you, he/she is likely to recognize that your interest in the job is quite serious.

Be careful not to overdo your follow-up activities. In your zeal to be noticed, you might create an impression of being overanxious. All of the above actions are appropriate; however each can be done to excess. An effusive thank-you note or too many reference callers will drive the interviewer in the opposite direction.

If You Have Been Eliminated from Contention

Why bother if you have been eliminated from the selection process? Because any employer can be a link to other job opportunities. Consider the following things that you can do:

Ask for feedback about your strengths and weaknesses   If you believe you had a decent interview, call or visit the interviewer to ask about how you presented yourself. Both the praise and the criticism are important to you. A little news of what you did right helps to keep you going, and criticism cues you about what you need to change. Often interviewers enjoy helping you improve what you are doing, especially if they want to encourage you to continue in their line of work.

Ask for referrals   "I'd like to continue seeking work in this field. Could you suggest who I might talk with, or where job possibilities might generally be?" While you may draw a blank on this, it is worth asking. Especially in tight fields where professionals know each other, you may get a strong lead if you made a good impression during the interview. At other times the interviewer can tell you the kinds of organizations best to approach, or give you other useful information.

Send thank-you notes   You're beginning to see the all-purpose value of reconnecting via the thank-you note. It is the best means you have of reinforcing a positive impression, so use it with anyone you hope to see again. A well-stated and friendly letter is remembered long after the selection process is over. If you write ten of these letters to interviewers you liked, odds are you will have some beneficial future contact with at least two or three of them.

The ability to follow up well separates the confident and enduring job hunter from those who are sticking their toes in the water but are ready to get out. Early interviews are just preludes to better interviews. Sometimes interviews circle back on themselves. The person you talked to three weeks ago (who rejected you, but you did some follow-up anyway) is the person you meet on the street who tells you about a new company she just heard of. The interviewer does most of his/her thinking about you long after your conversation is over. If you follow up well, they may give you the edge in the final selection, or they may call to tell you of another opening, or refer you to a good contact in the industry.

Follow-up also sharpens your persistence skills, your ability to keep moving toward a goal even when the initial signs are cloudy. There will be many moments when you want to give up or settle for less, but follow-up reminds you that every contact you make has some potential. It sounds corny, but the person you least suspect might help you can become the one who gives you the lead you're looking for.

There are memorable stories of follow-up told among job counselors and job hunters. One concerns a new college graduate named John who wanted a job with a financial newsletter on Wall Street, and wrote this letter after interviewing with ABC Company on his campus:

Dear Mr. Feinstein:

It was a pleasure speaking with you when you were here at the University of Pennsylvania last week to talk with me and other members of the graduating class. Your visit reaffirmed my interest in joining the ABC Company. I learned from you the importance of reading the key financial journals and how to sift the reliable information from other, more speculative data.

The job with ABC Company is still my first choice. I have been talking with other financial newsletters, but believe that yours is the best, because of its depth of analysis and professional growth opportunities. Even if I am not offered a job by your firm, I will improve my writing and analytical skills by following your many recommendations. I am also beginning my studies for the Chartered Financial Analyst examinations as you suggested, and will take key courses to help my preparation. I am quite convinced that this field is right for me, and plan to continue my efforts to do newsletter work in the Wall Street community.

Since you are an alumnus of the university, you may want to consider returning for Alumni Weekend on April 17–18. We will have a series of social and cultural events (program enclosed) that should interest you. I would be available at that time if you should wish to speak with me, since I am on the planning committee for that weekend.

Many thanks for your helpful recommendations regarding my career plans.

Sincerely,
John Sartoro
Class of 1987

Arlo Feinstein did return to campus for the alumni weekend, though he did not intend to meet with John Sartoro. He spent most of his time with old classmates, but, as luck would have it, he wandered into the university gymnasium during a few free hours and sought out a racquetball game. Standing around the gym, just having finished a game, was our man John. You know the finish of this story. Arlo remembered John's appreciative letter, they talked after leaving the gym, and John found himself a member of the newsletter team two months later.

John's letter was not a sales letter; he decided to take a different approach. He restated his strong interest in the job and backed it up with concrete evidence that he was determined to succeed in the financial analysis and newswriting field. He wrote a letter that stuck in the employer's mind. It seemed that luck worked in John's favor, but he did a lot to establish a positive image in Arlo's mind. He played the follow-up game in a deliberate yet professional manner, and it worked. Follow-up does not succeed every time, but if he had been this deliberate with other target employers, it probably would have shown results with one or more of them too.

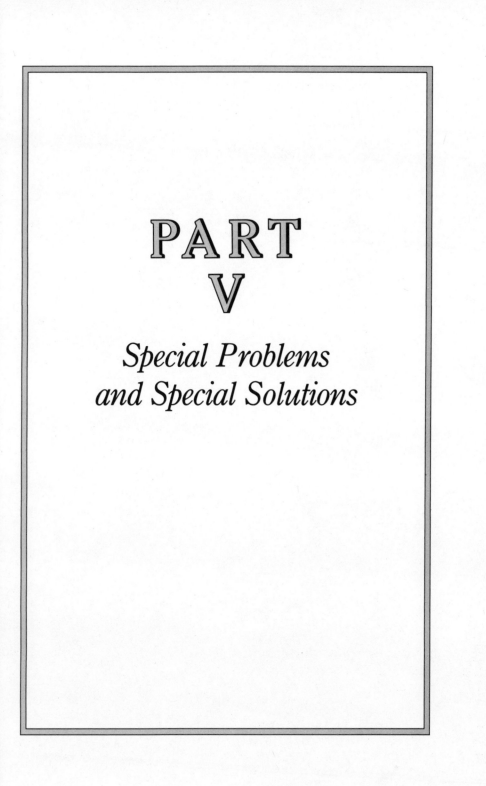

PART
V
Special Problems
and Special Solutions

21
Ways Job Hunters
Foil Themselves

Job-search manuals are written as though a reader can just absorb the advice and techniques that are laid out, and then go out and *do it*. Successful job seeking is not just a matter of practice, as in using dental floss, or persistence, as in keeping the garden weeded. Job hunting is more complex than that, and the forces that undermine it are darker and more mysterious.

I know hundreds of job hunters who tell me: "Everything you say makes good sense, and I have been doing most of it, but it is not working for me." They apply the methods honestly and diligently, yet something goes wrong or the results we both expect simply do not appear.

Apparently, understanding is not enough. Teaching concepts is helpful but this often fails to do the job. Other factors are playing into the formula, stifling people's best efforts. Perhaps you have had this experience yourself. You grasp the key ideas, follow the rules presented by the author, invest time in the process, and yet things do not happen the way they are supposed to. So, what is going on? Why the lack of results?

Career counselors have identified many factors which contribute to poor results in the job search. Most often the job seekers themselves are unaware that these factors are operating, so it is understandable that they are surprised and disappointed when their application of recommended methods does not succeed. An experienced counselor, once he/she recognizes that one of the factors below is involved, will try to bring it into focus and show a job seeker how it is affecting the whole process.

Regardless of how well you have done in the job search so far, I would recommend that you review the factors described here, to see if you recognize any that may fit your situation. Even if you don't have any of these problems, being aware of them may help you prevent difficulties in the future.

As many as 50 percent of all job seekers have a problem with one or more of the factors described below. Thus, these factors do not simply afflict oddballs who are out of the mainstream in job hunting. These problems strike *us*, the people at large, and we must take ourselves as we are, in our natural, rough-edged state, and do something to make ourselves as marketable as possible.

You cannot transform yourself into an entirely different personality. But you can reduce the impact of these hindrances if you know what they are.

One final word about these categories. Career counselors agree unanimously that all people who have problems applying the recommended job-search methods (and that's most of us) *will* succeed as long as they want to. None of these problems is genetic or intractable. Any problem can be worked with and overcome, and there are thousands of successful job seekers walking around who have proven the point.

People who are motivated enough to read a job-search book or meet with a career counselor are motivated enough to work on their weak points and move toward their career goals with positive results. The people who have these problems and do not acknowledge them are the ones who are in real trouble and will disappoint themselves without knowing why.

► 1. Career Obsessiveness ◄

You may be trying to break into a field of work that is too crowded or does not have enough opportunity for you right now. Yet, because you have been encouraged to pursue a dream, you keep pushing ahead. You experience mostly frustration and the nagging feeling that you are doing something wrong but do not know what.

Many job seekers are too quick to give up; they back out long before they have fully tested their potential. However, others stay too long at the fair, keep reaching for the brass ring, and go home with little but disillusionment.

You may be persisting toward a goal because it is on someone else's agenda ("Dad wants me to be a lawyer"), or because others have told you that you would be good at a certain kind of work. Other people's views of you usually do not pan out, if you do not fully agree with what they want for you or what they believe you can do.

Your career dream may be unattainable for now because you don't have enough data about yourself and how you can proceed toward your goal. Yet, your single-mindedness may be blocking your ability to see roads that are more promising. You probably need a "Texas two-step" strategy, which involves taking a job that is a possible bridge to a more desirable one.

What You Can Do About This Problem

I do encourage you to keep your dream alive. However, the best strategy for the moment may be to back away from the career you want and consider something else. Either take an interim job while you are still looking for your long-range goal, or broaden your options so that your career objective has a wider base.

For example, if you want to be an investigative reporter for a major newspaper, try smaller newspapers, magazines, trade journals, in-house publications of corporations or foundations, working in radio/TV, or being a research assistant for a publication. Any one of these jobs, even though it is not your ideal, allows you to position yourself for a future move.

Your current efforts may be unsuccessful because you lack ability or contacts or simply maturity as a news reporter. Rather than bumping your head against the *Washington Post* or the *San Francisco Chronicle* repeatedly, improve your skills while you are laboring at another job.

Career counselors meet many job seekers whose vision is too narrow. They think the desired job is the only one in the world, and believe that anything else is settling for less. This is a common error. Your best chance may be to take a related job that seems to be less, but keeps you in the ballpark. For example, someone who aspires to be a book editor for a major publishing house in New York may have to do clerical work for a smaller publisher in a smaller town before getting better opportunities. Or, a person who wants to be chief aide for a U.S. senator may have to work on local political campaigns or do research for federal agencies in Washington before hearing about a chance to move ahead.

By backing away from your goal, you may also discover that it was not really what you wanted. Stranger things have happened. In taking an interim job or simply a job that is available, you may find other abilities and motivations you were unaware of. It is better to be employed and feeling productive than continually being rejected in the marketplace.

So try a different kind of work for a while. A year or more later you may still feel that the original goal is what you want. That's fine. Now consider what new assets you can toss on the table when you reenter that arena. Improved abilities? More knowledge? Experience gathered on a part-time voluntary basis? An academic credential? Any of these may help, and the more the better. Time away from your original goal gives you time to improve your assets and make yourself a better candidate. Then, if that is what you really want, go after it again.

▶ 2. Low Self-Esteem ◀

Feeling "average" can get in the way of your best job-hunting efforts. Often people call this lack of self-confidence. No matter how much someone wants the job, or how much research he/she has done to prepare for interviews, he/she fails to project an "I can do it" attitude that is so crucial to being hired.

You may have some of those same feelings. Perhaps you feel you're a pretty respectable candidate for the job, but you can't seem to take that next step that would enable you to say: "I *know* I am the person you need. Just give me a chance to show you what I can do."

You may be aware that there are many people you are competing with, and it is hard to say *you* are the one to hire. You don't want to sound boastful or unrealistic about your abilities, so you scale them down to what you regard as a fair assessment. And, in doing so, you are projecting yourself as a middle-range candidate, *not* the one who will be noticed.

Perhaps you feel that none of your abilities is strong enough to crow about. You don't want to claim that you are superb, and then leave the employers disappointed if they hire you. Modesty is a reasonable, human feeling, but it will erode your confidence and make you a less effective job candidate. Such "modesty" is often low self-esteem in disguise.

What You Can Do About This Problem

Let's start with this understanding: it is not outrageous to say in a job interview, "I know that I can do the job you want done, and I have plenty of ability and experience to back up what I am saying." That isn't cocky. It is an honest expression of your belief in yourself, regardless of what the other candidates may have in their backgrounds.

Nobody is asking you to claim you are the world's greatest at a particular job. That *would* be bragging and very ineffective in any job interview. However, you must get straight with yourself that you have something to offer, and you must be willing to say it to anyone who needs to hear it.

If you are not sure you're good enough to do the job, one of four things may be holding you back:

a) *You have not done enough research to know how much ability or background they are looking for.* Before you subject yourself to being evaluated in an interview, do information interviews and other research. More often than not, you will discover that they don't require quite as much ability, experience, or knowledge as you imagined. It is common for the job seeker to exaggerate what is required. So, rather than reject yourself out of hand, talk to people who were recently hired, and be generous in your assessment of yourself.

b) *You don't have enough general confidence in yourself to make generous statements about your job potential.* If your confidence is low, explore with a counselor where your feelings may derive from. General feelings of low self-esteem will continually hamper your job search if you leave them unattended. Confidence problems can be dealt with and improved, if you are determined to address them.

c) *You have a stereotyped view of the occupation.* This can often distort your view of how likely you are to succeed. Many people believe that all lawyers must be great orators in the courtroom. While this is certainly a large part of *some* lawyers' jobs, many others do most or all of their work away from the courtroom, in quiet research libraries and small group meetings. Salespeople are not always high-powered, fast-talking types; sometimes the low-key approach works much better. There are college professors who do not act or sound especially intellectual, yet they teach well and their students like them. Not all accountants can move numbers in their heads with great facility. Advertising people are not always flamboyant. And so on. If you think you know what abilities are required in a job but have met few practitioners of it, you probably have at least a mild stereotype, and should clarify it by seeing these people firsthand and asking them about the abilities necessary for success in their field.

d) *You are unaware of your own abilities.* Job seekers are known for understating their own abilities or even being ignorant of them. If you have never made an inventory of your skills, be sure to do exercises such as those on pages 70–71. Perhaps with the help of a career counselor, you must assess your abilities well enough that you can talk about them. Much of the language of job hunting is the vocabularly of skills: "I am a good *organizer*; I have strong *writing* skills; I do *research* well; I have done a lot of *public speaking*; I have *planned* many programs." Armed with this vocabularly, you are in a far better position to tell an employer: "I can do this job, because . . ."

▶ 3. Self-Defeating Beliefs ◀

A person's job search can start with a self-assessment that makes progress very difficult:

Interviewers don't like me
I really don't have a sense for the business world
Computers scare me
I don't have the confidence to deal with that type of customer
I don't have enough class for that kind of place

And, like trying to move a bale of hay with a large cow standing in your way, that is where the project both begins and ends. Self-defeating beliefs, whether they are true or not, become true when the job seeker believes them.

A self-defeating belief can override the job hunter's positive research and growing knowledge of the field of work. If people feel pessimistic, they will interpret their data to fit their expectations. Now we know what some philosophers mean when they say there is no reality, just our own perceptions of it.

Self-defeating beliefs can be lurking around any corner, ready to pounce on your good, constructive job-hunting techniques. All the king's horses and techniques in this book cannot put you back together again if you fashion a negative image of yourself based on some "reason" you believe you won't make it.

What You Can Do About This Problem

Everyone can find one or more disadvantages in their backgrounds if they try hard enough:

- too old/too young
- too little experience/too much experience
- need more large-business experience/need more small-business experience
- too many previous jobs/worked for only one employer

Before you accept your self-defeating belief as fact, do these things:

Reality Check   Test your image of the occupation against a sample of people who are doing it. Do they have the characteristics that you believe? Allow for your inexperience before judging yourself too harshly. How did recently hired people penetrate this field? Were they once in the same position you are in?

Find Counter Factors   While you are reality checking, look for reasons that will *support* your presence in that kind of work. If you're going to develop a bias, it might as well be a positive one. Just as there may be areas where you lack something, so there can be ways that you will have the edge on your competitors.

Rewrite Your Self-Statements Based on better information, write a more accurate set of self-beliefs for yourself. Give yourself the benefit of the doubt. "I have good potential for this job because of these skills: ———, and it will be even better when I work on ———."

Fill the vacuum with data that you gather firsthand, and if it looks as though you have even a decent chance of being a good candidate, give yourself a try. Yes, rejections will occur in the natural course of job hunting, but this is better than rejecting yourself.

▶ 4. Other Income ◀
to Fall Back On

This may sound like an advantage in the job search, and certainly it allows you to eat while you are developing your grand strategy, but often the availability of outside financial support works perversely against your desire to forge ahead.

Many career counselors have reported that their clients are blocked or strangely unable to shape or move toward their goals when they have a steady or sizable income to keep them warm. Oddly enough, when money is there to free people to do whatever they really want most to do, they get stuck in their own trenches.

You may be having the same experience. Just when you are on the brink of doing what you really want, you seem to founder and feel unable to make up your mind. You are so taken with the idea that you can choose from the great candy store of careers that you become immersed in the process, and bog down in a morass of information, introspection, and creating still more ideas. Too much time and too much financial security can seduce you into exploring so many options that you begin to wonder: "If I make a choice, will I be overlooking something else that I would have found if I had kept looking?" We *could* look forever for careers, for marital partners, even for a new car, if we had enough time. But meanwhile, life goes on. Or, in the words of an unknown author: "Life is what happens while we're making other plans."

Career counselors note that this problem is a particularly tricky one; it *looks* as though the client is working hard, investigating, etc., and seems quite motivated. Often these are highly capable people who *do* have a lot of skills and awareness of their potential, who should be able to get a successful career underway. Yet, as time goes on, it becomes clear that these clients cannot mount the effort it takes to find goals that fire them up, and to move assertively and deliberately toward these goals.

What You Can Do About This Problem

If this problem seems to describe you, I will first give you credit for admitting it. This is a difficult problem to recognize.

You may be a new college graduate who is being supported by your parents. Or perhaps you are married, and your spouse's income is making it possible for you to develop a career path at your own pace. Or maybe you have an inheritance or trust fund that enables you to live comfortably while you are looking for a new job.

If you have been looking for your job for only a brief time, it's premature to consider that money is the problem. However, if you have been looking for six months or more, and you still don't have a clear goal in sight, or you have been unwilling to take steps necessary to move toward your goal, then you may be subtly undermining yourself with the comfortable pillow of financial support.

It may seem ludicrous to ask someone to surrender financial comfort, but you may want to consider some variation on that theme. So far, a steady income does not seem to have worked in your favor. Why not try cutting yourself loose for a while? Suppose you gave yourself a time deadline ("I won't use the money past a certain date"), or a financial limitation ("I will only spend $——— per month, so that I am forced to find employment by a certain time"), in order to build some urgency into your job search plans.

The presence of income support may compromise your efforts in subtle and complex ways. You may be thinking—perhaps unconsciously—"I have to find the perfect job," believing that your choice has to be *better* than the jobs of other people, because you have the so-called luxury of time to decide. In general, I believe that too much time and monetary support become liabilities, because they force you to think too much. You may spend so much time dwelling on the possibilities and gathering new information that you get weighed down with data. This makes it harder for you to pay attention to your intuition, your gut feelings about the direction you should choose.

Of course, money can also tie you to the needs, preferences, and wishes of the person who is supplying it. You may feel, without even asking, that you're obligated to choose a job or career that would please him or her. You may never have had such a conversation, but the influence can be felt anyway.

Thus, in many respects, it can help you to get clear of your financial support, if that is possible or you are willing to do it. Even if you are unable or unwilling to change your financial situation, ask yourself how it might be affecting your motivation. At the very least, you should do the following:

1. Identify a career goal that represents what you think *you* most want.
2. Talk with your family, spouse, etc. about your goal and do your best to draw out their feelings about it. If they disagree or are even lukewarm about it, hear what they have to say. Sharing your disagreement openly will help you to decide what is best for you and may lead you to a firmer decision.

How long do you want to continue contemplating your choice while the world beckons you to do something? I appreciate the need for research as much as the next person, but you may need to hit or get off the plate. If you *had* to find something worth doing by tomorrow, what would it be?

If you are bogged down in your job search, and you suspect that financial support has something to do with it, decide what you have to do to build a fire under yourself. Whatever direction you take, it is important that you clarify how your financial condition may be affecting you.

► 5. Bright But Scattered ◄ Ambitions

There are many job hunters who are a pleasure to talk with, who can think of lots of possibilities, and who are clearly brimming with intelligence, yet bounce around, unable to establish themselves or perform with distinction on a job. These people have lots of potential, but that's where it stops.

If intelligence and verbal facility could be cashed like so many chips in the marketplace, these people would do fine. But ease of conversation and an engaging manner are not the same as goal-directedness and determination.

Sometimes these bright but scattered people appear to feel "too good" for jobs they are offered, and their apparent aloofness simply adds to their problems.

What You Can Do About This Problem

We've all been scattered and uncertain at one time or another, so let's not consider this a social disease. Being restless can be a sign of constructive impatience. A certain amount of scatteredness is all right, as you are roaming the fields, looking for ideas. However, if you are continually unfocused and unable to find anything, then perhaps we'd better look a little closer at what's happening in your not-yet-brilliant career.

It is possible that regular, salaried jobs won't do it for you. You may be resisting the entire working-for-someone scene. If so, imagine starting your own little business, or working with a few other people in a small business, or developing a highly portable skill (photography, word processing, graphic arts, language translation) that allows you to avoid a nine-to-five, one-office desk job.

If self-employment won't work, and you need a secure salary, then you'll have to face squarely this problem of scatteredness. If you move from job to job, or you simply fail to be focused enough in job interviews, eventually you'll be typed this way and will find it a difficult image to overcome.

Where does your restlessness and uncertainty come from? I can think of two strong possibilities. First, you may still be on the trail of your real ambitions. If you have done little self-assessment (see chapters 1 to 6), you may not yet know the answers to important questions such as "What do I really want? What kinds of work would be most worth doing? Where can my abilities best be used?" If this is the case, be patient with yourself and take interim jobs while you are shaping your ambitions and career dreams.

On the other hand, you may be a person who will be perpetually unsatisfied with your paid employment, and the search for a fully satisfying job will largely elude you. Don't feel weird. This happens to a lot of people. No one ever said that paid work is the answer to everyone's prayers. Many jobs will provide only partial satisfaction, no matter how motivated you are.

If this is the case, consider how you can get fired up about some activity outside your paid work. Let your outside interests be your primary involvements, if possible, and regard your paid work as simply a job to be done, nothing more. Your outside interests may also offer clues for future career possibilities.

Bright people can have a hard time with career development once they have rejected the obvious "successful" career paths (doctor, lawyer, business executive, professor, scientist). A conventional career may not be right for you. Your career may be a floating circus of involvements, some of them paid, some of them unpaid, but with the program always changing. Don't settle for disillusionment or wallow in it. Find something good to *do*, whether it is paid or unpaid, temporary or permanent, promising or uncertain. Talking about it probably buries you deeper in the pit of inaction. Go ahead and do it.

▶ 6. Anger/Resentment/ ◀ Cynicism

It isn't hard to find something to be angry or resentful about when you are job hunting. Other people who have the inside track on jobs; lengthy selection processes that drive you to frustration; being rejected when you don't know why; being told you are overqualified; interviewers who say one thing and then do another; companies where it is impossible to penetrate the personnel department . . . the list goes on. Job hunting seems to manufacture frustration in great boatloads, and eventually that frustration will affect your feelings.

Such feelings are natural and expected, but they become a problem when they spill over to your behavior as you continue the job-search process. Career counselors are quick to spot people whose anger or resentment has affected their attitudes. They say to themselves: "If I were an employer, I would be reluctant to hire such a negative person." Alert counselors will tell their clients about this, because a bad attitude will undo almost anything else that a job seeker does right.

How much negativism are we talking about here? Not just the person who is obviously upset and would be rejected quickly, but also the small touches of anger and cynicism that you may think are not even noticed. You may not even be aware of the subtle feelings you carry with you from previous disappointments, but the occasional comment will give you away:

They don't really appreciate their workers over there.
I applied to some banks but I don't think they like older people.
That government system is designed to be hard to deal with.
I don't really know *what* they're looking for at that university.

While your feelings may be legitimate, prospective employers will often interpret them as negativism. Sure, it's fun to complain about things, but when you do it with an interviewer, you take the risk that he/she will view *you* as the source of the problem.

What You Can Do About This Problem

First of all, acknowledge your feelings—you're irritated at what's been happening to you, and probably feeling that "the system" is unfair, that you have a lot to offer, but the way things are set up, you're not getting a chance to show it.

Then, look more closely at how these feelings may be affecting your communication with others. Is your anger spilling into conversations, dominating everything else? Or is it just an undertone, but one that can be noticed by others who look for it?

If you are aware of negative feelings, then you probably are displaying them to others, including job interviewers. If you are not sure about this, get feedback from others. You may have a hard time seeing it in yourself. Do mock interviews with counselors or friends, or simply ask people how you are coming across when you talk about your job hunting.

Then, try to separate your legitimate gripes (yes, the application process at that organization *is* unnecessarily time demanding) from your just plain annoyance at being unemployed or underemployed and uncertain of what is going to happen next.

Identifying your gripes does not eliminate them. Life isn't always fair. Even though selection methods often put the job seeker on the defensive, you have to accept it.

Your task is to keep your own griping and grousing from hurting your chances for being hired. Find people at home to complain to, instead of interviewers and others you meet along the job-hunting trail. Negativism of any kind—including snide remarks, "funny" stories that make someone else look bad, ragging on former bosses, or just going along with the popular cynicism ("Ain't government bureaucracy awful?")—will almost always be taken by an interviewer to reflect badly on you. There's no escaping a general dictum of employers: "If you are negative in the job interview, you will probably be negative on the job."

That doesn't mean you cannot register an occasional snicker, or offer a constructive criticism at times, but whenever someone asks you "Why did you leave that job?" or "Why do you think you were not chosen for that job?" be careful to answer in terms that make both you and the employer look good. It will be very tempting to criticize ("I left there because that place really needs to get into shape" . . . "They didn't take me because everyone works a soft job there"), but resist doing it. Extract the positive from every situation and be prepared to talk about *that*: "I'm leaving to find an opportunity for growth. My present company (though you disagree with management and find certain people insufferable) has taught me a lot about this industry and enabled me to acquire many skills, such as . . ."

Angry or resentful job candidates often feel mistreated, overlooked, unrecognized for their talents. While their feelings may sometimes be justified, in other situations their negativism is a stand-in for another issue in their lives. If you're down on yourself or down on employers, check to see if there is something else bothering you. If so, don't use the job market as a whipping post.

A positive, sunny disposition, with as much optimism as you can muster, is perhaps the best asset you can have in job hunting. Smiling in the face of adversity helps a lot. Interviewers know you're having a hard time. If you can keep your head up despite it all, they will respect you for it.

► 7. Poor Work History ◄

Résumés require that you reveal your work history, and sometimes the story it tells does not work to your advantage. You may have changed jobs a lot, or had a gap of time when you were not working, or had an uneven record, perhaps including changes that would be interpreted as demotions. On paper, you may be far less than the perfect candidate for the job you are seeking.

Often it is not the work history itself that undermines you, but your difficulty in explaining it. If your work record does not have everything that an employer might want, you must make a strong case for yourself anyway. Many people have a hard time with this. They feel on the defensive and regard their past as difficult to overcome.

Don't be paralyzed by the past. While you do have to acknowledge what you have done before, there is much room for interpretation.

What You Can Do About This Problem

First of all, remember that employers do not expect to get the perfect applicants for their jobs. They write job descriptions as though it were possible to find perfection, but they usually expect to find someone who is short on one factor or another. So, don't eliminate yourself because your background fails to meet one or more of the specifications.

Second, be ready to explain any weaknesses in your work history that an interviewer might ask about:

I changed jobs twice because I was looking for the best place to use my writing skills.

I accepted less managerial responsibility there, because of the opportunity to work on a certain project.

I traveled in Europe that year, because I wanted to do it before starting my career.

I left the insurance business because I wanted a product area that had more potential for growth.

I lost that job because my technical skills were not as strong as others, but I have corrected that.

What if you have been fired from jobs because of bad personal relations, poor performance, or other conflicts that do not reflect well on you? There are two possible approaches:

1. Assume that they will not find out the full story. Create the most positive reason that you might have left, one that is within

the realm of possibility. Make sure you speak positively about the job and the people in it. I know that is not easy to do, but an upbeat attitude is essential. There is the risk they may already know you were fired when they ask you why you left, but that is a chance you can take if you want.

2. Tell them what happened, and explain what you learned about yourself from the experience, how you would handle that type of situation better in the future, and that you are convinced you can work effectively with everyone in this organization. Honesty may get you a lot of points here, particularly if you show you have grown and learned a lot since that time.

Whatever your work history, focus on what you learned from each past job or experience:

That job taught me a lot about supervising people who are unmotivated.

I was only there eighteen months, but I learned a lot about the government funding process.

That job in the state geological survey had nothing to do with my psychology major, but I learned how to organize data for a scientific research project.

Ultimately, you want your work history to be a catalog of the strengths you have to offer. Interviewers do not really care about your weaknesses, work gaps, or even uncertain motivation in the past. What they want to know is what you can *do*—now. Use your work record and present motivation to show why you are a good candidate for this job, emphasizing your strengths, your skills, and your experiences. Make a case for yourself and give yourself the benefit of the doubt. No, you won't sound like the perfect candidate, but neither will anyone else.

▶ 8. Overriding Emotional ◀ Concerns

In some cases, the job seeker's lack of progress derives from emotional issues that have not yet been resolved. The kinds of problems career counselors have found that may limit the job seeker's effectiveness include depression, performance anxiety, family conflicts, hyperactivity, obsessive/compulsiveness, and paranoia.

Many people with emotional problems hold jobs, so it is no surprise that job seekers have such problems too. If you have any of these concerns, you will have to attend to them. While you may not want to suspend your job search, you should recognize that any significant emotional issue will inevitably cloud your ability to be at your best in job interviews. Emotional issues have a way of taking over a person's ability to communicate and coloring all of his/her interactions. If you know you have psychological concerns that are affecting you, you must consider them a top priority, or else your career progress will continue to be hindered.

If you are not aware of any special psychological/emotional problems, but you cannot seem to control feelings or behaviors that are hurting your job-search strategy (possibly the "anger/resentment/cynicism" described above, or the "self-defeating behaviors" described below), you may have emotional concerns nagging at you under the surface.

What You Can Do About This Problem

Your first step is to acknowledge that the problem exists and is affecting your interpersonal relations in the job search. Often this is a judgment call, but even if you are not sure, it helps to explore the possibility.

These days professional help is widely available, from psychologists, psychiatrists, counselors, social workers, and various other therapists. You can take your choice, but it is usually good to develop a primary relationship with a single professional. Don't be afraid to consult a professional helper. You can initiate such contacts without being obligated to more than a single meeting.

For most job seekers, emotional concerns are not likely to be debilitating or force you to abandon your entire career strategy. In all likelihood, you can continue most of the job search while you are working on your other issues. However, you should probably slow down your timetable somewhat, because psychological concerns may keep you from being at your best when you identify the jobs you most desire.

While obtaining psychological help, continue the "detective" and "self-assessment" stages of job hunting. These stages often represent 70 percent or more of the time needed for a job-search strategy. Self-marketing skills are a good index of how well you have done self-assessment and detective work.

You can do self-marketing (have job interviews, etc.) while you are working on your emotional concerns, but you may be unhappy with the results. Self-marketing makes the greatest demand on your interpersonal skills. If the ways you behave with other people are affected by depression, anxiety, projected anger, or other emotional conflict, your ability to relate well will suffer. You can either steer clear of these experiences, or use them to test yourself to see how well you are doing.

Emotional issues do not bend easily, even when you are getting help and working hard to change your behavior. Don't expect overnight results. On the other hand, the fact that you have recognized the problem and are moving constructively toward change will have a positive effect on your attitude and expectations of yourself. You are moving in the right direction, and will be happy you did not ignore the emotional issue in favor of some illusory explanation.

▶ 9. Self-Defeating Behaviors ◀

Job hunting is hard enough without finding ways to inhibit your chances of being evaluated positively. Career counselors tell countless stories of individuals who compromise themselves by:

- being late for interviews
- not sending information that employers ask for
- not following up opportunities as soon as they are made available
- acting casually when they should be selling themselves
- sending carelessly prepared résumés
- failing to contact their references
- dressing badly for interviews
- failing to read the company literature before the interview

Any of these is a surefire way to get yourself eliminated from a job competition. And the importance of each of them seems obvious enough that you would expect a person to make sure they are covered well. Sometimes people don't know any better, but often they do. Despite knowing the Do's and Don't's, and having ample time to prepare, these individuals contrive to come in second place or worse every time, because they make one or more errors that could not be ignored but could have been prevented. Such people are a mystery to their career counselors, to their families and friends, and perhaps even to themselves. On the surface, they seem quite involved in their job searches, and willing to devote effort to the task, yet they have a piece missing in their puzzle and do not take full advantage of their abilities.

What You Can Do About This Problem

Self-defeating behavior, while it may sound ominous, is really pretty common among job seekers. We screw up and we don't know why. Sometimes it is just ignorance, and sometimes other priorities in our lives intervene, so that we cannot pay full attention to all the intricacies of job-search behavior. There *are* a lot of things to remember to do in job hunting and, just like forgetting to check the battery cells in your car, you are going to slip from time to time.

However, if you find yourself ignoring things repeatedly, or overlooking important details when you really wanted to remember them, you may have a more ongoing concern. Self-defeating behaviors are not incurable. In fact, they can be corrected pretty easily. But first you have to figure out where they are coming from. There are four possibilities:

You have not been coached well enough Through inexperience and general lack of advice, you may be doing things wrong without even knowing it. You may be mailing hundreds of résumés and waiting patiently by your mailbox for the job offers to come rolling in. This is self-defeating, because you will be frustrated to find nothing in your mailbox except rejections, and yet you may not know what you have done wrong. Or, you may be unprepared because you never knew that employers have literature you can read before applying for jobs.

Many job seekers get bad advice or little at all. If you are one of them, reading this book is a great start toward correcting the situation. I would also recommend you talk with a career counselor about your job strategy. You may find a counselor in one of your local colleges, a community career center, or a counselor who has a private practice.

You never had to look hard for a job before Once again, self-defeating behavior can be sheer negligence on your part. Maybe you have been contacted by someone else for all the previous jobs you have gotten, so you did not have to exert any effort to get them; unconsciously, you are expecting the same thing to happen again. While being chosen by others without deliberate effort on your part is an ideal to be sought (see The No-Search Job Search, pages 297–314), right now you will have to take more initiative. Following up job opportunities, doing research, contacting references, and all that may come as a rude awakening to you, but now is a good time to start new habits.

You may not want the job you say you want Self-defeating behavior—inattention to the details of an effective job search—may be a sign that you are walking down the wrong trail. You may have chosen a career goal but are ambivalent about it. Your uncertainty is perhaps reflected in your lack of follow-through and your casual attitude. People don't usually sabotage themselves unless there is an underlying reason. A person who is fired up about his/her job objective will typically take care of every item without being coaxed. If you are letting things slip, take a closer look at your motivation. Is there some other kind of work that you would really prefer but have been reluctant to admit to yourself?

Temporarily, try adopting a different job objective. See if you follow through on job search tasks more efficiently. If your self-defeating behaviors disappear, then you have learned something about the work you really want.

You may have ambivalence about succeeding in general   I know this sounds terribly psychological, but it does often happen that people act in self-defeating ways because they are reluctant to succeed. In job hunting, lateness for appointments, inabililty to prepare, casualness of attitude, etc., can be signs that someone is setting him/herself up to fail, certainly to not get the job he or she is supposedly seeking.

If you think you have a touch of "fear of success," or perhaps a major case of it, I encourage you to explore that theme within yourself (with the help of a counselor or psychologist if you choose) before you do yourself any more damage in job hunting. If your job search is disorganized or uneven, you will not get much benefit from it, only frustration.

Regardless of where it comes from, if you see a self-defeating pattern in your own behavior, I encourage you to break the pattern while you are aware of it. If you have to get out of the game for a while, do it. Jump back in when you can see what you did wrong before and your motivation is more clear.

► 10. I Don't Want a ◄
Nine-to-Five Job Where All I Do
Is Sit at a Desk

This one is a bit of a mystery to me. Most jobs have desks and regular hours. Is this an unwillingness to join the adult world? No, I think it is just a stereotype that Work Is Dull, and being "chained to a desk" is like prison. Furthermore, some people are afraid of being "locked in," unable to change to a different kind of work if the first proves to be unacceptable. The image of being tied down immobilizes the job seeker, preventing him/her from moving toward anything because it might shut the door on future exploration.

What You Can Do About This
Problem

As you continue your detective work, you will come to feel one of three things:

1. *My Kafkaesque fears are unfounded.* The desk jobs I observe aren't so bad after all. They do let one walk around and get out

of the office, and people have a good time working with each other. My image of a faceless functionary is not confirmed. Many people believe in what they are doing and are eager to tell me about it.

2. *I am better suited to some situations than to others.* Some desk jobs *are* bad, but I can also find a few that have the variety and challenge I am looking for. I have to be careful to choose my work environment, but by seeing a lot of different places, I am developing antennae for the jobs that will fit me best.

3. *I don't have to be company president in a week.* My hopes and expectations for immediate responsibility and rapid advancement were a little unrealistic. There's a lot of room between the awful desk job and the seats of ultimate decision making that I aspire to, but I can live with a progression of responsibility. I also know that I will not be bound to a job if it gets bad. I can change, because a lot of other people have done it.

Don't rule out careers sight unseen. Once you stare them in the eye, if they still look unpromising, move on to something else. Don't accept boredom. You will probably work nine to five, or eight to six, or ten to seven, and you will almost certainly have a desk, but the rest is up to you.

22

Unattractiveness, Personality Flaws, and Other Impossible Obstacles

Hidden somewhere in many of us is the fear *"something about me* will slow down or halt my job search progress, even if I do everything right." Maybe you have felt this before. You were qualified for the job, you applied correctly, had all your paperwork in order, presented yourself well in the interviews, but they still didn't hire you, and you suspected you were boomed because of—how you looked, how your spoke, your personality, your size, or something else that should have nothing whatsoever to do with the hiring decision. You don't really know why you were rejected, but you fear discrimination nonetheless. And these factors, of course, are never mentioned in the interview or afterward in any evaluation or feedback you may receive.

► Physical Appearance ◄

Physical appearance is a major concern of a lot of job hunters. Imperfect diamonds that we are, there is usually something that we worry will detract from our marketability. What should you do about it, if you feel you are at a disadvantage in this respect?

1. Leave Well Enough Alone

The first strategy is to do nothing at all; that is, nothing different from the rest of your job-search strategy. Recognize that there are many physical attributes you can do nothing about, and just sit back and appreciate the way you are, trusting that others will too. Qualities such as:

270

Shape of body, height, size of body
Facial features, body features (nose, ears, eyes, elbows, skin, etc.)
Type and amount of hair, complexion, ways you walk
Speech pattern, accent, vocal qualities

All of these are things that define you; you've been living with them for a while and will have a few more years to carry them around. Don't get obsessed with trying to change these, because you probably cannot do much about them, and will only create frustration for yourself when you say: "If only I were a little taller (smaller/less awkward looking, etc.)." It's better to focus on things that you can change and want to change, because there are certainly enough of those to occupy your attention.

If you are concerned that an employer is judging you on one of these physical attributes, and you would like to say something about it, you may consider doing so, but don't feel that you must. There is room for you to make comments such as the following, if you feel they are necessary:

> EXAMPLE ▶ You may be wondering about the fact that I am very small, and may think I look immature for this job, but I can assure you that I will present a strong image to the customers, and that I will do as good a job as anyone—probably better.
>
> I know that my speech is a little different and that sometimes I talk too slowly, but I am effective at getting my points across and can handle myself in any situation.
>
> People sometimes comment on the fact that I walk funny, and think that I can't keep up, but it's not a problem for me, and I'm sure you'll see that if you hire me to work here.

Letitia was never a "looker" and had a name to match. She was scrawny, wirehaired, bookish, and inclined to withdraw from personal contact. As an adolescent she suffered the abuse you would expect. Eventually she learned that her feeling of presumed "inferiority" had to be dealt with. She decided: "I can't let my body keep me from doing what I want to do." She made the unlikely metamorphosis from withdrawn scarecrow to salesperson of computer equipment and eventual computer manager, because she wanted to make it big in the world of technology. Though still not a great beauty, Letitia grew more attractive with her business successes and learned that her so-called physical liability was minor indeed.

2. Things You Might Do
Something About, But You Would
Prefer to Leave Alone

This is another do-nothing strategy, concerning physical attributes that you might change if you wanted to, but you prefer to leave intact. There are hundreds of big and little physical qualities you might alter if you chose. They include:

Body weight, style of clothing, grooming, hairstyle
Clarity of speech, vocal qualities, personal habits (smoking, etc.)
Speaking vocabulary, casualness of dress

Looking at those aspects you might change, but prefer not to, is a way of looking at the hiring equation: "How much do I believe that weight/dress/speech, etc., are considered in the hiring decisions?" Are your other attributes—job competence, personality, previous experience, etc.—enough to compensate for the physical aspects that might be considered? In most cases, physical attributes will not matter as much as experience, skills, motivation, and credentials. You will decide that your appearance is plenty good enough, and that even though some competitors may be a little better looking than you, you have qualities they don't that will beat them out in other ways.

3. Situations in Which You Can Change, You Want to Change, and You Should Change

Now we're left with the situations where you feel you're going to be one down in a selection process because of one or more physical attributes, and you would like to do something about it. There are several situations in which you should probably consider some changes:

a) *You feel bad about it yourself:* Bad results in job hunting sometimes come from the feelings you carry around inside you. If you feel that being overweight—or talking differently, or dressing differently from others, or your unusual laugh—or other physical factors are casting you in a bad light, and your self-belief is undermining your general confidence, then you should consider some changes.

b) *The norms of that job setting call for you to change:* If you have done enough investigation of the job and the organization where you want to work to see that most of the people there look different from you, and you would like to fit in better, then you ought to consider some changes. Perhaps they wear different clothing, or everyone in the office is trim and fit, or they all have better diction than you do, or they speak more forcefully. Egad! The stereotype of this profession is coming true, and your physical qualities are going to put you at a disadvantage.

Yet, you would like to work there very much. There *are* jobs where appearance is important. Sometimes this factor is openly stated, and sometimes it isn't. If your research reveals that physical attributes are important, you'd better do whatever you can about them.

▶ Personality Traits ◀

This is another reason many people are rejected from jobs without knowing why. Some people with the worst personality flaws will approach this section and move on, thinking that it could not possibly apply to them.

Evaluation of personality characteristics is highly subjective. One person's ogre is another's hard-driving hero. However, there is still room to say that certain personality characteristics will tend to work against a job candidate in many situations. These traits are common enough and amenable enough to change. You may want to consider whether any of these may be hurting your success in the job market: overbearing behavior, timidity, sneakiness, rigidity, negativeness, aloofness, faultfinding, or talkativeness.

While we can think of situations in which such traits would be useful (for example, the aggressive personality can certainly pay off in courts of law; as a newspaper reporter; to sell certain products), in other job-hunting situations such traits are going to subtract from one's overall effectiveness.

We are not talking here about the wonderful variety of personality differences that make people interesting. There is great room for individual styles, senses of humor, ways of interacting, personal mannerisms, etc., in life as well as in job hunting. Here we are concerned about those traits that will most often be perceived as negative, because they will make you a less effective worker. Often the interviewers will not tell you that you have exhibited one or more of these but proceed to "ding" you, "boom" you, or otherwise short-circuit your job prospects because of them. What should you do?

1. Identify Specific Behaviors That You Can Try to Change

The more specific you can be about a personality trait, the more likely you are to be able to change it.

EXAMPLES ▶ I need to learn not to interrupt people when they're talking. I want to learn how to talk about my good qualities clearly and concisely. I must learn not to make negative comments about my previous jobs.

2. Hold Mock Job Interviews

Eventually you must put into practice what you are learning and changing. Practice job interviews give you a good opportunity to hear yourself talk and interact, and allow you to get feedback without the pressure of knowing you're being evaluated for a job. Mock interviews can be arranged with college career-planning offices, high school counselors, professional counselors or psychologists, your friends, or people in the working world who may be willing to role-play situations with you.

In a mock interview:

- Prepare yourself to answer the questions you would find most difficult
- Tell the "interviewer" in advance about the personality traits that concern you, and ask him/her to test you firmly on these, even try to trap you into showing some of those traits you've had trouble with before
- Allow enough time to get feedback immediately after the practice interview
- Choose "interviewers" who are not particularly easy, so that you have to face pressure similar to that of a real job interview

Personality Traits Are Touchy Business

Nobody likes to have anyone else mess with their personality, least of all, perhaps, a job interviewer or author of a job-search book. Telling you that you don't act right is an invitation for "Same to you, buddy." Nonetheless, interpersonal skills are critical in hiring decisions. If you're doing something that makes you less likeable than other job candidates, or interviewers are concluding that you may not get along well with others, then you need to change your behavior enough to show the best sides of your personality and your most positive potential for the job.

► Taking Advantage of Your ◄ Disadvantages

We all know people who are overweight, rude, look funny, or act oddly but seem to benefit from their differences rather than suffer from them. Some are covering up their difficulties, but others truly use their peculiar ways or features as departure points for making their lives work. You can be one of them too. If you decided long ago "This is the way I am," then you can go forward with confidence.

Certain attributes, such as rudeness, I do not advise you to maintain. But others—casual style of dress, little attention to fitness and body image, talkativeness, brashness, low-keyness, and others—may work well for you.

EXAMPLE ▶ I know I dress oddly and look a little funny, but that won't stop me from doing a good job as a graphic artist for you.

I talk a lot, but I believe that is necessary in this field of fund-raising.

Unusualness can often be turned to your advantage. As long as you are comfortable with yourself, you can use your individual features as your "calling cards."

23

Stuck on the Job-Search Merry-Go-Round

"Stuck" is how you feel when you've followed the experts' advice, worked harder than you have in any job, examined and summarized your skills, pounded pavement like a jackhammer, but still you see few signs of progress. A stuck needle . . . a broken record . . . I'm getting nowhere . . . getting nowhere . . . Are these interviewers trying to tell me something? Wouldn't anyone else have a job by now? Maybe I was meant to stay where I am.

These are the thoughts that haunt you. But you're not through with the job search yet, and it's not through with you. You're spinning in the dryer of your own mind. You can break this cycle once you know that you're in it.

Welcome to the world of the Advanced Job Hunter. You have been through the mill a few times, know the principles of job searching backward and forward and, as a result, you are more choosy about what you will accept. You are facing the complicated problems of a more demanding job seeker.

It does not make any sense for you to recycle the same methods, reciting a litany of "these are my values, these are my skills, if I don't get hired, I'll start taking pills." It's time for you to look past the first principles and develop a strategy that fits your situation. You may want to seek the assistance of a professional counselor, a job-search support group, or other competent services in your area.

On the other hand, you may be able to solve your own problem. Your complaint of "nothing works for me" may be a temporary feeling if you can identify and attack the problem that you're having. For the advanced job seeker, here are some special problems you may be experiencing, and specific solutions for getting yourself unstuck.

▶ **Problem 1:** *"My Network Goes Round and Round, Oh-Oh-Oh-O, and It Goes Nowhere"*

My network list is all thumbed and worn out, and so are the people I have been contacting. Some of them have heard from me for the third time. I'm getting into the Pest Zone and don't know where else to go. People like to help me, but after a while they begin to wonder about me, and why I haven't gotten a job yet. I'm tired of being on the outside, looking in. Am I back to ground zero? Where do I find a new network, on another planet?

Networking gets wearisome for both you and your contacts. You are stuck in a rut of your own making, and you have to leave these people alone for a while.

Don't make the mistake of assuming that networking is the end product of the job search. It is merely a method, an imperfect one. It's like being a salesperson and assuming that talking to a lot of people will lead to sales. Not necessarily so.

Don't network till it hurts. If you really don't want to make that next contact, don't, because you'll just be going through the motions. Like mass mailing of résumés, such production-line networking will yield very low returns. Numbers seen, hours spent, and calls made do not translate to results.

Take a close look at *how* you have been networking. Are you making friends, or are you making poor use of people's time? Are you doing anything that might turn people off? Are you asking them questions that you could have answered for yourself by reading their literature? Are you asking for more help than they can reasonably provide? Networking and information interviewing are the fine arts of getting help from people in ways that feel painless to them. Your technique may be a little rough around the edges. Maybe because you are fatigued, you are not concentrating anymore, just rushing from one contact to the next one.

Get away from networking for a while. Go back to making direct applications. You may have been relying too heavily on "help" from others. Such help can sometimes lead you to relax and expect that others will be doing the work for you. Direct application will force you to sell yourself more strongly. Refer to your target list and make a beeline in their direction. Don't ask anyone to help introduce you.

Broaden your range of potential employers. Perhaps you've been too narrowly focused on a single field. If you like to sell, try other products, such as computers, insurance, real estate, financial services, hospital supplies, stocks and bonds, or other areas of the marketplace. Even if you prefer a particular industry, give the others a chance, to see if they would like to use your abilities too.

▶ **Problem 2:** *The Case of the Trailing Spouse*

My wife got the job, and my career took a nosedive. She's doing fine, but I am stuck with the leftovers. This town really does not have a lot of opportunity for me. I'm trying to make the best of it, but it's harder than I ever thought it would be. My job in Detroit had me right on track, but now I wonder what my future is. It does not seem fair, but I guess I'll recover, as soon as something opens up in my field.

This could be you. A 1985 Merrill Lynch survey showed that by 1990 75 percent of corporate moves will involve dual-career couples.[1]

When you succeed in job hunting as a trailing spouse you will be awarded highest honors in this job-search game, because this is a most difficult test. You are limited to one town or city, yet you do not want to settle for less. And you're looking for work under the watchful eyes of a lot of people who know your spouse already has a job, and who keep asking you "How's it going?" until you'd rather they disappear.

You should spread your wings to cover a much wider variety of possible jobs. Now is a time to be the most creative and imaginative. Don't let yourself be tied to your résumé. Investigate fields that are related in some way to your intended field.

Consider part-time work more seriously. This is an excellent way to start in any field, particularly if you have little or no experience. You'll get paid a lower rate, but don't consider it a pay cut. The idea is to get front-end experience that you might want to market for better opportunities later.

Look carefully at how your personal interests might be converted to income production. In the service and information age we live in, self-employment is easier than it used to be, because it requires little capital investment. Often only a business card and telephone will get you started.

Let's say that you know a lot about canoeing. The possibilities for a small business include:

- marketing equipment to local canoeists
- organizing canoe trips
- organizing canoe races
- writing a newsletter

- writing a book describing conditions on lakes and rivers in your region
- contracting your services to scout troops and other organizations

You may be discounting the emotional dimension of this problem. Trailing spouses seldom take kindly to their fate, no matter what they say. Are you irritated at your partner for having made this move? Do you feel second-best in the family right now? Are you wondering what your friends and family think of all this?

If you don't feel some resentment, you are probably burying it somewhere, and it will come back to bite you both later. Talk it out with your partner as best you can, ask for the kind of support you need, and tell him when to leave you alone, too.

Join community and social groups, even when you have no job leads at all. Rather than do deliberate networking, just get involved in some things (canoe club, Jaycees, Kiwanis, volunteer firemen, barbershop quartets, whatever suits your fancy) to connect with people. Go to these meetings *without* your spouse, so that you can develop relationships on your own and not have your employment situation compared to his/hers by everyone you meet. Many of your job ideas will come from these associations, as you meet people and hear about their work and other involvements.

▶ **Problem 3:** *Skills Overload*

I have a lot of transferable skills but they do not add up to job opportunities. I feel like that couple on the *Twilight Zone* episode where they endlessly ride a train to nowhere. My skills are tickets, but where do they take me?

Piling up skills can mask other problems in the job search. There is no such thing as having too many skills, but you are probably overlooking other aspects that are dragging you down. First, check the Problem categories (pages 252–269) that have been identified by career counselors. Are you displaying negative traits in job interviews (resentment, cynicism)? Are you scattered in your motivation? Are you slowed down by the cushion of other income available to you? Are you doing some self-defeating things and you don't know why? These are common sources of difficulty, ones which the job seeker is often unaware of. You may be undermining yourself. If you are, the skills won't compensate.

Second, you may be looking at the wrong end of the train. Instead of loading up your skills in the freight cars, go to the engine up front and see what's pulling this train, that is, where is the train going? Your goals, the kinds of work you are seeking, may be unclear. What are your key work values? What goals reflect these values best? Identify your goals first, and then determine which skills are necessary. You can work on the skills that need help, but only once you know where they are taking you.

Third, skills do not necessarily equal knowledge of a field of work, and employers prefer people who have a knowledge base, who are familiar with their field. You can acquire such knowledge either through (a) formal schooling, or (b) on-the-job experience. These two categories break down this way:

Formal Schooling

Degree Programs   Associate, Bachelor's, Master's, or Ph.D. programs in areas of study that relate to specific job markets.

Nondegree Programs   Specialized training programs that offer certificates or other credentials that apply to certain fields of work. These include physical therapy, occupational therapy, paralegal training, and many others.

To learn which fields of work require degrees or nondegree credentials, check the *Occupational Outlook Handbook*, the *Guide to Occupational Exploration*, and other references in a high school, college, or university career center. Many of these books can be found in the reference sections of libraries.

"Retooling by schooling" is often oversold as a method of career preparation. Colleges and other schools will often try to persuade you that their degrees or certificates are preferred or required for entry into certain jobs, when in fact the field may be more fluid than that. Check with a good sample of practitioners first, in addition to the above reference books, to determine how important formal schooling might be.

On-the-Job Training

Company Training Programs   You must be hired first to enter such training programs. Many organizations prefer to train their own employees, and will recruit you on the basis of potential demonstrated by previous jobs or experiences. This sounds like a catch-22 (no experience, no job; no job, no experience), but read pages 55–71 and 209–218 to learn how to translate your previous activities into salable skills.

Internships   Profit and nonprofit organizations offer work experiences in exchange for your services, typically at a low rate of pay. These usually have a defined time period of a year or two. Review the *Directory of Internships* to see whether there are internships which would enable you to acquire the knowledge you need. It is also possible to negotiate an internship with an organization which has not previously had such arrangements.

Volunteering Working for a person who can teach you about a field used to be called apprenticeship, and it has a rich history. Though the concept is not as prevalent today, you can still apply it. Look for a person who would like to help you learn about a field, and in exchange you will help him/her do the work. It's possible to do this part-time or full-time. The arrangements are strictly between you and the other person, who may be self-employed or working for an organization (your choice).

Part-Time Work Any kind of part-time employment may offer you an opportunity to get started in a field, when full-time jobs are scarce. Part-time or temporary work is valuable experience and will be respected by an employer when you look for the full-time position you are more serious about. Take what you can get and use it as a bridge to future advancement.

► **Problem 4:** *Overdosed on the Job Search*

I'm tired and beat and feeling like a jerk. I am weary of putting myself on the line, being evaluated, scrutinized, chewed up, and spit out. The energy and enthusiasm that you recommend is nice in theory, but it just feels like a poor acting job now. I've ruled out drugs or a facelift. Got any brilliant ideas about how to revive me?

Fatigue, of course, is the backwash of rejection. You're bound to lose energy after a certain number of nos. However, there may be other things you're doing wrong, and certainly there are things you can do to improve your attitude. I would recommend any one or more of the following:

Incubation If sheer overexposure is your problem, then a certain amount of "incubation time" is in order. This means backing off the job search and allowing your mind to rest. Any of your favorite leisure activities will do nicely—even a few mindless late-night movies, the more awful the better.

Incubation activities rejuvenate the spirit, and your mind can ease into reflection without your forcing it to THINK. You will get some better ideas, believe it or not, while your mind is far away from land, preoccupied with picking up shells or watching a bird. You should build some incubation time into any week of the job search, but now you may need a bit more.

Break the Cycle   The job market you want may be exhausted, though be careful of using this as a convenient excuse. To break the cycle of looking everywhere for the same kind of work, try either (a) an interim job (see pages 219–224), which allows you to get working and still keep looking, or (b) changing the focus of your search to a slightly different kind of work, because you may be beating a dead horse.

Don't Lone-Wolf It   Fatigue can come from keeping the whole thing to yourself, exaggerating your woes, and perhaps entering a state of depression. To counter these forces, develop a support group of some kind and even give a party for everyone you know who is job hunting. Shared misery helps, and you'll probably scale down the enormity of your problem by hearing how others are fouling up too.

Get Off the Production Line   Overdosing can come from an excess of job-search activity, from sheer quantity of time spent, appointments made, research done, and phone calls returned. Too much quantity and not enough quality. Three good conversations (whether they are formal interviews or information gathering) may be worth a whole week of racking up appointments.

Dig Out of Your Ruts   Fatigue may come from your doing things that undermine yourself. If you're unaware of your errors, you will keep making them. When you feel overdosed it's a good time to get some feedback from a counselor or a friend about what you are doing and how you come across in a practice job interview. Review the categories of problem clients that career counselors talk about, and see if your behavior might fit any of these. Sure, it may be hard to admit that there's some way you're messing up, but now is not the time to stay frozen in your past ways.

Breaking the fatigue cycle will probably require a combination of the remedies mentioned above. Fatigue is temporary. All of these remedies involve changing your angle of approach. Like a sailboat tacking for better wind, you will find the right angle eventually and move ahead.

▸ **Problem 5:** *Too Much Competition*

There is too much competition for the jobs that I want. I have good interviews, but someone else is always better qualified. I can do everything I am supposed to do in job hunting, but still come in second best. Why beat my head against the wall? I knew I should have picked an easier field to get into.

You may very well be faced with a highly competitive field. In that case I advise you to broaden your search in one of several ways: (a) geographically—widen the territory in which you are making contacts; (b) by level—maybe you are shooting too high, try the next level down to see if you can get hired and then promoted; (c) organizations—try employers that do similar work, perhaps smaller companies or firms in related areas.

If all this still leads to blank walls, decide what you must do to become competitive in that occupation, set those steps in motion (e.g., formal education, part-time experience, acquisition of skills, volunteer work) and seek an interim job while you are building your case for the longer-range goals. You haven't lost the competition. You're simply going to enter the game at a later date.

If you are just starting out or have not covered the field yet, you may be exaggerating the depth of the competition. It is easy to get scared off by other people. Don't take secondhand information. Go directly to the "experts" and ask them what they think your chances are and how you can best prepare for successful entry.

Don't be deterred if you lack a particular degree or credential. Check to see if there are people hired recently who did not have the credential that relates to their work. Ask them how *they* got hired.

I suppose if you looked hard enough, you could always find someone who is better than you. But not everyone is out job hunting at the same time you are, not everyone is as motivated as you are, not everyone is in the same location you are, and even people with "better" qualifications often conduct the job search poorly.

Remember, for any given job, most people don't want it, most don't have the talent for it, and even fewer are willing to make an effort to obtain it. Thus, if you have ambition and talent the odds are almost always in your favor for any career.[2]

If your assessment of the competition is accurate, that simply means you must position yourself for the next move. You must decide what you lack, find a strategy for correcting the situation, and then while you are getting yourself into shape, make yourself visible to those people who may be interested in you or in the near future.

▶ **Problem 6:** *They Should Be Finding Me*

I am experienced in my field, I have a good work record, my bosses have thought well of my accomplishments. Why then do I feel like I am starting over? By this time I should not have to be doing a job search the way I did when I was younger. They should be coming to look for me, for gosh sake.

You're right. It doesn't seem fair. Since you have done well in your field and you're looking to stay in this line of work, you might reasonably expect that people pick you out of the crowd now and then. So, let's see what you might be doing wrong, and what to do about it.

Perhaps you are not visible enough in your profession Do you attend meetings with people who do your type of work in other organizations? Do you publish anything or give talks to professional groups? Do you show your work around at all? How would anyone else in your field find out about your work? Are you encouraging that in any ways?

Maybe you are shy about blowing your own horn This personality trait can work against you. Modesty can be a way of hiding, and protecting yourself from criticism or what you think is the sharp glare of publicity. It's hard to get job offers if you are diligent about keeping your best work undercover. See if someone else will be assertive for you, somebody who likes to talk and knows what you are capable of doing.

You haven't gotten excited about anything in your work lately, and it's showing If you're bored by what you are doing, and the challenges have run out, others will notice and it will be hard for them to get excited about you. Nobody wants to offer a job to a person who seems burnt out. Therefore, you've got to light a fire under yourself somehow. Find at least one aspect of your present job that you want to dive into, and then tell a few folks what you are up to.

See The No-Search Job Search (pages 297–314) for other clues about getting noticed and appreciated for your work. You're right—the *ideal* is to never have to look for a job again. If you can learn how to position yourself as competently as you perform your present job, you can approach this ideal.

24

Pursuing Your
Career with the Wrong
Set of Qualifications

The *biggest step* you will take in the job search is the first one—getting yourself to apply for a job. More people trip themselves up here than any other place in the job hunting process. Deciding not to apply is so easy. You just think of some reason you're "not qualified." As Krumboltz says in *Private Rules of Career Decision Making*, "when a reason is needed, any reason will do."

Almost everyone can tell you why their backgrounds are "wrong" for the jobs that they want—or why they are working in fields they were initially "not qualified" for but got anyway, or "just lucked into," as they often say.

EXAMPLES ► I'm working in the finance department, but only have an English degree.

I'm an editor at a book publishing house, but I was in insurance sales for three years, studied biology in school, and never wrote for the school paper.

I'm head of a small historical library, but took only one history course, and used to be in the car repair business.

I studied classics in college and now I'm entering the artificial intelligence field, even though I'm just learning about computers.

No doubt you can explain why you have a missing piece or two for the field of work that you want to enter. Your differences may not be as broad as those described above, but you have an image of the ideal candidate, and you don't believe you fit that profile.

People are champs at pulling themselves out of the race. More individuals disqualify themselves from job possibilities than are ever rejected through job interviews. Why does this happen? Because you do not want to apply incorrectly for a job, and then wind up looking foolish—or being embarrassed—and eventually getting rejected.

Believing yourself to be an inferior candidate, you may refuse to apply, or apply halfheartedly, or apply to only one place and forget the others, or give up halfway through the process and conclude, "I was right all along, they did not want me." Then you drop back and limit yourself to only those safe job possibilities where you know you have a good chance and will not face more rejection.

Feeling discouraged and being rejected in a job search are inevitable. You have to take your lumps with the rest of the job hunters. But, before you make the situation worse by pulling out of the hunt, consider this:

- Personnel departments, which write the job qualifications for many job openings you hear about, are notorious for inflating the job requirements beyond what they expect to hire. They do this in order to attract the best possible candidates, knowing that the eventual decision maker will usually settle for less, for someone who fits some of the criteria but not others. Personnel departments are not alone in this. Anyone who writes a job-candidate profile likes to include everything they might want from applicants, recognizing that it will be possible to back off when they review the candidate pool.
- Most employers will admit that job-candidate profiles are written in order to screen applicants, to keep out the driftwood, to discourage people who truly are not in the ballpark. What they are looking for is not someone who fits all the criteria on paper, but "the best possible person," "a candidate who fits *some* of the basic criteria, is highly motivated, is nice to work with, has good learning skills, and has potential for staying and growing in this field." But they can't put that description on paper, because it sounds too loose. Thus, your task is to get into the interview, based on having *some* of the right criteria, and then in person try to demonstrate that you are motivated, ambitious, willing to learn, likeable, and want to be given a chance to show what you can do.

You won't have a chance to impress people in job interviews if you eliminate yourself at the front end. Deciding to apply in the first place is the biggest decision you will make in the job search. Without it, you are nowhere. As research consistently demonstrates, direct application is the single most successful method used in obtaining jobs, across the entire spectrum of the job market.

You are probably wondering whether you should pay any attention at all to job requirements when reviewing job notices or job descriptions. Of course you should. Try to choose those jobs that best fit your background and experience. However, do not make the mistake of reading "qualifications" statements too literally. There are two main areas of concern here: *education* and *experience*.

Education Do not limit yourself to only those jobs that request your particular academic background. While in some cases the academic degree required will not be flexible (e.g, you have to show an engineering degree for an engineering job), most of these are in the technical fields. In many other cases, the degree requirements are looser than you think. For example, many liberal arts graduates are hired for business jobs and elsewhere, even though they don't have academic majors that fit the jobs. If you are not sure whether the educational requirement is strict or not, check with people who have been hired recently in that kind of job and see what degrees they have.

Experience Do not eliminate yourself if you don't believe you have the experience called for. The experience requirement is a typical screening device used to discourage candidates who are less motivated or who truly know little about the field and don't have the capacity to learn it. While in some cases the experience requirement will be strict and unbending, be sure to inquire first and, once again, talk with people recently hired in that field. In many cases you can stretch some experience you have had to be relevant to the job, or discover skills you have developed that will be useful in this job. "Relevant experience" is open to much interpretation. For example, if you want a job as a museum worker, but have not ever worked in one, your experience as a library assistant (information gathering), or your theater background (set-designing skills), or your history courses can be described as related experience, at least enough to get you in the door.

Thus, in deciding whether or not you are qualified for a particular job, keep these principles in mind:

1. Go ahead and apply. Even if you lack something compared to the requirements on paper, go ahead and apply if you believe you have relevant background, and especially if you are highly motivated. The best that can happen is that they will respond well to your enthusiasm, look closely at your positive features, and give you a chance to sell yourself. The worst that can happen is that you don't match up to other candidates, but you will learn what the job is about and may be referred to other job opportunities.

2. Focus on what you *do* have, not what you don't have. Concentrate on those abilities, experiences, and areas of knowledge that you believe do fit the job, and sell these as well as you can. Don't waste any time talking about what you don't have, because you'll just sound defensive and will fritter away valuable interview time. Even when they ask why you don't have certain "qualifications," answer concisely and truthfully and then use this as an opportunity to clarify your positives.

3. Don't oversell yourself. Do not be arrogant, disrespectful, or overly general in stating your attributes and qualifications. You might be tempted to say: "Just show me any job. Whatever it is, I can do it." That's going too far. Instead, pay attention to what is needed in the job, and explain patiently why you believe your skills and experiences will enable you to perform well. This shows you have respect for the job and the person who wrote its description, at the same time you are displaying confidence that you are a good candidate.

4. Learn how to "package" yourself. Your particular combination of experiences, education, skills, interests, and knowledge can be appropriate for many different kinds of work, because they can be "packaged" and repackaged in different ways. Résumé writing is a form of packaging. So is your verbal presentation in the interview. Learn to complete the statement "I am a good candidate for this job because————," or "I believe that I can learn this job and do it well, because————." For one job, you will emphasize certain features of your background, for a different job you will emphasize other features. That is what packaging is all about.

Your marketability is affected greatly by how much you *believe* you are marketable for that kind of job. I am not suggesting that you apply inappropriately for jobs where your missing qualifications cannot be overcome. But give yourself the benefit of the doubt. If you have some reason for believing that you can do that job well, give yourself a chance to express that belief. Turn the Krumboltz dictum on its ear: "When a [positive] reason is needed, any reason will do."

"I think I'll be a good stockbroker because I don't like money, and I want to help other people who don't want to deal with it either, but are forced to, and we can talk about how to minimize our involvement with investments, and still get good results."

Not the usual reason one might hear from a prospective stockbroker, but this person can sell it if he/she believes it and thinks that approach will appeal to prospective customers. Whatever works for you works for you. Don't be afraid to tell someone about it.

▶ What Is Your "Wrong Set ◀ of Qualifications"?

How are you undervaluing yourself? What beliefs do you have about your marketability that are slowing you down, perhaps keeping you from making contacts or applying directly in fields where you would like to have a chance?

I am not saying that all lack of progress in job hunting is self-induced. Certainly many of the market requirements are realistic and many fields are off limits to you. However, I would estimate that a typical job hunter disqualifies him/herself from 33 percent of the job possibilities that might be available if he/she pursued them. One-third of all job opportunities represents a lot of lost chances. Let's take a look at the main themes of self-disqualification.

"I have the wrong college major"

I majored in sociology, so I can't get a job in business
I studied biology, so I guess I'll be eliminated from job possibilities
  in journalism, which is where I really want to work
I majored in economics, but I really think I'd like personnel work,
  and I suppose that's for psychology majors

College graduates unnecessarily eliminate themselves on the basis of perceived qualifications for certain jobs. Believing that college studies are like vocational training, they often assume they have missed the boat, and therefore cannot enter certain fields of work. On the contrary. For all fields except those which are technical (engineering, architecture, pharmacy, nursing, etc.), college graduates having the "wrong" majors will be considered and welcomed if they have: relevant experiences, some coursework in related fields, strong interest, or relevant skills. Many of the "wrong" graduates are hired and perform well on the job. Liberal arts graduates, though not the only examples, are often the best proof of this, in that their majors seldom denote any fields in the world of work. Yet they obtain good jobs and advance satisfactorily, often to higher levels of responsibility than those "trained" in certain vocational areas. Studies by the University of Texas, the University of Virginia, and Pennsylvania State University have confirmed the career progress of liberal arts graduates.[1]

Many employers recognize that technical information is best learned on the job rather than in prior schooling; hence they are little concerned about a graduate's major field of study. They seek individuals who have general learning skills and high motivation, so they can provide training themselves, within the organization. This attitude has led recently to a trend away from hiring costly M.B.A.'s in businesses, and toward hiring bachelor's graduates who can be trained according to the company's needs and sent later for graduate study, if necessary.

EXAMPLES ► Desired field: journalism; "wrong major": medieval history
Solution: This history major applied her writing and research skills developed in many history courses to the tasks of a journalist, and recognized that her understanding of history would help her to write good news stories and features. She "packaged" herself as a person with skills relevant to newspaper/magazine journalism, and got a job with a foreign affairs newsletter in Washington, D.C., and then used that experience to become a correspondent with the *Baltimore Sun.*

Desired field: social work; "wrong major": music
Solution: This music major had been a counselor at a music camp and had volunteered in social service agencies during college, including Family Planning and the Rape Crisis Center. She applied to the local mental health clinic as a beginning caseworker and was hired on a trial basis. Her talents were evident and she was soon promoted to a job as social worker, and has used this experience to change jobs to social work positions having greater responsibility.

Desired field: corporate finance; "wrong major": radio/TV/film
Solution: This RTF major decided he did not want the communications field after all, even though he completed the degree; he took his two accounting courses and a summer job in a bank to the finance department of a large corporation. He convinced them to give him a junior financial analyst job based on his interest in the company, his high score on a company aptitude test, and his willingness to take finance courses at night from a nearby college. Obviously, he did a "sell job," but it worked. He is now Vice-President for Financial Affairs in the same corporation, having proven himself through on-the-job performance.

"I Have the Wrong Combination of Experiences"

Career development is supposed to look orderly on paper. Résumés are supposed to "make sense," but often they do not. You may have an odd jumble of experiences and education, and furthermore they may differ from the field of work you now want to enter. Despite what you have done or studied in the past, you cannot predict what you will want to do in the future. Thus, the unexpected career change is born, and you are forced to justify this odd progression to future employers.

How do we account for the biology major who works successfully for a computer company (as a service representative) for several years and then goes on to start an eventually profitable music publishing company? How do we explain a stockbroker who quits her job, enrolls in law school, then quits that to become a successful director of a summer camp? Or a retailer who leaves that business behind him to become a happy leader of river-raft tours, and then leaves that field after several years to become a successful fund-raiser for his alma mater?

Careers are expected to be predictable and "logical" but they seldom are. Most people have a set of experiences that make them ideal candidates for almost nothing, but respectable candidates for more jobs than they think.

Perhaps you know what you would like to do next, but are pessimistic that the marketplace will let you do it, based on your unlikely combination of past jobs, education, and other experiences. You may not be the ideal candidate for the job you want (hardly anyone is), but you can make a strong case for yourself if you look closely at what the job needs. Let's take a look at a few case studies.

These examples are especially relevant to (a) Career changers, who want to leave one field for another; (b) Liberal arts graduates, who are not in any fields of work that they can apply for; (c) Anyone who has "done many different things" and is not sure how they all add up.

EXAMPLES ► *Goal: To be a recruiter for a major corporation*
"Unlikely Combination" of Experiences: Arthur has been a librarian for ten years, has a personal interest in sailing, changed jobs to become an auto mechanic for three years, and volunteers his time at the local dog pound.

Strategy: This sounds like a tough one, doesn't it? You would not expect this guy to want to become a college recruiter. But the motivations of the individual cannot be predicted that easily. Arthur takes a job as a production assistant with a large company, then applies for a transfer to the personnel department, where he becomes a pension analyst for two years, but then an opening occurs in the college relations section of personnel and he applies for the job, gets it, and becomes part of the company's college relations team. His past experiences did not help in particular, but he might have used his library experience to show that he knows how to develop a computer system for keeping track of job candidates, offers made, trips completed, etc. He did use his contact with one of his sailing buddies, a vice-president in the corporation, to get the initial job in the production department.

Goal: To start a graphics design business
"Unlikely Combination" of Experiences: Ann was a secretary for a construction firm for six years, has a college degree in biology and home economics, spent three years as an insurance agent, and does community work with the Humane Society.

Strategy: Ann has some raw talent in graphics work, and believes she has a feel for magazine and book layout, for brochure design, for using graphics to dress up publications. But she has the ol' bugaboo, No Experience at All Whatsoever. So she volunteers to "apprentice" with a friend of hers for a year, discovers her instincts were pretty sound (she does have talent for graphics work), and then starts part-time in acquiring clients. How does her past experience help her? Work as an insurance agent helps her in dealing with the public, secretarial work helps her to keep the new business orderly and take care of the correspondence, and community work has given her contacts for potential clientele. Where do biology and the Humane Society come in? Who knows? But it's quite possible that one day Ann will design layouts and promotional materials for books and magazines about the animal world. And where, pray tell, could they find somebody better?

Goal: To manage a state or local program providing job training for the unemployed

"Unlikely Combination" of Experiences: Bill has a college degree in philosophy and history, six years' experience as a trust officer at a bank, is a carpenter in his spare time, and worked two years with two partners, trying to develop a new kind of hardware store (it didn't work out; the idea flopped and the partners fought).

Strategy: Bill had heard the community was trying to attract funding for helping the unemployed and school dropouts; he wanted to become involved, but had no idea who did such things or how they did it. He checked with his banking friends, one of whom is a member of the city council, and learned that a new group was forming, called the Private Industry Council. He applied to be a community representative on the P.I.C. Board, served for a year, and learned that an opening existed on the P.I.C. staff. He applied for the job and got it. How did he sell himself? Bill knew a lot about low-income housing (carpentry experience) and the unemployed people who need it; he had been a good administrator at the bank and figured those skills would transfer to coordinating employment training programs; and he said that he could figure out how to tap into federal and state moneys available for this purpose. He used his analytical skills and research skills (remember the philosophy and history majors?) to figure out the latter. He did not have nearly the ideal résumé for a P.I.C. staff member, but he reasoned that he could do the job as well as the next person, and gave it a shot.

Goal: To become a financial counselor on a private basis

"Unlikely Combination" of Experiences: Judy has an Associate of Arts degree in Textiles and Clothing. After that program, she enrolled in a paralegal school, and she works presently for a large law firm. She does gardening in her spare time and is a board member of the Y.W.C.A. Judy has been taking accounting courses at night, but finds she is bored by that field and would prefer to help people manage their money. She has no experience in the field, but reads a lot about financial decision making.

Strategy: How does a person become a financial counselor these days? Some work for banks, others are glorified stockbrokers, still others hang out a shingle and hope someone will respond. Some are certified (C.F.A.- Chartered Financial Analyst), but most are not. How can Judy get on this train with little relevant background? The same way that most people market a product or service successfully to the public—they offer it, and people vote with their dollars. Judy intensifies her reading, attends seminars, has long conversations with friends who are in related fields, reads some more, takes courses, does some mythical investment planning of her own, tries her skills with family and friends, and then finally goes public. Gathering clientele is slow at first, but some people are pleased with her ability to organize their whole financial picture and offer patient, low-key opinions about how to reallocate their money. Word of mouth begins to work for her. She quits the law firm when there is enough steady business to believe her long-term prospects are good. Her income is less steady and often lower than what it was in paralegal work, but she likes it better and sees greater earnings ahead, as the concept of "financial counselor" becomes more familiar to people and gains greater public acceptance.

Goal: To work as a lobbyist for a state education agency
"Unlikely Combination" of Experiences: Rich has a college degree in physics, worked for several years as a service representative for a firm that sells equipment to eye doctors, and then moved to Washington, D.C., to work for the National Science Foundation. He left that job to start his own company raising bees for honey production, and now is unemployed. He knows a lot of teachers who have gripes about their jobs, but what makes him think he can become one of their representatives in the state capital?
Strategy: Rich is a resourceful guy. He has had his fill of science, and figures the way to be a good lobbyist is to be good at talking to people. He takes an interim job as an equipment repairman (physics background helps), but devotes his primary energy to volunteering his time with the local teachers' union. He learns what their needs are, develops friendships with union leaders, and gets introduced to the lobbying staff. One thing leads to another, his view is confirmed that successful lobbying is getting your ideas across to people (in this case, legislators), and he applies for a job on the staff. Can a physics major find happiness on Capitol Hill? The rest is history.

What do we make of all these examples of people whose careers take new twists and turns, and yet they come up breathing and find new ways to succeed? Life's a mess and make the best of it? Are these oddball examples that really do not fit the great majority of people? Do we really want people to bounce around like this, instead of getting into a field and staying there?

These examples are real people, and any one of them could be you. Take note of the ways they have dealt with their situations, because career development is the challenge of reacting to your present circumstances and making the most of what you've got, not settling for less. If you're bored, move on. If you're unemployed, stitch together your assets and find someone who wants you. If you're looking for a new challenge, repackage yourself for a different market. The examples above reflect these key principles:

1. Your life and career are essentially unpredictable You have to take what develops in your needs and the shifts of the labor market, and find something different to do, whenever circumstances change, and they will. The work that excites you today may be old-hat tomorrow. The industry you are part of may lose its grip on the public. Your spouse may get an offer he/she can't refuse in another city and you can't find your present job there. Or, your money needs may change, upward or downward, and that will dictate a different kind of work. Expect the unexpected, and don't fret if the work you're seeking next does not seem "logical" based on what you have done before. If careers were that predictable, we could all get our heads stamped when we take our first jobs. But, they are not. The economy changes, family situations change, jobs and careers change, and perhaps most of all, so do you.

2. Anything can be combined with anything Any job experiences, educational credentials, and personal interests can be combined and made useful toward a particular career goal. Now that is a tall order, or quite a strong claim. Yet, whether you have farming and calligraphy, or playing the drums and real estate, carpet cleaning and auctioneering, or auto mechanics and bird watching, *any* combination of experiences in your life can be hung together to contribute toward the work that you want to do next.

The magic of combining is that, in some way, all things can relate to each other if you look closely enough. This is because generic skills underlie most jobs, and these skills can be applied in new contexts. For example, the drummer knows about pleasing people, working odd hours, and networking with others. He/she can apply these experiences to work as a real estate salesperson. Wherever you go, you take the tools in your kit with you. You may not be the perfect candidate for the job you want, but you'll stretch every last bit of knowledge and experience to fit the new job description. And, if they give you a chance, you're a pretty good bet to show that you can learn the job and do it well.

3. Your imagination and general ability to learn are often more powerful than labor market qualifications Now certainly there are plenty of jobs you cannot apply for, and others for which you would need formal training to enter. However, there are many other jobs where formal qualifications are less important than the desire to succeed. If you imagine that you could do the work (everyone who has never done a job before has begun by *imagining* it) and draw on your general learning skills to help you, then there are many jobs and careers available to you. I could fill this book with examples like those above, but I would prefer that you talk to friends, neighbors, and others to hear their real-life stories of how they learned *on the job*, en route to advancement and satisfaction.

4. The job market is not as rational as it claims to be   Employers are supposed to hire people with the best qualifications, but they do not always do so. For many reasons, they hire individuals with unorthodox backgrounds, people whom they like, people who happen to show up the week they really need to hire someone, people who have more promise than past performance, and people who are recommended by friends. It's almost impossible for an employer to figure out which job candidates are the best, based on paper credentials. Thus, if your qualifications for the job sound reasonable, and you're standing there in front of them, and you're pretty likeable too, they say to themselves: "Why should we look any farther?"

► Self-Disqualification Can ◄ Ruin Your Complexion

If you disqualify yourself from job possibilities, it can be dangerous to your job-hunting health. The dropout syndrome affects your job hunter's immune system. If you eliminate yourself arbitrarily, you will have less ability to fight the infection of rejection, not to mention the trauma of post-interview depression. A healthy job hunter is one who keeps exercising the exploratory muscles, and exposes his/her body to the rigors of job market workouts. Self-disqualification is like checking into the sick bay at summer camp on the chance that you might come down with a cold. Don't do it. Keep yourself in the hunt. There is a place for your combination of experiences and ambitions.

The Job Hunt Is a Crapshoot

Sometimes employers hire the most qualified individuals, but other times they take whoever is available, because they don't have the time and resources to look further. More importantly, they have imperfect judgment about who is best for a given job. Thus, sometimes you will be hired when you are not the best candidate (but you got there first), and on other occasions you *are* the best applicant but someone else got hired for some irrelevant reason. And other times you're a strong candidate and you happen to show up at the right time, and you make a good case for yourself, and it all hangs together. But, don't count on the pieces always falling into place, even when you work hard and apply to employers who should want you. Chance rears its head, and sometimes smiles on you, and other times it is ugly.

Roll the dice and keep rolling, because in this game the losses do not count against you. Sure, the jobs-not-gotten cost time, energy, and sometimes money, but the standings of your wins and losses do not appear on the sports pages. An employer does not care if you have applied for thirty-eight other jobs and lost them, if you are the one he/she wants. Good things happen to people who keep their beliefs going in the face of uncertainty. As Tom Jackson says, job hunting is a bunch of NO's waiting for a YES.

If you disqualify yourself, you're out. If you succumb to the myth that every job has a right candidate and you're not it, then you're doubly out. But, the game still goes on and all kinds of "wrong" applicants are getting jobs out there. You know some of those less-than-perfectly-qualified people yourself, don't you? They must have had "pull," you think. In some cases perhaps they did, but in most situations they just went ahead and applied and the crapshoot worked in their favor.

Don't wait around for the right job for you. Go ahead and apply for a few of the wrong jobs where your background doesn't quite fit, but what the heck—they deserve a chance to find out who you are and what you can do. With a little extra effort, you can be as "qualified" as the next person.

25

The No-Search
Job Search

How would you like never to have to look for a job again? That is probably the nicest gift this book could give you.

No matter what the books say—be optimistic, be persistent, organize yourself, do this, don't do that—the whole job search is an injury in search of a victim, a knee-deep pile of rejection, an endless set of chores, a sure way to raise your blood pressure and lower your self-esteem. You've heard "finding a job is the toughest job you'll ever have" until you want to croak. That message does not encourage you to get started. It makes you want to hide and pray for redemption.

Ever run into people who have jobs offered to them? People who seldom have to send out résumés, pound the pavement, or wonder about where their next job offer is coming from? Don't you wonder how they do it? Are they just lucky, do they have great connections, are they extraordinarily talented, or simply in the right place at the right time? Wouldn't you like to be one of them? They are engaged in the No-Search Job Search. These people have learned how to function so that job opportunities occur in the natural course of their lives. There are more such people than you think. This approach is also within your grasp. Many of the principles in this book, when followed faithfully and done well, lead logically to the No-Search Job Search. In this chapter, I will describe more deliberately how you can set yourself up for future job offers and understand what it means to say: The best job search is no search at all.

► Why Not Look for a Job? ◄

First let's examine what can be wrong with the ordinary job search. While no one can eliminate entirely the need to initiate a formal job search, there are three key reasons why it is better to avoid it whenever you can.

1. Perhaps the worst place to be evaluated for a job is in a job interview You have had very little prior contact with the interviewer. The interview is guesswork, and you both know it.

It is difficult to go for interviews where you have to perform your act in thirty minutes. You're downright lucky if the interviewer happens to divine most of what your capabilities are. We teach people interview skills, but it is always a struggle to portray your key experiences, motivations, and talents when the interviewer has no other information about you.

2. The process of the job search can be debilitating No matter how much we dress it up and equip you with tools and tips for success, a formal job search, where you are the supplicant and the jobs seem to continually elude you, is a grinding experience. The formalities of job hunting deserve some attention, but I maintain that, as Finch says regarding the Company Mailroom in *How to Succeed in Business Without Really Trying,* "It is a place OUT OF WHICH YOU MUST GET." I have suggested ways in this book to recapture some of the enjoyment of job hunting, but I believe the most pleasurable job search is one you conduct without résumés, without formalized interviews, and without the wearisome planning and record keeping that most job-hunting books urge upon the reader.

3. Given the choice, most employers would rather recruit you informally than through a formal search process The more employers know about you prior to an interview, the happier they are. They know that formal interviews are a guessing game too, and it's harder for them, because they have even more at stake. The worst that can happen to you is a bad interview, but if they make a bad hire, they can embarrass the company and possibly lose their livelihood.

► The No-Search Job Search ◄

You are doing your best job hunting when you are engaged in something else besides job hunting. And, job opportunities pass in front of you every day, even though you may not think about them. Consider these two ideas:

1. Everything you ever do is noticed by somebody Every nail you hammer, memo you write, or job you complete affects someone, and a great number of people see you at work as you are lining things up, working toward your goals, and putting the final products out for inspection. Even though nobody asks them, all of these people form judgments about you and how you do your work. Since it is a small world that we live in, any one of these individuals might one day have the chance to comment about your capabilities, and your potential for doing the next job you might be seeking. In other words, everyone you run across is in a position to help you with your future aspirations.

2. Your next job may be right in front of your eyes   Often the job you will seek next is one you are only dimly aware of when you first see it. You don't know you want to be manager of that department across the hall when you first walk in there. Your awareness develops over time. You don't know you have a flair for association work the first time you call them up to get some information. It may only hit you later after repeated contacts. Often we are drawn naturally and unconsciously to the areas that interest us, and we may fail to recognize their potential.

The No-Search Job Search does not happen automatically. Many people will miss their chances, either by not recognizing them, or because they act too passively. Learn to make use of these three principles of the No-Search Job Search:

▸ **Principle 1: Positioning**

It is one thing to do a good job. It is quite another to do the job well and have key others know that you have done it. Adele Scheele[1] calls this skill "Positioning," and it is crucial to the no-search job search. Positioning means finding a way that you can be useful in that "place where I want to be," and then getting them to let you do it. People who aspire to political positions and volunteer to work on election campaigns are veterans at positioning. If I work at a local college but covet a position at the largest flower shop in town, and I give the flower store information about how to appeal to students needing flowers for formals and other special events, then I am positioning myself for future possibilities.

▸ **Principle 2: Timing**

The earlier, the better. Positioning and other aspects of the no-search job search work better if you practice them long before you ever think of changing your work. Doing these things three months before you want to make a change is less effective. It is too little and too late. People with whom you have contact will not offer you jobs at first sight. Their knowledge of you and confidence in you will grow over a period of time.

▶ **Principle 3: Genuineness**

Positioning doesn't mean much when you are trying to get someone's attention in a deliberate, manipulative way. If you want a job with me one day, be interested in what I am doing without regard for what I might do for you. Don't just try to "win points" with me, because I will figure that out before long.

▶ An Example of the ◀
No-Search Job Search

Let's suppose you work way uptown for a small bookstore, but you really want to have a management position with the Metropolitan Transit Authority, the city agency that deals with bus systems. One job has nothing to do with the other. How can you possibly position yourself to be offered a job with that agency? Thinking as far ahead as possible, you might do any of the following:

- attend the public board meetings of the MTA, where you can learn more about what they are doing, where their activities draw the public's attention
- request informal meetings with anyone in the agency who will talk with you
- volunteer to do some informal research in your neighborhood regarding use of the bus system, complaints, patterns of commuting
- compile a listing of current books (remember, you work in a bookstore) that illuminate the problems of cities and their public transportation systems; then abstract these publications and request a meeting with one of the MTA managers to present the information.

   Surely you could think of even more things to do. No one of these by itself will necessarily yield a job offer, but each brings you in contact with key officials of the MTA, and each gives them an opportunity to know more about you.

   If anyone asks you, in the above example, why you are doing these things for the MTA, you can answer: "I am very interested in public transportation and think I would like to get into this kind of work one day." You are admitting your career inclination without making formal application for a job. If any members of the MTA want to encourage you along these lines, they are free to do it.

► Will You Never Have to ◄ Look for a Job Again?

The no-search job search may only be an occasional reality for many people, but it always pays to strive for it. You *can* increase the number of job offers made to you, even though you still have to initiate job searches when necessary. Time pressure and economic necessity may force you onto the streets, but that does not undermine this basic principle of the no-search job search: people who know and respect your work, your work habits, and your motivations best will create opportunities to work with you, because it is to their advantage to seek known quantities rather than take their chances with people from the vast, anonymous labor pool.

While résumés, job interviews, application forms, and job-notice boards will never disappear, you can become less dependent upon them. The no-search job search emphasizes that job seeking can and should be a natural and informal process of people getting to know each other, not a parade of hoops an applicant must jump through to attract an employer's attention.

I believe that three themes make the no-search job search possible and practical for anyone who wants to use it:

► Theme 1: The Jobs That Are Appealing to You and a Good Fit for Your Talents Are Definitely Out There Somewhere

This is one article of faith I will ask you to accept in this book. If you can assume that a job is out there which appeals to you, and you have a decent chance of being hired for it if you make yourself available, then you have reason to stay involved.

Detective work is easier than you think. The "small world problem" (see page 121) explains how you can find *anyone* in the working world, any job no matter how remote, faster than you thought possible.

An important corollary of the above theme is this: *A potential job opening can be anywhere, often in a job that is currently occupied by someone else.* You should look at any job, no matter who is in it, regardless of whether or not the job is "open." Because a certain amount of *turnover* (people leaving their jobs, sometimes unexpectedly) occurs continually in all sectors of the working world, what appears to be a filled job may become vacant before too long. It has been noted[2] that 30 percent of the American work force has been in their present jobs one year or less. Thus, if you can find it, you might get it. If you don't get it, you'll probably be put on the trail of something similar. If you still don't get it, you have learned more about your job market than if you sat home and hoped for the best. It saves you the wear and tear of sending letters and résumés and waiting by your mailbox in frustration. Detective work keeps you active rather than passive, and puts you closer and closer to your goals. Your job(s) are waiting out there for you, but someone else will find them if you don't.

▶ **Theme 2: Many of the Most Effective Job-Hunting Skills Are Not Thought of as Such**

It will interest you to know that you are doing some mighty effective job hunting even when you have no idea you are doing it. How is this possible? Because the job search is not like specific mechanical skills, or computer skills, or gardening skills, for which specific, structured manuals can be written. The job search involves people, and the decisions people make about hiring are not scientific, structured, or done with laboratory equipment. People are on display every day, at various times, not just in job interviews. Thus, there is much daily-life activity that introduces the job seeker and the jobs to each other, long before an employer evaluates a job candidate. As a result, these skills can be viewed as job-search-related:

1. Partying Social skills contribute greatly to successful job hunting, and where is socializing more obvious than at party time? Fraternity boys and sorority girls have known this instinctively for a long time, and in fact make many of their job contacts through such socializing. These opportunities are available to you as well.

I am not trying to make your playtime into pressure occasions, where you have to worry about how many people you are meeting, or whom you are impressing favorably. I don't want you to feel like an actor who must always be "on." If you get used to parties as natural points of contact, the benefits to your job search will accumulate without unnecessary pressure or forcing.

2. Reading As in reading books and journals that relate to the fields of work that interest you. If you want a job in advertising, you should be reading *Printer's Ink*, *Advertising Age*, and a couple of the best books on the topic. Jobs will not jump at you from these publications, but they will give you valuable background on the field. Reading is an indispensable skill in job hunting, because you can learn so much about a field through easy access to a library. Without such information, you are a sitting duck in any job interview. Reading also can give you names of people you may want to contact—authors of journal articles, newsletter editors, etc.

3. Cleaning Up Your Room/Your House Getting the drawers unstuffed, sweeping up, finding things you thought were lost forever, going through the books, magazines, and papers lying around. Why is this helpful? It's time to get a little organized, to see what names, addresses, materials, files, books, or other things you might have that will help your job search. Looking through your belongings also helps stir your memory about what your interests are. Cleaning up your home helps to clean out your mind, and gives you a fresh start for deciding what your job direction will be. It's good therapy, and doesn't cost anything. Try it. You'll find it's a form of unconscious job exploration.

4. Painting a Few Rooms Or getting involved in some other project around the house that takes a few hours and takes your mind off your job-search troubles, giving you a chance to mull over job or career ideas without having to do anything about them. Creative thinkers call this "incubation time," time when ideas can be shaped slowly before they appear in a sensible form. Let your mind relax. Paint the kitchen . . . fix the bicycle . . . even clean the oven (ugh), and you'll come up with a few thoughts you did not expect.

5. Watching Television Often construed as a waste of time, TV watching can be another form of incubation time for you. If you spread yourself around, you will see almost every kind of work portrayed in some fashion, though sometimes a bit stereotyped. Local news programs may also tell you about plant openings, new kinds of jobs available, and emerging trends in the local economy. For better or for worse, television is an eye to the world. The problems it highlights (crime, politics, social services, schools, etc.) may trigger your interest toward areas where you feel you can make a contribution.

6. Walking Around the Neighborhood Or any neighborhood where you might see things that spark your curiosity, and talk with people about their work or their opinions on anything at all. You need access to a wide variety of people whose work differs from your own. You're probably in your own rut—you see the same people every day, and hear the same opinions. Check out your neighborhood or someone else's and be sure you meet people whose work is different from yours. Think of this as outdoor partying, without a formal invitation.

7. Writing Letters Especially when you are at a distance from the work that you would like, this can be a useful skill. Sending résumés is not an especially successful method, but writing personal letters can have a greater payoff. For example, get acquainted with the author of an article that you read about gardening. Or, send for the literature of a new company that you heard about. Get the name of a department head before you write, so that he/she may give you a personal reply. Or, write to a friend who works in another town or city to find out what his company is like. Or, write to a professional association to get advice about how to enter that profession. Or, write a personal letter to someone whose work you admire, and ask her for a lead or advice.

I am not talking here about the stiff, formal "letter requesting a job interview" that appears in so many job-search books. I am suggesting a more informal letter saying something like: "I have heard/read about your work/your organization and would like to know more about———. Could you tell me? Can you suggest other materials I might read? Many thanks . . ."

8. Playing Sports Like anything from volleyball to racquetball to body building to aerobics to sailing. Or any other recreational pursuit that you might prefer, ranging from bird watching to needlepoint to skydiving. Recreational activities are great places to meet people, and chances are they represent a wide variety of kinds of work. You are not joining the group deliberately to make "contacts," but they will happen naturally if you do. Even if you prefer not to talk or even think about work when you are doing your favorite sports or other pastime, you will unconsciously gather valuable information from listening to group members talk.

► **Theme 3: There Are ways to Attract Job Offers Without Résumés, Job Interviews, Reference Letters, or Application Forms**

This is the heart of the No-Search Job Search. It's the art of considering what kind of work you think you want next and then using your present circumstances—present job, community activities, professional activities, personal and recreational interests—to set yourself up for future job opportunities, without embarking on a formal job search. Advancing your career is often much more effective when you are not submitting yourself for formal evaluation (as in job interviews). Instead, you are simply going about your business, doing what you do. All the while, you are using some of the detective skills in this section, but *you are not job-hunting*. If you use these informal methods well, the formal job search will become just that, a mere formality, because your informal activities can produce the same results.

Perhaps you are imagining that these informal methods are ones that high-powered, well-placed people use, but how could they possibly be relevant for little ol' you? Yes, informal job hunting *is* common among people who have advanced in their organizations, but you do not have to be a high-level honcho to use them. These approaches apply to anyone in any job field at any level.

You have probably not used these informal methods before, because you mistakenly believe that in order to look for a job, you have to look for a job. "Looking for a job" refers to all the formalities of the job search (résumé, etc.), but in fact many jobs are learned about, people are evaluated, and job offers even made long before a formal search process is begun and completed.

Each of the following is a powerful means of advancing your job and career opportunities. Note that each of these is potentially more beneficial than formal job-seeking behaviors, because it allows a job seeker and a possible employer much more intensive contact with each other than would ordinarily take place in a formal search process or brief job interview. Integrate as many of these as possible into your habitual activities. The more you use these methods, the less you will have to depend upon job search formalities.

► 1. Be Active ◄
in Your Profession

Whether choosing steers at the marketplace, shoes for hiking, or employees for hiring, a person will always prefer a known quantity over an unknown.

Professional involvement is the easiest way to become known to a large number of your colleagues, some of whom you may want to work for one day. This does not mean that you must run for elective office, chair committees, or do other heavy work involved in leading an organization. Attend programs, go to conferences, choose a committee or two if you are interested, present papers, get to know people in your local area who do the same work you do. Keep up with new information, through journals, programs, and meetings. Much of the best information in a profession passes by word of mouth. Friendships made at meetings become trusted contacts later. Treat your profession like a fraternity/sorority, in the best sense of that analogy. Get to know your brothers and sisters, break bread with them, and you will find that you hear about job possibilities long before they are advertised. It is no accident that so much job hunting occurs at conventions and conferences. Face-to-face meetings make it easier to evaluate people. Résumés and the usual formalities become less important.

▶ 2. Become Active in ◀ Someone Else's Profession

Other people's work can be terribly remote and foggy until you meet the people who do it in person. It can be enjoyable to acquaint yourself with a new profession by attending one of their meetings and being there to talk with their practitioners for a few days. Read their journals before you go there. Be familiar with the current issues and theories in the profession. Ask questions about them, and you'll feel connected to this group soon enough.

If possible, find some reason to be there that relates to your present work. You're an accountant and you are curious about the National Association of Social Workers? Let's say you want to become acquainted with accounting procedures in nonprofit agencies. Any excuse will do. Or if you're thinking of changing professions, just go ahead and admit that. You're not job-hunting. You're just learning about a new profession. But, if someone happens to mention a job possibility—or a good graduate program, or an internship opportunity—you're there to hear it.

▶ 3. Volunteer Your Services ◀

You cannot try every job in the world, but the next best thing to being there as a paid employee is being a nonpaid worker in your spare time. Sure, you don't have much free time, but if you want to sample a new kind of work, there's no substitute for doing it. The word "volunteer" has come to have overtones of hospital aides, and various people referred to as "do-gooders," but don't let that image derail you. Many fields of work have opportunities for offering free help. If you work there, you get a taste of the challenges involved, make contacts with key people, and probably hear about openings when they occur.

Volunteer positions are easier to get than paid part-time jobs, and the employer is usually grateful for your services. A volunteer worker can often have all the responsibility that a paid employee would have, because the job is there to be done, regardless of the pay involved. Some fields of work and certain organizations are more receptive to volunteers, but don't make any assumptions about who might want you. Inquire in person and, if that one doesn't work out, try another.

EXAMPLE ▶ Marc wanted a job as a writer with *Philadelphia Magazine* in the worst way. He couldn't land anything paid, so he volunteered to do office work for them. After three months, the magazine gave him a trial writing assignment; he did a good job and the piece was published. He contributed six more articles (all unpaid) in the course of the year. Finally, a staff writer job came open and you can guess who was first in line for the position, and had the credibility and experience to be hired, so that a more elaborate search was not necessary.

▶ 4. Do a Project with ◀
Someone in the Profession

What better way is there to know someone's capabilities than to work with that person closely on a project for several weeks or more and count on his/her contribution to get the project done?

The old concept of an apprenticeship was a sound one, and it looks positively brilliant today next to the chancy and impersonal methods of personnel selection. Though we do not call for apprentices anymore, it is still possible to develop such an arrangement for yourself in almost any field of work. Sometimes we call these internships, or collaborations between professionals, or research projects. It doesn't matter what you call it, just find a way to assist a person with some of his/her work, and that person will learn more about you and your capabilities than could be learned in a hundred job interviews.

In scholarly fields, doing a paper with a colleague can be a good route upward. Or, if you help a person build a house, he/she will probably remember you too. Wanna work for the local newspaper? Help a reporter write a three-part series about your neighborhood or the company you work for. Wanna work for the local historical society? Assist them in organizing and mounting a fund-raising campaign, and I assure you that you won't be forgotten.

In many cases, this can be job hunting at its finest. Yet nary a résumé changes hands, and it would insult the other person to think that you are being interviewed. Just the same, if a job opens in his/her setting, you will be in a great position to hear about it and should be a prime candidate.

▶ 5. Find a Link Between ◀
Your Present and Future Jobs

Your present job can be a bridge to different fields of employment, long before you may decide to make a change. Let's say you're working as an insurance underwriter, but you really want to be in the recreation and leisure fields. Check out the insurance needs of some parks and recreation departments or leisure organizations. Make yourself useful to your present employer while looking into possible new ones. Let's say that you are a technical writer for IBM, but you have your heart set on managing a plant nursery. Review some gardening manuals to see if their style and approach might help you in designing the manuals that are used to train computer workers.

Suppose you are a bank loan officer, but you would prefer to be in the music business. Investigate and review loan applications for music publishers, learn something about their financial situations, and gather some information that will help you to decide when and how to pursue a change of jobs. With a little stretching of your imagination, your present work can be made relevant to almost any other occupation that you might want to enter. You can help your present employer in the process by either looking for new business there, or exploring connections between your job and theirs, or by getting data that will be useful to your company.

▶ 6. Information Interviewing ◀

You might get the impression from some get-a-job books that a rash of information interviews is the main avenue toward discovering job opportunities, and that this should be the centerpiece of any job-search strategy. Not necessarily so. It *is* accessible, but information interviews are brief and sometimes lead to frustration when relied upon too heavily. Thus, I recommend that you use information interviews only in combination with the other, more intensive methods described here. To get the best informal exposure to people whose work interests you, you need more than a forty-five-minute conversation.

▶ 7. Do Your Present Job Well ◀

Often the best advertisement for yourself is a job well done. That may sound old-fashioned and trite, or like a page out of the Scout Handbook, but it is still true. When you perform your job, others see you do it. They form an impression of you, and many of these individuals are connected to other job possibilities that you might want. *Everyone* you meet and work with is a possible link to the next position that you may want to be considered for.

The methods I am describing here may help you to eliminate the use of résumés and other job-search materials, and may help you to minimize the number of formal job interviews you must endure, but they will probably not allow you to sidestep the reference check. Regardless of how much you may dislike your present work (and sometimes you even feel you're being treated unfairly), this job can help you make progress toward a future career if you impress the people around you. Good words from them will always work in your favor ("He's a class guy. He didn't like it here, but he always got his job done").

▶ 8. Write and Speak ◀ About Your Work

Do you know which people are most likely to be remembered in any profession? Those who speak publicly on a variety of occasions and those who write books and articles for professional journals or popular publications. If you want visibility for your views among other professionals or members of the general population, go public with your ideas. From such visibility job opportunities will develop.

They won't be interested in you if they've never heard of you. Other than having worked with you, the only way a prospective employer might have an impression of you is through your speaking or writing.

EXAMPLE ▶ Clarissa worked as a staff member for a member of the City Council, but always wanted to move to the Mexican-American Chamber of Commerce. However, she could not figure out how to meet a member of that board and make a good impression. She decided to write a newsletter for her council member and send it to various civic groups, including the Mexican-American organization, and also spoke to civic groups whenever possible. She used her role as newsletter editor as an excuse for requesting an interview with the board President; her name recognition got her in the door and gave her the chance to request an interview. Two months later she was offered a job and a chance to use her writing and speaking skills.

Look for opportunities to become a spokesperson for your employer, in your professional organization, and in your community work. Be interviewed in the newspaper. Write for journals, newsletters, or other publications. People who represent themselves or their organizations in print or in public speaking are presumed to know a lot about their field. Often you will be accorded the role of "expert" on a given topic simply because you have been quoted, invited to speak, or receive a byline for your writing.

Now I know that many of you are deathly afraid of writing or speaking or both. You may view these as the two quickest ways in the world to make an instant fool of yourself. Perhaps you have avoided these activities for years and see no reason to get friendly with them now. All right, it's not easy, but people who know far less than you have taken the plunge and are getting some of the credit and visibility that you deserve.

Put your little toe in the water. Try writing anything, for an audience you are comfortable with, such as your family newsletter, or your church bulletin, or a lengthy memo to your coworkers. For public speaking, try joining a Toastmasters' group to practice your skills in supportive surroundings. Or speak up when your tennis club has meetings; talk to coworkers about a topic you know well; anything to get yourself started.

Volunteer your services. Don't wait for someone else to ask you. It is not cocky or presumptuous to do so. All publications are looking for new material to publish, and many groups need speakers to stir the interests of their members. In terms of potential career advancement, one well-placed article or speaking engagement is worth ten reference letters. Be the one they're talking about when someone says: "Oh, yeah, I've heard of him," or "I read something she wrote, just the other day."

▶ 9. Do Community Work ◀

There is no general category of activity that offers a greater range of contacts and experiences than community work. This category includes anything you do outside of your employment that contributes to the betterment of the town or city where you live. Service organizations (Rotary, Kiwanis, Jaycees), hospitals, boards of directors of businesses and other organizations, United Way, Salvation Army, youth groups, recreation departments, private industry councils, humane societies, child guidance clinics, and many others all need help.

We all know that community work is for the good of your fellow man or woman, and certainly that is the main reason you do it, but there is nothing unkosher about getting some benefit from it yourself. How does doing community work help you? (1) It exposes you to an excellent cross section of people in a wide variety of professions and fields of work, people who can introduce you to new career possibilities. (2) Community involvement provides you numerous forums for becoming known to others. Without having to ask them for job interviews, you have many chances to show what your skills are, sell your personality, and show that you are responsible and hard working. (3) It gives you many reasons to get closely involved with people without being overtly engaged in the process of job hunting. (I would much rather consider you for a job if I had shared committee tasks or other projects with you, than if you are simply a name on a piece of paper.)

► Is All This ◄
"Sneaky Job Hunting"?

All of the nine methods above are highly useful in opening up job possibilities for you, and they all can be done at any time, not just when you are looking for a job. Furthermore, they are more effective when you are happy in your present job but exploring possibilities for the future. Thus, they constitute the No-Search Job Search.

However, these methods may have a distinctly unpleasant flavor to you. They may strike you as being sneaky, aiming at career progress even though you are not saying so. You may prefer to be more open about your intentions. Do not discount these approaches as deceptive, because they are not. You are doing all of these things because you want to do them for their own sake—attending professional meetings, writing articles, contributing to projects, etc.—to broaden your thinking, to expand your range of experience and information. Sure, they are good public relations for you, but your involvement grows out of your genuine interest in your profession, the work of others, and the problems of the community. If you weren't drawn to these activities, you could not sustain your interest simply for career points. Get involved in these things, because a lot of others are already doing them. Don't hide your light under a bushel. If you would rather be up-front about it, then tell everyone: "I'm doing this to set myself up for a future job." This may release someone else to say: "Well, bully for you, so am I."

The No-Search Job Search Is
Compatible with the Rest
of This Book

The normal job-search process and the no-search job search approach are integrated with each other. Self-assessment skills, detective skills and communication skills (Parts 1, 2, and 3 of this book) are all used in the NSJS approach, and all are used in the deliberate job search as well. The more you can put these informal methods into practice, the less you will have to devote time to the formalized job search. Detective skills in general carry the flavor of the NSJS, since they emphasize that 80 percent of your job-search progress can be made before you engage in the formalities of applying for jobs.

I recommend that you incorporate the no-search job search as a continuous part of your routine, because these involvements will generate more and better job opportunities for you than a metric ton of résumé writing, job interviews, and application forms. When you hear a person say: "I did not actively seek this job. They found me," odds are that person has been using several no-search job search methods as a regular practice.

▶ Doing It Your Own Way ◀

This book is full of structure, advice, and rules, like most other job-search books. You know you're not going to do half of what I say. Oh, you'll agree with enough of it to get inspired for about two hours, and then you'll settle back into your usual routine, saying "How am I gonna DO all this? . . . It's harder than I thought . . . I never liked school anyway."

Well, let's just say all rules are off. I don't want to set you up for frustration and disappointment in yourself. Don't worry about the way it is *supposed* to be done. Don't follow any programmed approach (do this, then do that). The only way you will do a job search successfully is your own way. Use your own unique, maybe even funky, methods, because you have learned some good ways to get things done in life and you should not abandon them now.

No two people do job hunting the same. You will choose the parts of this book that you like and incorporate your own strategies, whether they are efficient or not. You'll do some things the right way, and others you will finesse or sidestep, because that's the way you are. I'm not going to try to change you and you shouldn't either.

Here are just a few of the individual ways that certain people go about their job search. Some of these may even apply to you. More likely you will add your own special approaches to the list.

Each of these strategies is a distortion of my advice in this book and a lopsided view of any textbook job-search model, but it *works* for the particular individual who uses it, and it works a lot better for them than "doing everything right." Therefore, I encourage you to find the lopsided or skewed strategy that works for you. Be creative, and above all, ignore the parts of this book or any other job-hunting book that look too tedious or awful to do.

EXAMPLES ▶ **No phone calls** I hate the telephone. It's too impersonal, and it makes me nervous. I would rather deal with people face to face, which is more natural. So, I just walk in and talk to people or I meet them someplace, and one thing leads to another and . . .

All phone calls The telephone is my ally. I keep on the phone for days and weeks until I get ten solid leads or interviews. No pavement pounding for me; this is more efficient.

I only go to parties I don't do anything else to look for a job. I have a good time. I know where the people hang out. I check things out, lay back, listen, talk some more, until someone gives me a job lead. I'm patient, and it happens. It sure beats making phone calls, answering ads, and all that other stuff that's just a pain.

I offer to work for free   I figure out who I'd like to hire me, and I give them some free help. Not everyone takes me up on it, but eventually I strike a deal. Then I can prove myself through day-to-day work, instead of going through the artificial messiness of applying for jobs.

I go to the mountaintop   I go directly to the head of the organization where I want to work. I want the person in charge to know who I am, and I need to find out what his/her priorities are. If the leader likes me and what I have to offer, then I don't have to fool around with anyone else.

I send letters or make phone calls to my most trusted contacts   These are the only people I ever tell that I'm looking to make a change—the people who know me best. This is all that I do. If I threw myself onto the open market, it would be a waste of time. I tell my friends and contacts what I am looking for, they give me a few leads, and I eventually plug into new possibilities.

I never talk about jobs   I seek out projects with people whose work I like. Sometimes these projects are related to my present job, other times they are side interests. Usually I do this while I still have a job that I plan to leave. Lo and behold, people offer me new jobs. It doesn't work right away, but this is more fun than the résumé-rejection scene.

I research a field of work to death   I find out everything there is to know about a new field, through library research and in-person detective work. I read annual reports, study industry trends, know key statistics, and recent happenings in the companies where I want to work. I get all this in my head before I ever show up for a job interview.

I contract my services on a part-time basis   I want them to know about me before I go for the full-time appointment. So I offer them a sample of my work through part-time contracting. If they buy it, they usually like it and I'm in a good bargaining position for a more permanent connection.

Each of the other methods makes sense for the person who uses it. Most of these methods are not so oddball after all. Each takes advantage of a job seeker's strength.

Notice that many of these methods seek to reduce the amount of time spent in the formalities of job searching. These are wise people, because they know the 1-2-3 methods are wearisome and frustrating. The less time spent in sending résumés, completing applications, or suffering through screening interviews, the better.

You probably know some people who seem to hear about jobs without even trying. Some of these folks practice the so-called oddball ways described above. They're not dumb. They would rather dig a tunnel to China before doing everything recommended in a job-search manual. You can find and cultivate your own more efficient methods too.

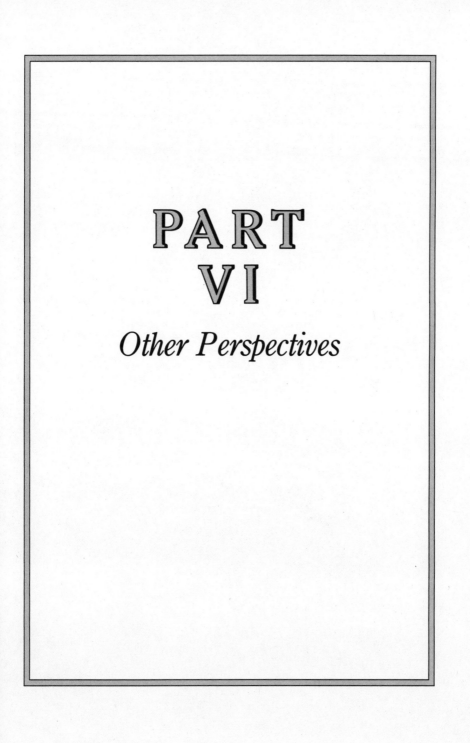

PART
VI
Other Perspectives

Liberal Education
and Careers

I Tell Them I'm a Liberal Arts Major

"And then, of course, they say:
'How quaint; and what are you going to *do* with that?'
. . .
Well, I thought perhaps I'd put it in a cage
to see if it multiplies or does tricks or something
so I could enter it in a circus
and realize a sound dollar-for-dollar return
on my investment.
Then, too, I am exploring the possibility of
whipping it out like a folding chair
at V.F.W. parades and Kiwanis picnics.
I might have it shipped and drive it through Italy.
Or sand it down and sail it.
What am I going to *do* with it?
. . .
You don't understand—
I'm using every breath to tread water
in all-night swimming competitions
with Hegel, Marx, and Wittgenstein;
I am a reckless diver fondling the bottom of civilization
for ropes of pearls
. . .
What am I going to *do* with it?
I'm going to sneak it away from my family

317

318 · *Other Perspectives*

gathered for my commencement
and roam the high desert
making love to it."

—Carol Jin Evans[1]

Many readers are people whose education is general rather than specific vocational preparation. You are relying on your generic learning skills to help you get a job. You may either have chosen "liberal arts" (this is a term I will use to apply to any nonvocational general education) deliberately, or you may have completed a specialized program, but now are seeking work in a different field. All of you have contemplated how your general education will help you in your pursuit of a career.

There is a pervasive misunderstanding about the relationship between education and jobs, and it goes something like this: Many people believe that the main purpose of going to school is to become trained for a vocation or a career. Thus, those who direct their schooling toward this end, and choose the "right" fields of study (those that have good job markets), are the presumed winners of the labor market game. Those who miss the boat either studied the "wrong" fields, or chose liberal arts education and therefore never got themselves "trained" for anything.

Following this reasoning, it seems ludicrous that anyone would consciously choose liberal education, because they would seem to have no chance of success in the labor market. But colleges of liberal arts (both private colleges, which have *only* liberal arts, and universities with large liberal arts colleges) continue to enroll thousands of students. In fact, approximately 1,000,000 college graduates receive liberal arts degrees every year. You may be one of these graduates or may expect to become one. Thus, you would wonder: "What *does* a person do with a general education in the job market?"

► Is Education Vocational ◄ Training?

There are numerous examples of education that is preparation for certain jobs or careers. Many high school programs or vocational schools available to high school graduates are specifically designed to provide such training.

Furthermore, many college and university programs are career oriented as well, and a person who wants to enter certain fields of work must have such training as a basic minimum. The most prominent examples of such career programs include engineering, pharmacy, architecture, physical therapy, and nursing.

Careers Which Do Not Require Academic Credentials for Entry

There is no question at all that the above fields require an academic credential for entry. However, the confusion starts when we look at many other fields for which there *are* college programs—business, journalism, social work, city planning, public administration, radio/television, computer science, etc., but where it is *not* absolutely necessary to have a degree in this field in order to enter the field of work. While many college graduates do receive the degree, even a casual study of these fields of work would reveal that liberal arts graduates are working alongside and performing equally as well as the so-called "trained" graduates. Then there are other careers for which educational programs seldom exist; thus they can be entered by anyone, though often a college degree is preferred or required. A sample of such fields includes retailing, banking, insurance, public relations, book publishing, and advertising. In all, we can generate a long list of career fields that are available to the generally educated individual:

Career Areas for the Generally Educated

Advertising	Magazine and newspaper publishing
Art	Marketing research
Banking	Nonprofit associations
Book publishing	Personnel
Computer services	Public relations
Entertainment and music	Real estate
Fashion	Retailing
Film	Sales
Government	Social service
Insurance	Television and radio
Investments	Travel
Management	Writing

Ivar Berg, in a book entitled *Education and Jobs: The Great Training Robbery,* pointed out that there is always an imperfect relationship between schooling and jobs available. No matter how closely an educational program may attempt to follow the job market, its "training" may still not be what employers want, and the demand for such graduates may shift by the time the individual completes his/her program. Thus, those who use schooling for career training are often left unsatisfied and must then rely upon their general learning skills to find a job.

How Do Liberally Educated People Get into All Those Careers?

In the face of schooling the purports to "train" an individual for certain careers, the interesting question remains: "How *do* the 'untrained' but generally educated compete effectively for these jobs?" If you are one of these, what do you have that you can throw on the table that can compete with the person who has an academic credential in management, journalism, marketing, radio-television-film, or some other field that you hope to enter?

In fact, the liberally educated graduates have many assets they can call upon other than specialized academic credentials.

I call this the "Tools in Your Kit" approach to marketing yourself, and it looks like this:

"Tool Kit" of the Generally Educated Who Seek Jobs and Careers

General Learning Skills The ability to become competent in a wide variety of jobs, through having learned how to learn. Courses that emphasize analytical thinking, research, writing, and communication skills are valued because they can be applied to any new learning situation.

Specific Academic Courses While a person may not have an academic degree relevant to the career he/she desires, it is possible to have taken certain job-related courses, such as accounting, computer systems, statistics, expository writing, etc.

Experience General exposure to a field of work outside of the classroom can include internships, work experience during summers, volunteer or part-time experience during the school year, etc. Such experience often provides greater knowledge of a field of work than what can be gained from academic courses.

Motivation Your sheer desire to succeed, drive to become involved in a given field, and level of enthusiasm will contribute greatly to your overall job and career potential. Often motivation is the factor that distinguishes one good job candidate from another, because such drive colors everything that you will do on the job.

Skills Employers seek generic skills to enable a person to perform well. Such skills—which can be acquired in either academic courses or outside the classroom—include research, writing, planning, supervising, organizing people or data, budget management, and many others.

Interpersonal Skills   Often referred to as "getting along with people," this set of skills can be acquired anywhere, and is highly valued. The ability to engage people, work cooperatively with them, motivate them, and deal well with conflicts can be demonstrated in the job interview itself, or by reference to past jobs, campus activities, community work, or leadership experiences.

The importance of interpersonal skills was underlined recently by the *Wall Street Journal*:

> SOCIAL LOUTS: That's one assessment of today's corporate trainees. Fresh hires in management training programs have above-average intelligence, but most lack tact, diplomacy, and understanding of people. . . . Business school graduates are rated especially brash.[2]

Thus, we can begin to understand why the liberally educated find places in the job market, even though their academic credentials do not show any "training." While the "tools" noted above do not provide you any guarantee of being hired for the jobs you may want, these factors enable you to compete effectively with others having academic credentials.

► What Is a ◄ Liberal Education?

While it is becoming more clear that a liberal education is highly valued in jobs and careers (see pages 327–335), you may wonder how you will know if you have such an education. You don't have one just because it says so on your transcript. In fact, some liberal arts graduates do not have a liberal education, and some graduate or specialized programs do. You are most likely to acquire the broad learning and communication skills that characterize a liberal education if you do the following:

a) Take as broad a selection of courses as possible.   This means you cannot afford to avoid courses in *any* of these areas: science, mathematics, humanities (English, philosophy), foreign languages, social sciences (political science, history, psychology), and fine arts. Each of these course areas teaches you to study the world in a different way. The overall effect is that you become comfortable with any form of learning and are not afraid to tackle any new body of information. Also, your perspective on problems and how to solve them is broadened by studying a variety of arts, political philosophies, sciences, and views of life.

b) Take the courses that make demands on you. You cannot afford to take the "easy" courses in any of the liberal arts disciplines—and we all know which courses these are when we're in school—because your mind will not be stretched and challenged. Sure, it is more painful at the time, but you'll thank them later, because your learning capacities expand only when demands are made upon you to stretch your ideas and grapple with solutions to difficult problems. After studying slavery in America and assessing what you might have done if you had been Abraham Lincoln—taking into account economic factors, belief systems, the U.S. political system, and the psychology of key leaders' personalities at the time—the problems of a job may well seem both intriguing and manageable.

c) Study a field in depth. Of course, this is usually known as a major field of study. It is important not only to have a major, but to invest yourself in it, to take the most challenging courses and learn how it feels to investigate and understand an area of knowledge at some of its deepest levels. You will do equally intensive investigation of certain subjects when you are on the job.

d) Acquire the skills of a liberal education. A truly broadening education brings with it certain skills that are highly valued in the workplace and everywhere else in life. Liberal arts courses encourage these skills, and you should be conscious of their importance even though they may seem abstract. You will call upon these skills every time you meet a new, unfamiliar situation in your career, which will be often. The most marketable skills of a liberal education tend to be:

- *Research*—the ability to gather information on a new topic
- *Languages*—the ability to communicate in languages of other cultures and understand the views of other people
- *Speaking*—the ability to express your ideas orally, and argue your viewpoint
- *Critical thinking*—examining ideas closely, to determine their truth and broader meaning
- *Imaging*—using your imagination to develop new solutions to problems
- *Analytical thinking*—the ability to understand ideas, grasp concepts, think abstractly, assimilate new bodies of information
- *Writing*—expressing yourself in written communication with clarity and precision
- *Artistic understanding*—the ability to see the world as artists see it, to gain fresh understandings of our culture and others

e) Become attuned to differences in people. It is often said that the "ability to work effectively with a wide variety of people" is one of the hallmarks of a liberal arts graduate. Courses in anthropology, languages, political systems, history, literature, and others help make you more sensitive to the reality that the world is filled with people very much unlike yourself. You soon learn that much of your success in a career will depend upon your ability to work productively with people who think differently from you, value different things, have different backgrounds, and often even speak different languages. A liberal education encourages this sensitivity, so don't try to tune it out. As Lee Iacocca notes in his autobiography:

> In addition to all the engineering and business courses, I also studied four years of psychology at Lehigh. I'm not being facetious when I say that these psychology courses were probably the most valuable courses of my college career. . . . I've applied more of these courses when dealing with the "nuts" I've met in the corporate world than all the engineering courses in dealing with the nuts (and bolts) of automobiles.[3]

► A Liberal Education Is ◄
Important for the
Vocationally Trained Too

If you think you're going to gain entry to a career simply because you have an academic degree that says you learned all about it, guess again. Employers do not hire academic transcripts; they hire people who have the greatest potential to become productive in their organizations. They have learned that workers are productive for a variety of reasons, among them, general learning skills. Employers know you cannot be trained in school to face every problem that you will encounter on the job. So, they want your mind to be as well trained as possible.

Those who study career-oriented curricula cannot afford to ignore liberal learning. If they concentrate only on their career-preparation courses, and believe mistakenly that knowledge of a career and its technical concepts are what matters, they will suffer from a lack of analytical, writing, research, and other generic skills. Perhaps even more important, a career-focused student may ignore the importance of interpersonal skills, of understanding other cultures, or of learning to think imaginatively. The short-run, "bottom line" mentality of business school graduates is a deficiency in present and future business leaders. Robert Callendar has said:

> In my opinion, a liberally educated person is still the type of individual needed at the highest levels of corporate life. . . . The real

issue in the banking sector is not how to get out of Mexico . . . It is how to play a constructive role in Mexico's development. To our young bankers, we give such a challenge, and we sorely need those minds that are well grounded in history, politics, language, sociology, and psychology.[4]

The vocational courses may look good on the transcript, but they are long forgotten once an organization looks to you for leadership of people, strength of ideas, and the breadth of thinking to be able to manage an organizational ship in uncertain waters.

Career-focused courses *can* be taught with general learning skills in mind. However, you must look closely at your courses to see what skills are emphasized. Does the course require you to express your ideas in writing? Do you have to handle abstract concepts and think broadly about problems? Are you required to express your ideas in class and be challenged by others? Do you have to exercise your research skills? Does the course sensitize you to different cultures? Move toward schooling that emphasizes these broader skills, because you will need them in whatever job or career you enter.

► Where Does the Generally ◄ Educated Person Fit in a High-Tech World?

Those who are skeptical about a liberal education often point to the increasingly technical nature of our world, and claim that you have to be technologically prepared to have the best chances of success in a career. While there is no doubting the onset of technology, the proportion of jobs that require technological training is still relatively small:

High technology occupations, as a group, will account for only 7 percent of all new jobs between 1980 and 1990. The general educational requirements for creating good citizens and productive workers are not likely to be altered significantly by high technology. Everyone should acquire strong analytical, expressive, communicative, and computational skills, as well as extensive knowledge of political, economic, social, and cultural institutions.[5]

This study by Henry M. Levin and Russell Rumberger also makes clear that for every new job created by so-called high technology, there are four or five other jobs needed that are not technological in nature. This makes sense if we look at the introduction of a new technological product to the marketplace. Let's suppose the engineers at IBM get together to create a new product. What kinds of people are necessary to get this product sold and delivered to its potential customers?

Salespeople—Individuals must sell the product to other organizations or individual customers

Trainers—People must instruct employees of IBM to understand what the product is and how it can be used

Customer Service—Other workers must be available to tell customers how best to use their new product

Marketing—Staff members must figure out how best to attract potential customers, and distribute it to them most efficiently

Production—Individuals must supervise the manufacture of the new product, which involves organizing people and stimulating them to work most effectively

Thus, it would seem for every engineer there is probably a salesperson, a trainer, a marketing person, a production supervisor, and a customer service representative. While sometimes these people have technical backgrounds, often they do not, because these jobs require interpersonal skills that technical people may lack. This is why Levin and Rumberger conclude that most jobs are not technological, and why there is considerable room for the liberally educated to find employment in a high-tech job market.

Though you need not obtain an engineering or other technical degree to join the world of high tech, it is important that you become comfortable with the language and concepts of technology, because your career will very likely involve communicating with technical people. You can accomplish this familiarity either through taking certain technical courses (such as computer science), completing enough natural science courses (physics, chemistry, etc.) that you are comfortable with scientific ideas, getting part-time jobs where you work closely with technological people, or all of the above. Once again, the key is to not be afraid of people who are different from you. Learn to speak their language and appreciate the things they regard as important, and you will work effectively with technological people.

► The Short-Run Problem of ◄ the Liberally Educated

The liberal arts graduate has a public relations problem. The public is continually bombarded with stories about the poor souls with liberal arts degrees who cannot find jobs, so they must drive taxicabs, be woefully underemployed, or live off their parents. These fates fall to other graduates as well, but somehow the world comes to believe it is the special dilemma of the generally educated to be underpaid and overlooked in the job market. The stories of beleaguered liberal arts graduates, portrayed as "unprepared for job market realities," make each new graduate feel defensive and expect the worst when they embark on the job hunting trail.

However, the problem that looks so ominous is only a brief transition problem in which new liberal arts graduates must leave one world for a very different one, and adjust to the new demands in their lives. Typically the new graduate must:

- move from studying the world and its problems on the grand scale to occupying a specific place in the grand order of things
- shift from having no vocational focus to choosing among a seemingly unlimited number of options; liberal arts graduates must create this focus from their own mind, rather than having it handed to them on a college transcript
- leave the comfortable financial environment of home for a more tenuous but independent financial state

While these transitions are small dots on the scale of an entire life and career, they loom large at the time the graduate is moving through them.

The inevitable fallout of adjusting to new goals and a new life context is that it takes a bit longer to find the first job than anyone might hope or expect. One to three months of job seeking is not unusual, and sometimes it takes even longer. So what? In the meantime there are interim jobs to be had, career possibilities to be explored, and a sense of invigoration that comes from knowing you're going to find something new and stimulating to do.

The first job may also create some initial disappointment, because it does not match the intellectual excitement of a liberal education. "Yesterday I pondered the fates of capitalistic and socialistic societies, and today I am concerned with negotiating contracts as an insurance underwriter." It takes a while to make this transition. You can still think about Descartes and Freud in your spare time, and you may well find some connections between great thinkers and your job, but for the most part you are dealing with concrete, earthly matters, and it takes a while before that grows into a feeling of commitment.

You may not even find that really great job on the first try. It may not come until your second or third job, but you take the first job to keep your personal finances in order and get your first taste of the working world. That is enough for now, while you stay on the lookout for a more enduring career opportunity.

So, if you are a new, generally educated graduate, you can expect some discomfort during this initial transition from studies to the working world. But rest easy in knowing that after the initial weeks or months of transition from school to work, you will have a greater number of job and career options than other graduates, and you will take advantage of these when you are ready. Life ain't easy for the new liberal arts graduate, but the best is yet to come.

► The Long-Run Advantage ◄
and Leadership Potential
of the Liberally Educated

Liberal arts graduates may be initially disadvantaged by their less specialized and less career-oriented training. But . . . as liberal arts graduates climb the corporate ladder, they often become advantaged. The immediate employment gains of a practical course of study may come at the sacrifice of ultimate career gains.[6]

Most liberal arts graduates do not know at the time they graduate— at age twenty-one without any work history—the benefits they will get from their education as they progress through their careers. The virtues of general education do not unfold until after some years have passed, jobs have changed, and the graduate can reflect upon the skills and attitudes that made a difference in his/her career. Such insights are not available to the new graduate, nor should we expect them to be.

Nonetheless, it is becoming increasingly clear that the liberal education provides a critical base for those who desire to advance to positions of leadership in their careers, whether in small organizations or large ones, in the profit or nonprofit sectors.

The higher one's level of responsibility in a career, the more important are the generic learning skills and interpersonal skills that tend to characterize a liberal education. The ability to solve complex problems for which you have not been "trained," to communicate effectively, and to understand different views are going to be crucial qualities for any organizational leader.

As Rawles Fulgham, president of First International Bancshares, Inc., explains it: "We've found that too often young people have difficulty expressing themselves, even though they are well schooled in technical matters such as finance, statistics, and accounting. It's

328 • *Other Perspectives*

been my view that these people did not know much about history, psychology, the humanities, or foreign languages. Many had not had public speaking in college. They are often men of character and expertise in their fields, but they lack leadership qualities."[7]

The skills employers are looking for in graduates are not specific to a machine or industry; they want young workers who can read, write, compute, pick up new skills quickly and eagerly, and interact cooperatively with others. These are the adaptive skills of a liberal education, not the specific skills of vocational education.[8]

These statements are not mere lip-service testimonials. They grow from business and other leaders' increasing recognition that liberal arts have been abundant in their own midst. *Fortune* magazine found that 38 percent of CEOs have liberal arts degrees. Nine of the thirteen top executives at IBM, the prototype high-technology company, have liberal arts degrees.

Executives are frustrated by new graduates of business schools and other career-focused programs who cannot function well beyond the level of mere technicians, and who communicate poorly within their organizations. A senior vice-president of First Atlanta Corporation says, "If I could choose one degree for the people I hire it would be English. . . . You can teach a pack of cub scouts to do portfolio analysis."[9]

Furthermore, several research studies have demonstrated the long-run merits of a general education, and the leadership qualities evidenced by liberal arts graduates:

- AT&T, the largest employer of college graduates in the United States, studied the college backgrounds of employees who, after twenty years, had advanced to senior management positions. It was found that 43 percent of them advanced to senior management, compared to 34 percent of the business school graduates and 28 percent of the engineering graduates. In a highly technical company such as AT&T, one might have expected the reverse. The president of AT&T, Charles Brown, offered an explanation: "The humanities and social science majors were most suitable to change—the leading feature of this kind of high-speed, high-pressure, high-tech world we now occupy."[10]
- Chase Manhattan studied the effectiveness of its people as "relationship managers" and learned that 60 percent of the liberal arts graduates were regarded as high performers, while 60 percent of the MBA graduates were evaluated as "low performers."[11]

George Klemp, in a study entitled "The Three Factors of Success,"[12] found that knowledge of the job was less important than the following factors in distinguishing highly successful performers from average performers across a wide spectrum of kinds of work:

▶ Klemp's Three Factors ◀ of Success

Cognitive Skills

- the ability to see thematic consistencies in diverse information
- the ability to understand many sides of a controversial issue
- the ability to learn from experience

Interpersonal Skills

- a positive regard for others, a belief that people are capable of doing good things with a bit of support and encouragement
- giving assistance that enables another person to be effective
- the ability to control impulsive feelings of hostility or anger that make that other person feel powerless and ineffective

Motivation

- a need to do something better than it has ever been done before
- rewards lie primarily in the satisfaction that comes from accomplishing something unique, rather than in the money that may be earned in the process

Klemp's success factors bear a close resemblance to the skills that are most commonly attributed to a liberal education. While certainly liberal arts graduates would have no monopoly on these factors, one would expect a liberal arts graduate to be somewhat more likely to have them than graduates of other programs. A liberal education need not be limited to liberal arts graduates. A student of business or any other specialized program can acquire the advantages of a liberal education through wise selection of courses, teachers, and out-of-class experiences.

▶ Graduates Comment About ◀ Their Liberal Education

After some years of perspective between graduation and their emerging careers, five former liberal arts students offer interesting comments about the value of their liberal learning:[13]

> *Executive Assistant to Vice-President of Production, Universal Studios* (Major: American studies): "My broad generalist's approach to American civilization has been valuable in helping me understand the tastes of American film audiences. My broad background gave me confidence I could successfully perform in any job I desired."

> *Commodities Broker, Saul Stone and Company* (Major: Geography): "It is a fantastic advantage to be able to carry on a conversation on almost any topic with almost any person. In my career, personal contact is vitally important."

> *Computer Systems Analyst, Bureau of Labor Statistics* (Major: Government): "While technical skills are necessary, an ability to communicate effectively (orally and in writing) can give one the edge over others with the same technical skills."

> *Vice-President and Part Owner, Graphics Design Company* (Major: English): "After ten years I just realized what I really learned at the University of Virginia unbeknownst to me while it was happening—i.e., how to think and solve problems. This is the single most important factor in my current success."

> *Bank Vice-President for Marketing and Development* (Major: Biology): "A liberal arts background provided me with an overall understanding of people, politics, and society, which are most important to the understanding of marketing."

▶ Problems to Avoid ◀

Notwithstanding all of the virtues of a liberal education, there are certain traps that liberal arts graduates fall into, which make it more difficult for them to achieve their goals. These problems are likely to occur for the person who has emphasized a general education:

Vague Goals   A world filled with career options sometimes leads the graduate to resist focusing on a particular area, and instead resort to statements such as "I want to start a company that is developing some great new product" (What kind of company, what kind of product?) or "I want to work with people in a management context" (Management of what? what kinds of people?).

Vagueness is usually the result of too many options and an unwillingness to settle on the one that seems best. However, you must focus your attention, if only for the sake of knowing whom to talk with first. A tentative goal is not a commitment. "I want to look into the arts administration field" does not mean you will stay in it "for the rest of your life" (as new graduates often fear), even if you try a first job in that area. Vagueness gives you little to talk about. Try on several different hats (goals) before you discover which fits best.

Unrealistic Expectations   While it has been said of M.B.A. graduates that they want to run the company within a week of being hired, this same criticism sometimes applies to liberal arts graduates. Having been educated to think in broad terms, the graduate will almost immediately view him/herself as a prospective manager or leader of an organization when applying for a job. Thus, the first job—an entry-level position with little responsibility—is almost a sure bet to be disappointing. Even in a small organization, it takes at least a year or two before responsibilities increase and the job becomes more exciting. In a large organization, it probably takes even longer. Liberal arts graduates sometimes do not cope well with this delayed gratification. If you are one of these, be patient if you like the organization you're working for. If you don't, then try somewhere else, but don't ruin your prospects for advancement by demanding too much too soon.

Snobbery or Ambivalence   A liberal education sometimes produces in the graduate a disdain for the working world. Mere jobs seem pedestrian, too utilitarian, or downright boring as you contemplate becoming part of them. This is an attitude problem, and it will hurt your chances for getting hired if it gets the better of you.

Liberal arts majors make poor sales pitches for themselves. They expect the interviewer to guess how wonderful they are.[14]

If you want a surefire way to get eliminated from any job, have an indifferent or even mildly snotty attitude about the employer, the industry, or about work in general.

Your transition from intellectual life to the working world may not be an easy one, but you can do it. It is important that you have respect for what a business or a nonprofit organization is trying to accomplish, even if it does not satisfy in the same way that your higher education did. As you look more closely at the challenges of a career, you will find their problems stimulating in their own right. If, the closer you get, the more ambivalence or disdain you feel, you should probably be in higher education or some other field that feels more compatible.

► Questions Asked by ◄ Liberal Arts Graduates

As they embark on the job search, liberal arts graduates seem to have certain questions that stump them and make it difficult for them to express full confidence in themselves:

1. "How do I answer 'Why did you study liberal arts and not business'?"

"I felt that I would get a better set of learning skills in liberal arts, and that I could demonstrate my interest in business in other ways, through my part-time work experience and membership in business clubs on campus. I learned (in my liberal arts courses) the analytical, writing, and research skills that I'll need to be a good financial analyst, and have also taken a few business courses so that I am familiar with the problems that occur. I am confident I can do this job."

Any variation on these themes will express your confidence in yourself, your education, and your career goals. Employers want to know that you take your career goals seriously, and want to hear your rationale for your educational background. It would also help to identify any experiences you have had that reveal potential for a career in business.

2. "Must I go to graduate school?"

Liberal arts graduates often enroll in graduate and professional school programs, but they can also get many jobs without additional education. In fact, the majority find employment immediately after graduation, rather than continue their schooling.

There are many fields of work that have corresponding graduate programs but can also be entered with a bachelor's degree, such as business, social work, journalism, public administration, city planning, and many others. Does that mean that people with the advanced degrees will get the better positions? In some cases, perhaps that is true, but in many others it is not. For example, a Bachelor of Arts graduate can go just as far on a newspaper as a Master's of Journalism. Or, as the Chase Manhattan study demonstrated, Bachelor of Arts graduates have often done even better than the M.B.A.'s in their company. So, before you decide that a graduate degree is necessary or preferred, talk with managers in the field of work itself, to see what their experiences have been with bachelor's and advanced-degree holders.

3. "How important are my grades?"

Much less important than you think. While grades are a good measure of your performance as a student, they tell an employer little about how you will function on the job. If your grades are low, don't be defensive about them. Your best reponse is something like: "I am proud of my degree, and would have made better grades, except that I chose to be involved in other activities, such as ———, which enabled me to develop skills that will help me on this job, such as ———." Draw some advantage from your grades if they are good, but don't ever depend on a grade average to sell yourself as a job candidate.

4. "How do I compete with a 'trained' graduate?"

If, for example, you want a job in business and you are competing with people who have B.B.A. degrees, (a) Show some evidence that you have had business-related experience, such as a part-time job, or business-related skills you have developed in a campus activity; (b) Do enough research that you know exactly what these business jobs are about; (c) Show evidence of your leadership capabilities; (d) Be enthusiastic about the jobs you are applying for; and (e) Point out the business-related courses you have taken in your academic program.

This approach toward job hunting was outlined more fully in the "Tool Kit" section on pages 320–321. It emphasizes that your college major is just one of many tools that you have to offer in the marketplace, and that you should be sure to make all of your assets known, rather than relying only on your academic transcript.

5. "How much should I know about computers?"

Know as much about them as seems advisable, in terms of your specific job goals. Since most jobs today have some involvement with hardware and software, you probably ought to have had a computer course or two or gained some exposure in other ways. You probably don't plan to be a computer specialist, but you will be working closely with computer people on your job and will need to know what the equipment can accomplish for you. It is not necessary for you to major in computer science, unless you plan to be a specialist. However, you should understand the computer terminology that is widely used, regardless of what career you plan to enter. You will acquire much of your computer literacy after you are employed. Be prepared to learn a lot about computer capabilities. Many of the decisions you make in your job will depend upon the tasks a computer can perform that will help your operation function more smoothly and productively.

Here are six levels of computer-related experience that you may consider. Most jobs available to college graduates will not require you to know more than Level 3, though knowledge at higher levels would give you some advantage in certain competitive situations.

► Levels of Computer-Related ◄ Experience

- *Level 1*—Little or no understanding of anything dealing with computers
- *Level 2*—Understanding of the general uses to which computers are put in our society
- *Level 3*—Facility with basic computer applications, including accounting, word processing, database, information transmission and retrieval, and graphics software applications
- *Level 4*—Programming language familiarity; ability to design, write, and debug programs
- *Level 5*—Programming language fluency; understanding of programming principles leading to efficient, fast programs. Some knowledge of computer hardware design
- *Level 6*—Practical experience in product development[15]

6. "Why do liberal arts graduates get paid so little?"

Starting salaries for liberal arts graduates average lower than those for engineers, business graduates, and others, because employers are willing to pay more for technical skills at the entry level. The potential for a liberal arts graduate is more uncertain at the start; therefore the employer prefers to give raises after he/she has shown some productivity. Also, certain industries that are popular with this group (publishing, banking, insurance, advertising, and others) are known for starting new college graduates at low pay; this applies to both LAGs and other graduates. The pay increases as graduates advance through their organizational hierarchies. To the extent that a liberal arts graduate attains positions of leadership (which they often do, according to various studies, pages 327–329), he/she will have earnings that exceed other graduates. Thus, the liberal arts graduate may often start lower in terms of pay and responsibility, but become higher over time. In general, starting salary is a poor predictor of future earnings, because the employer has no evidence yet of the graduate's ability to perform.

At Penn State we followed a sample of LAGs from 1955, 1960, and 1965. . . . We found that they started at lower salaries than those trained in such occupations as computer programming, sales, marketing, and administration. Over a period of time ranging from three to fourteen years, however, they outdistanced the field in every one of those occupations in salaries and presumably in value to their organizations.[16]

7. "If I have a liberal arts major, should I take some 'marketable' courses?"

It is probably a good idea to take some courses in college that relate to the field of work you hope to enter. If nothing else, such courses give you some exposure to that field and a knowledge of its vocabulary. The importance of coursework can vary according to the field. For instance, if you want to be an accountant but you are a liberal arts major, you are well advised to have two or more accounting courses. However, there is much difference of opinion about whether taking marketing courses helps very much in applying to be a marketing representative for a company. Check with people working in the field to see what they would recommend. In any event, if some coursework helps you to feel more comfortable about job hunting, then that is reason enough to do it. On the other hand, if you are confident that you can perform well based on your past experiences and/or your general education and general intelligence, and you feel you don't need relevant courses, then there is no reason to burden your educational program with courses you do not want.

27

Zen of the Career Search

Copernicus had no motive for misleading his fellow men as
to the place of the sun in the solar system. He looked for it
as honestly as a shepherd seeks a path in the mist.
—George Bernard Shaw,
Man and Superman

Our culture is predominantly a scientific one. In our eagerness to validate
the power of the scientific method, we have assumed that a career field
is no different from a wheat crop, an engineering problem, or the solution
to an algebraic equation: it can be observed, measured, and brought under
control. We then apply our optimism to the individual and compound the
scientific arrogance by proposing that his or her career journey can be
charted, planned, and understood in advance. Fortunately, we are learning
from experience that a career is far more subtle and complicated than we
had imagined.

It is too easy to graft the mentality of the Western Hemisphere onto
the processes of the work search. All the convenient props for rational
thinking are available. A Western mind would have us think about alternatives, weigh the pros and cons, assess probabilities, and predict outcomes. In short, Western thinkers do everything possible to impose
crystalline logic and rational thought on a set of decisions and processes
that may be highly illogical, unpredictable, and perhaps even impervious
to rational inquiry.

Rational thinking has been so successful in solving modern-day problems—how to place human beings on the moon, how to control inventories
of billions of units—that we assume such thinking can accomplish anything.
We conveniently forget that rational thinking succeeds best only when
the relevant variables are under our control, observable, and objective in
the sense that any two observers agree about what they are seeing. We
must recognize that the work search is not a highly predictable process,
many of its variables are not known or observable, and certainly many of
them are not subject to the individual's complete control. Hence, scientific,
rational methods of inquiry may be of dubious value.

The problems of the work search are closer to the subtle, unfathomable realm of human relations than they are to the scientific realm of rational inquiry. Though we admit that scientific problems and human relations problems are different in character, we continue to believe that scientific methods can be applied to nonscientific matters.

All our efforts to impose reason on the individual ignore that life choices—career, marriage, and the like—are essentially irrational, perhaps even unconscious, acts. By attempting to introduce order into a disorderly process, we disturb a highly effective but murky process by which an individual makes life decisions.

When we talk about an interpersonal process that is as highly complicated as the work search, the intellect has severe limitations. Powers of reason have to yield ground to other forms of inquiry. In short, until we can demonstrate that Western rationality explains work-search behavior in a way that illuminates our career decisions, we must allow for the possibility that Eastern modes of thought have something to teach us. This is what the Zen master D. T. Suzuki has to say about the intellect:

Let the intellect alone, it has usefulness in its proper sphere, but let it not interfere with the flowing of the life-stream. . . . The fact of flowing must under no circumstances be arrested or meddled with, for the moment your hands are dipped into it, its transparency is disturbed, it ceases to reflect your image which you have had from the very beginning and will continue to have to the end of time.[1]

Suzuki tells the story of a son who asks his father to teach him how to be an expert burglar. The father says nothing until one night he takes the son to a house to be burgled, goes to the attic, locks the unsuspecting son in a trunk, and then leaves the house. The son devises a way to escape the trunk and the house, returns, and asks the father breathlessly why he did that. The father replies: "Be not offended, my son. Just tell me how you got out of it." When the son describes his adventures in the house, the father says: "There you are, you have learned the art of burglary."[2] "The idea of the [burglary] story is to demonstrate the futility of verbal instruction and conceptual presentation," Suzuki says. If we apply this idea to our views about the work search, we may conclude that conceptualization and the intellect have no place in our learning. In fact, this entire book would seem to disturb "the flowing of the life-stream." It is true that this book deals heavily in the description of concepts. Nevertheless, I feel that the skills approach to the work search is compatible with Eastern views because these skills are offered to illuminate the search process rather than proscribe it, to give you ways of approaching it rather than telling you a specific set of rules that must be obeyed.

These skills liberate you from the bonds of immediate decision making by showing you ways of gathering data that render decision making unnecessary. As you use the skills, you may discover that tentative and even more enduring decisions occur naturally in the context of your activity. This is the Zen way.

> Zen proposes its solution by directly appealing to facts of personal experience and not to book knowledge. The nature of one's own being where apparently rages the struggle between the finite and the infinite is to be grasped by a higher faculty than the intellect . . .

> By personal experience it is meant to get at the fact at first hand, and not through any intermediary, whatever this may be. Its favourite analogy is: to point at the moon, a finger is needed, but woe to those who take the finger for the moon.[3]

The purpose of this book is to describe skills you can use to maximize experience in the work search and minimize the need for intellectual and analytical thinking. You are more likely to understand yourself and what you want by direct experience (and a review of your past experiences) than by making arbitrary choices based on criteria external to your own feelings.

My friend Julie loved to dance and move from the time she was a child. However, like most young dancers, she did not have enough talent to develop a professional career. Her parents were puzzled about how to advise her, her boyfriend tried to interest her in business (it was the furthest thing from her mind), and her schoolmates just gave up on her. Julie continued to dance, took lessons when she could afford them, and read books about dance in her idle hours. In her early twenties, Julie became aware of the healing aspects of movement and the many benefits she had received from dance. She began to read about psychotherapy with great enthusiasm. She formed small creative-dance classes during college. It wasn't long before Julie discovered a tiny band of people doing what they called "dance therapy," an exciting, brand-new profession. She became one of the first therapists registered with the American Dance Therapy Association. By following her best instincts, not what people advised for her, Julie found her career direction.

Suzuki encourages a semiconscious or unconscious flow toward those people and activities that feel comfortable for you. He encourages a "let it happen" mentality and suggests strongly that there is greater wisdom in trusting your inner instincts than in *thinking* about what you should do. "The master [Tenno Dogo] said, 'If you want to see, see right at once. When you begin to think you miss the point.' "[4]

► Direction by Indirection ◄

As nearly as I can determine from applying Zen concepts to what is essentially a Western process—the formalized search for better work— Suzuki and other Zen masters would advise us to focus our energies by not organizing them. Are these senseless riddles that only confuse you? I believe Zen ideas have some promise for us, and that they can be translated into our work-search language as follows.

First, let go of judgments. Begin by forcing yourself not to assign external ratings to the work possibilities you explore. If a job pays $20,000 and all your friends say it is a good opportunity, forget that. Explore without making judgments or assigning ratings. Let yourself experience how you feel about the work. Tim Gallwey's brilliant book about the applications of Zen principles to teaching tennis urges a close consideration of the word *abandon*:

> "Abandon" is a good word to describe what happens to a tennis player who feels he has nothing to lose. He stops caring about the outcome and plays all out. This is the true meaning of detachment . . . It is caring, yet not caring; it is *effortless effort*. It happens when one lets go of attachment to the results of one's actions and allows the increased energy to come to bear on the action itself. In the language of karma yoga, this is called action without attachment to the fruits of action, and ironically when this state is achieved the results are the best possible.[5]

You will note this principle of deferred judgment is echoed in the section that explains how to use creative brainstorming (see Chapter 4). Osborn's view that the best things happen when the mind surrenders its power to evaluate is essentially a Zen idea.

Second, try by not trying too hard. Zen assumes that the best things occur when you turn off your conscious mind and let the unconscious take over. Hard effort is usually associated with hard thought; Zen masters insist that such effort intrudes upon the life-stream and inhibits the ability to act.

> As soon as we reflect, deliberate, and conceptualize, the original unconscious is lost and a thought interferes. . . . The arrow is off the string but does not fly straight to the target, nor does the target stand where it is. Calculation, which is miscalculation, sets in.[6]

Perhaps this is why it is said that great poetry is born in silence. Great music and art are said to arise from the quiet depths of the unconscious.[7]

All this means that your collective unconscious has stored considerable knowledge about what you want in your work, and much of your work-search effort should be arranged so that you let the unconscious have its way. Grafting mechanical procedures or formulas onto your instinctive (unconscious) pursuit of compatible work will probably disrupt the process.

A Zen master once asked an audience of Westerners what they thought was the most important word in the English language. After giving his listeners a chance to think about such favorite words as love, faith, and so on, he said, "No, it's a three-letter word; it's the word 'let.'" Let it be. Let it happen. Though sometimes employed to mean a kind of passiveness, these phrases actually refer to a deep acceptance of the fundamental process inherent in life. . . . In the more general sense it means faith in the fundamental order and goodness of life, both human and natural. . . . [Let] problems be solved in the unconscious mind as well as by straining with conscious effort.[8]

Third, remember that insights occur at the times you least expect them. It was Pasteur who said: "Chance favors the prepared mind." The more you have been trying to decide what to do about your work, the more likely you are to find a solution when you are least prepared for it, if you let your unconscious roam freely.

I was struggling with my preparation for a talk to a group of counselors and made little progress when I sat down to think about it. Time overcame me, and I had to depart by car for the conference site four hundred miles away. En route, I parked in New York City, had my car towed away, spent several exhausting hours tracking it down, learned that I didn't have sufficient cash to rescue the car, and had to trundle my belongings to a late-night bus bound for the conference site. By the time I plopped into a bus seat, I was physically drained and, I reasoned, mentally exhausted as well. During the four-hour bus ride, I discovered my thoughts falling into a most coherent pattern and was prepared to talk the next morning at half-past eight.

The unconscious picks its own times and places. Some time ago a group of research chemists were asked where and how they got their scientific ideas. Here are some of their answers:

"While dodging automobiles across Park Row and Broadway, New York."
"Sunday in church as the preacher was announcing the text."
"At three o'clock in the morning . . ."
"In the morning when shaving . . ."

"Just before and just after an attack of gout . . ."
"Invariably at night after retiring for sleep . . ."
"While resting and loafing on the beach . . ."
"While sitting at my desk doing nothing, thinking about other matters . . ."
"After a month's vacation, as I was dressing after a bath in the sea."[9]

So, prepare your mind for the task at hand by reading about the skills described in this book and then let your unconscious take over; it will orchestrate the process, put the pieces together, and provide the insights you are seeking in the moments you are least prepared for them.

Fourth, notice clues in your tiny experiences. As you flow into your work search, assume that every event has meaning for you, perhaps especially events that seem to have no meaning at all. When you review your broad areas of experience—major field of academic study, the job you have now, the project you completed last year—you will have a marked tendency to overlook the small events, the tiny ones that contain the clues with deeper meaning.

An acquaintance of mine spent many years after his graduation from college trying to figure out what to do with himself. He ignored his engineering major because it didn't excite him enough; he refused his father's offer to enter the family business for a similar reason; he turned down graduate school offers because he had no idea what to study. His frustration came out indirectly with his family; he fell into the habit of criticizing their speech, grammar, and spelling in family letters. All concerned dismissed his behavior as the angry rantings of an unemployed, unmotivated loafer, until finally it dawned on Jim that he unconsciously focused upon *words* in all his idle interactions; these tiny events in which he released frustration revealed an important clue to his future work—he became a copy editor at a publishing house and is prospering in that work today.

What are the tiniest experiences you can focus upon in your daily life? Can you discover any meaning in them? Do you like to plant the garden a certain way? (How do you arrange tasks?) Do you have a preference for the color green? (Do you like working with money, outdoor life?) Do you accomplish your best thinking standing up? (What occupations does this suggest for you? Teacher?) Do you frequently read maps incorrectly? (Do you prefer a sense of adventure, of not knowing where you are going?)

▶ How to Apply Zen Principles ◀

The foregoing discussion suggests that you cannot apply Zen ideas to your work search except by trying *not* to apply them, that you will be penalized for any conscious effort, that thinking is disqualified. Certainly Zen prin-

ciples caution you to minimize the extent to which conscious thought interferes with the flow of your life-stream. However, I believe that certain conscious processes are implied and that you can reorient your mental activity to take better advantage of your unconscious knowledge of yourself, in the following ways.

Think of Pictures Instead of focusing on words (job titles, job descriptions) or numbers (salary, number of people supervised), use your imagination to envision scenes and situations where you would like to work. Pictures are more powerful than words and can tell you a great deal about what you desire. When you picture yourself at the peak of your capabilities, what do you see? Do you see yourself wandering around your room alone, thinking of solutions to difficult problems? Do you see yourself standing in front of a crowd, persuading your audience of an idea? Are you surrounded by children, teaching them, nurturing them? Are you orchestrating a process even though no one can see you? Do you imagine yourself drinking great draughts of ale, laughing into the night?

Defer Judgment Every authority on creative thinking (Osborn, DeBono, Crawford, and others) insists that the best ideas occur when a person is not inhibited by evaluation or judgment of goodness or badness. Thus, Zen insists that the mind roam freely, without concern about popular opinion, judgments of relatives, or the wisdom of one's meanderings. Creative ideas about work possibilities occur more frequently in an environment of *acceptance*.

Focus on the Present Decisions made for tomorrow require that you pay close attention to how you feel today. Perversely, you may think too much about the past ("What have I done before, and how should this relate to what I do next?") or the future ("If I do this, what will happen five years from now?"). Such backward and forward thinking can help you avoid pitfalls, but it can also seriously inhibit your sense of risk taking, your willingness to respond to what you feel is right for you now. Zen masters would persuade us that the present is our only reality.

Consult Your Senses The intellect has its particular way of judging the worth of a career plan; the body and its visceral senses have other ways of viewing the situation. The next time that you explore a career possibility, ask your body whether it feels comfortable. Do you tighten up when you are at the work site? Do you feel in the hands, abdomen, and back of the neck that this place and these people are right for you? The senses have a lot of information for you, if you will allow it to be presented.

Work and Play Together   A powerful test of compatibility between you and your career is the extent to which you can view it as *both* work and play. You can view *work* as all effort that you expend toward a set of desirable outcomes, while *play* is an inherently enjoyable activity, done for its own sake, without concern about outcomes. The most intrinsically rewarding work has elements of play within it, so that you can look forward to what you are doing on a moment-to-moment basis in addition to anticipating the ultimate rewards.

What educator Bill Harper has to say about play expresses the attitude I have tried to communicate about how people should work and try to get better work:

> Play, I think, is very close to being an innate characteristic of man, and for that reason as long as man is man, it is never going to be forgotten or abolished. But there are times when we get very grim and serious, and the whole style of society tends to make it harder for people to play. When this happens—and we are in that kind of period—people languish, become spiritually spindly as they might physically if they did not have sufficient or proper food. I think play is an essential element for spiritual well-being.[10]

Notes

Chapter 1

1. Gail Sheehy, *Pathfinders* (New York: Bantam, 1981), p. 15.
2. Louis E. Raths, Merrill Harmin, and Sidney Simon, *Values and Teaching* (Columbus, Ohio: Merrill, 1966), p. 6.
3. Howard E. Figler, *PATH: A Career Workbook for Liberal Arts Students*, 2d ed. (Cranston, R.I.: Carroll Press, 1979), pp. 77–79.
4. Sidney B. Simon, Howard Kirschenbaum, and Leland Howe, *Values Clarification* (New York: Hart, 1972).
5. Ralph Mattson and Arthur Miller, eds., *The Truth About You* (Old Tappan, N.J.: Revell Press, 1977), pp. 34–46.
6. Merrill Harmin, Howard Kirschenbaum, and Sidney B. Simon, *Clarifying Values Through Subject Matter* (Minneapolis: Winston Press, 1973), pp. 32–34.

Chapter 2

1. John W. Wright, *American Almanac of Jobs and Salaries*, 1987–1988 (New York: Avon, 1987), p. 275

Chapter 3

1. Joseph Luft, *Of Human Interaction* (Palo Alto: National Press Books, 1969), p. 13. The Johari Window gets its name from the first names of its inventors, Joseph Luft and Harry Ingham.
2. Sidney A. Fine, "Nature of Skill: Implications for Education and Training," *Proceedings*, 75th Annual Convention, American Psychological Association, 1967.
3. Ibid., pp. 365–66.

346 · *Notes*

Chapter 4

1. Edward DeBono, *Lateral Thinking* (New York: Harper and Row, 1970), p. 14.
2. Alex F. Osborn, *Your Creative Power* (New York: Scribner, 1972), p. 269.
3. Alex F. Osborn, *Applied Imagination* (New York: Scribner, 1953), p. 284.
4. Adapted from DeBono, *Lateral Thinking*, pp. 91–99, 131–40, 167–74, 193–205; and from Osborn, *Applied Imagination*, pp. 212–14, 217, 261–62.

Chapter 7

1. Sanford L. Jacobs, "Expect Big Things from Little Guys," *Wall Street Journal*, Nov. 5, 1986.
2. David L. Birch, "The Atomization of America," *Inc.*, March 1987, pp. 21–22.
3. Robert Wegmann, Robert Chapman, and Miriam Johnson, *Looking for Work in the New Economy* (Salt Lake City: Olympus, 1985), p. 33.

Chapter 8

1. John C. Crystal and Richard N. Bolles, *Where Do I Go from Here with My Life?* (New York: Seabury Press, 1974), p. 188.
2. Stanley Milgram, "The Small-World Problem," *Psychology Today*, May 1967, pp. 290–99.
3. Kirby Stanat, "How to Make the Interviewer Want You," in *Careers Without Reschooling*, ed. Dick Goldberg (New York: Continuum, 1985), p. 46.

Chapter 10

1. Austin Marshall, *How to Get a Better Job* (New York: Hawthorne Books, 1964), p. 55.
2. Lee Ash and Denis Lorenz, eds., *Subject Collections: A Guide to Special Book Collections in Libraries* (New York: Bowker, 1967).
3. Marshall, *How to Get a Better Job*, p. 49.

Chapter 11

1. Theodore Reik, *Listening with the Third Ear* (Moonachie, N.J.: Pyramid Publications, 1972).
2. Lawrence M. Brammer, *The Helping Relationship* (Englewood Cliffs, N.J.: Prentice-Hall, 1973), pp. 81–82.
3. Gerard Egan, *The Skilled Helper* (Monterey, Ca.: Brooks/Cole, 1975), pp. 65–66.
4. Paul J. Moses, *The Voice of Neurosis* (New York: Grune & Stratton, 1957).

Chapter 12

1. Alfred Benjamin, *The Helping Interview*, 3d ed. (Boston: Houghton Mifflin, 1981).
2. Ibid.

Chapter 13

1. Gordon Bower and Sharon Bower, *Asserting Yourself* (Reading, Mass.: Addison-Wesley, 1976), p. 60.

2. Philip G. Zimbardo, *Shyness: What It Is and What to Do About It* (Reading, Mass.: Addison-Wesley, 1977), pp. 13–14.

Chapter 14

1. Zimbardo, *Shyness*, p. 5.

Chapter 15

1. Ernst Jacobi, *Writing at Work* (Rochelle Park, N.J.: Hayden, 1976), p. 4.
2. J. Mitchell Morse, "The Age of Logophobia," *Chronicle of Higher Education*, May 16, 1977, p. 40.
3. Thomas S. Franco, "In Answer to Your Ad. . . . ," *Public Relations Journal*, Feb. 1977, p. 24.

Chapter 16

1. Jack Falvey, "Developing Party Skills," *Managing Your Career*, Dow Jones Co., Fall 1986, p. 39.
2. Ibid., p. 40.

Chapter 18

1. Adapted from Figler, *PATH*, pp. 145–46.

Chapter 20

1. John L. Lafevre, "A Peek Inside the Recruiter's Briefcase," *Managing Your Career*, Dow Jones Co., Fall 1986, p. 32.

Chapter 23

1. Karen O. Dowd, "Relocating the Dual-Career Couple," *Journal of Career Planning and Employment*, Winter 1987, p. 28.
2. James O'Toole, "How to Forecast Your Own Working Future," *The Futurist*, Feb. 1982, p. 11.

Chapter 24

1. "Liberal Arts Graduates Move Ahead in the Job Market," *Career News Network* (Austin: University of Texas Career Center, 1984); Richard S. Benner and Susan Tyler Hitchcock, *Life After Liberal Arts* (Charlottesville, Va.: University of Virginia, Office of Career Planning and Placement, 1986); and Stanley Paulsen, "The Liberal Arts Graduate in the Job Market: Spring of Hope or Winter of Despair," paper delivered to College Placement Council, Chicago, May 22, 1980, p. 4.

Chapter 25

1. Adele Scheele, *Skills for Success* (New York: William Morrow, 1979), pp. 28–33.

2. Robert Wegmann, Robert Chapman, and Miriam Johnson, *Looking for Work in the New Economy* (Salt Lake City: Olympus, 1985), p. 113.

Chapter 26

1. Carol Jin Evans, "I Tell Them I'm a Liberal Arts Major," *Chronicle of Higher Education*, June 9, 1980, vol. 20, no. 15, p. 48.
2. "Social Louts: That's One Assessment of Today's Corporate Trainees," *Wall Street Journal*, Oct. 21, 1986, p. 1.
3. Lee Iacocca, with William Novak, *Iacocca: An Autobiography* (New York: Bantam, 1985).
4. Robert J. Callendar, "Liberal Learning and the World," keynote address, Association of American Colleges meeting, New Orleans, Jan. 9, 1986, p. 5.
5. Henry M. Levin and Russell Rumberger, *The Educational Implications of High Technology* (Palo Alto, Ca.: Stanford University, 1983), p. 5.
6. Michael Useem, "What the Research Shows," *Educating Mangers*, ed. Joseph Johnston (San Francisco, Ca.: Jossey-Bass, 1986), p. 71.
7. Bill Sloan, "Back to the Liberal Arts!," *Dallas*, Mar. 1979, p. 29.
8. James O'Toole, "The Reserve Army of the Underemployed," *Change*, June 1975.
9. "The Money Chase," *Time*, May 4, 1981, p. 61.
10. Robert E. Beck, *The Liberal Arts Major in Bell System Management* (Washington, D.C.: Association of American Colleges, 1981), p. 13.
11. Stanley Burns, *From Student to Banker: Observations from the Chase Bank* (Washington, D.C.: Association of American Colleges, 1983), p. 16.
12. George O. Klemp, "Three Factors of Success," *Relating Work and Education*, ed. D. W. Vermilye (San Francisco, Ca.: Jossey-Bass, 1977), pp. 103–8.
13. The first three quotes are from "Interviews with Graduates of the College of Liberal Arts," *Career News Network* (Austin: University of Texas Career Center, 1984), p. 7; the last two are from Richard Benner and Susan Tyler Hitchcock, *Life After Liberal Arts* (Charlottesville: University of Virginia, 1986), pp. 6–8.
14. Carol Murphy and Lynn Jenks, *Getting a Job: What Skills Are Needed?* (San Francisco, Ca.: Far West Laboratories for Educational Research and Development, 1982), p. 3.
15. The six levels are from Andrew Carson, *Career Development and Computer Skills for Liberal Arts Students* (Austin: University of Texas Career Center, 1987), pp. 4–6.
16. Stanley Paulsen, "Liberal Arts Is Useful Training for Management," *The Evening News* (Harrisburg, Pa.), Oct. 2, 1981.

Chapter 27

1. Daisetz T. Suzuki, *Essays in Zen Buddhism* (New York: Grove Press, 1949), p. 19.
2. Daisetz T. Suzuki, *Zen and Japanese Culture* (New York: Pantheon Books, 1959), pp. 9–10.
3. Suzuki, *Essays in Zen Buddhism*, pp. 1–19.
4. Suzuki, *Zen and Japanese Culture*, p. 13.
5. W. Timothy Gallwey, *The Inner Game of Tennis* (New York: Random House, 1974), p. 138.

6. Daisetz T. Suzuki, in foreword to Eugen Herrigel, *Zen and the Art of Archery* (New York: Random House, 1971).
7. Gallwey, *The Inner Game of Tennis*, p. 31.
8. Ibid., p. 135.
9. Rudolph Flesch, *The Art of Clear Thinking* (New York: Barnes and Noble, 1951), p. 146.
10. Bill Harper, quoted in Bil Gilbert, "Play," *Sports Illustrated*, Oct. 13, 1975, p. 90.

Selected, Annotated Bibliography

Chapter 1: Values

Figler, Howard E. *PATH: A Career Workbook for Liberal Arts Students*. 2d. ed. Cranston, R.I.: Carroll Press, 1979.

Offers an integrated sequence of exercises for assessing your work-related values, attitudes toward work, and ways that play correlates with work.

Green, Thomas F. *Work, Leisure, and the American Schools*. New York: Random House, 1948.

A philosopher's keen understanding of the definitions of job, career, labor, work, and leisure. Green helps us understand when a job is not a career, what "good work" is about, and why leisure is not simply recreation, but a serious complement to productive work.

LaBier, Douglas. *Modern Madness: The Emotional Fallout of Success*. Reading, Mass.: Addison-Wesley, 1986.

The author focuses on two groups that have found their way to his psychoanalyst's office, as a result of values conflicts they experience in their work: (a) highly successful people who have adjusted to values they do not like and are troubled as a result; (b) the Working Wounded, who have had severe conflicts in trying to adjust to the demands of "success."

Miller, Arthur, and Mattson, Ralph. *The Truth About You*. Old Tappan, N.J.: Roselle Park Press, 1977.

States the importance of key motivating factors in your career and explains how they can be detected and defined through close scrutiny of your patterns of life experiences.

Sher, Barbara, with Gottlieb, Annie. *Wishcraft: How to Get What You Really Want*. New York: Ballantine, 1983.

A thorough and entertaining look at the emotions that inhibit people from aiming for their highest values in their work, and ways that these emotions can be managed and creative forces tapped in the job-search process.

Chapter 2: Money

Slater, Philip. *Wealth Addiction*. New York: E. P. Dutton, 1983.

A provocative look at the ways in which money affects and often rules people's lives. Once money is given a favored position in the person's values hierarchy, other values are slighted or distorted. The author explains how such choices occur unconsciously and what an individual can do about them, if desired.

Chapter 3: Skills

Bolles, Richard N. *What Color Is Your Parachute?* Berkeley, Ca.: Ten Speed Press, 1987.

Describes a clear philosophy for the self-initiated job search, in which you learn that identifying your main skills is the central strategic element; the better you know and can talk about your skills, the more effective your search will be.

Chapter 4: Creativity

Adams, James L. *Conceptual Blockbusting*. 2d ed. New York: W. W. Norton, 1979.

A guide to thinking more creatively by breaking conceptual habits. Focuses on perceptual, cultural, emotional, and intellectual blocks.

Figler, Howard E. *PATH: A Career Workbook for Liberal Arts Students*. 2d. ed. Cranston, R.I.: Carroll Press, 1979.

Explains and gives many examples of how your values and skills can be creatively combined into several careers you probably never imagined before.

Osborn, Alex F. *Applied Imagination*. 3d rev. ed. New York: Scribner, 1963.

Gives hundreds of examples of creative thinkers and how they developed their ideas; includes an outline of the nine fundamental creative processes and demonstrates how you can nurture them.

Chapter 5: Decision Making

Yost, Elizabeth B., and Corbishley, M. Anne. *Career Counseling: A Psychological Approach*. San Francisco, Ca.: Jossey-Bass, 1987.

The authors explain how career counselors assist individuals in developing career alternatives and choosing among them. The reader can gain much insight into the decision-making process by examining how counselors guide the process without influencing one's decisions.

Chapter 7: Prospect List

Jackson, Tom, and Mayleas, Davidyne. *The Hidden Job Market*. New York: Quadrangle, 1976.

Explains how the simplest forms of job market research can be done by combing numerous publications that are widely available to anyone.

Chapter 8: Personal Referral Network

Crystal, John C., and Bolles, Richard N. *Where Do I Go from Here with My Life?* New York: Seabury Press, 1974.

Gives a detailed plan for building and expanding your network of personal contacts through use of systematic targeting. Your geographical preferences, personal goals, and chief skills dictate which targets to include on your list.

Chapter 9: Information Interviewing

Bolles, Richard N. *What Color Is Your Parachute?* Berkeley, Ca.: Ten Speed Press, 1987.

Gives a detailed rationale for using the field survey method in a career search and explains how to use it most productively in all stages of your search.

Figler, Howard E. *PATH: A Career Workbook for Liberal Arts Students*. 2d. ed. Cranston, R.I.: Carroll Press, 1979.

Includes a format for interviewing when you are researching a target employer.

Chapter 10: Library Research

Todd, Alden. *Finding Facts Fast*. 2d. ed. Berkeley, Ca.: Ten Speed Press, 1979.

Explains methods and materials used by librarians, scholars, reporters, and detectives to get information with relative ease. Tells how you can use printed sources to research your target employer before you present yourself for interviews.

Chapter 11: Listening

Egan, Gerard. *The Skilled Helper*. Monterey, Ca.: Brooks/Cole, 1975.

Clarifies the essential qualities of a good listener—the verbal, nonverbal, and emotional components of fully attending to the messages of another person. You can use these listening skills to improve your communication in any formal or informal career-related interview.

Chapter 12: Questioning

Benjamin, Alfred. *The Helping Interview*. 3d. ed. Boston: Houghton Mifflin, 1981.

Explains how to ask effective questions and how questions can be misused. You can learn ways to use questioning to maximum advantage in your career search, types of questioning, and common errors.

Chapter 13: Assertiveness

Alberti, Robert E., and Emmons, Michael L. *Your Perfect Right*. San Francisco: Impact Publishers, 1974.

Distinguishes assertiveness from aggressiveness and explains how you can build assertive responses into your everyday life. It shows that you need not be especially gregarious or have a dominant personality in order to be assertive.

Chapter 14: Self-Disclosure

Zimbardo, Philip G. *Shyness: What It Is and What to Do about It.* Reading, Mass.: Addison-Wesley, 1977.

Explains the factors that may inhibit you from talking about yourself and recommends many ways to overcome being self-conscious. These methods will help you to talk easily about your skills, values, and relevant life experiences during job and career interviews.

Chapter 15: Writing

Jacobi, Ernst. *Writing at Work.* Rochelle Park, N.J.: Hayden, 1976.

Outlines and explains the numerous subskills and self-attitudes that characterize clear and readable writing. You can apply the many principles and examples to your communication with prospective employers.

Strunk, William, Jr., and White, E. B. *The Elements of Style.* New York: Macmillan, 1979.

Offers the last word on the written word and gives rules and advice regarding syntax, grammar, composition, style, usage, and form. You should always consult this reference when you are unsure about what you have just written.

Zinsser, William K. *On Writing Well: An Informal Guide to Writing Non-Fiction.* Rev. ed. New York: Harper and Row, 1985.

A superb set of guidelines for clear writing. This book demonstrates the simplicity and power of saying what you have in mind without excess words to muddy it. It tells you the importance and warns against the overuse of verbs, adverbs, adjectives, and other parts of speech. The book is its own best example—cleanly written and a persuasive advocate of plain talk.

Chapter 18: Interim Jobs

Terkel, Studs. *Working.* New York: Pantheon Books, 1974.

Personal interviews from the entire panorama of the working world, revealing glimpses of people and how they feel about their jobs. As you tour this book, you will generate ideas for interim jobs that can afford you broad access to career alternatives.

Chapter 26: Liberal Education and Careers

Bennett, Steven J. *Playing Hardball with Soft Skills.* New York: Bantam, 1986.

The author is a refugee from an academic Ph.D. program. He explains how a person with "soft" (nonvocational) skills can prosper as an entrepreneur in a high-tech world; describing how to develop, fund, and market new ideas for products and services.

Collard, Betsy. *The High Tech Career Guide.* Palo Alto, Ca.: Women's Resource Group, 1985.

A detailed compilation of job titles and job descriptions in technological organizations. This book identifies hundreds of jobs in "functional areas" (engineering, marketing, sales, operations, finance, personnel, graphics, etc.). The author has balanced the areas of work that liberal arts graduates know most about (e.g., public relations and personnel) with those they know little about. The sum is an excellent compendium of job opportunities.

Figler, Howard E. "Liberal, Not Vocational Skills." *Alumnus Magazine.* Dickinson College, Feb. 1976.

Describes the skills (communication, thinking, human relations, valuing, investigating, interviewing) and attributes (making decisions based on partial information, interpreting foreign languages, mediating between interest groups, dealing with the unknowable) that are most crucial in job and career success. Explains how these skills and attributes can be acquired from a liberal education.

Flores-Esteves, Manuel. *Life After Shakespeare: Careers for Liberal Arts Majors.* New York: Penguin Books, 1985.

A compact yet detailed compilation of jobs for liberal arts graduates. It defines numerous jobs in advertising, airlines and travel, business management, cultural organizations, finance, foreign affairs, international service, lobbying, opinion polls and surveys, personnel, politics, publishing, radio/TV, recreation, research, social service, and many other fields. The book gives ample evidence that there is a virtual candy store of possibilities for nontechnical and nonspecialized graduates.

Jackson, Tom. "Wake Up, Corporate America!" *Business Week's Guide to Careers.* March–April 1984.

A leading consultant to business and industry asserts that a good liberal education is "an essential ingredient in the formation of an effective, productive leader of American business in this post-industrial era." Jackson notes: "Nothing kills sales more than dull products. People lead with their senses. We live to touch, feel, listen, and see. . . . Scholastically, these senses are in the domain of the liberal arts."

Munschauer, John L. *Jobs for English Majors and Other Smart People.* 2d. ed. Princeton, N.J.: Peterson's Guides, 1986.

This book makes the important distinction between "professional work"—which must be trained for in law school, medical school, architecture school, etc.—and "trait-oriented work," in which people are hired because they possess the right traits, such as communication skills, sound judgment, reasoning skill, and imagination. The author tells insightful stories about liberal arts graduates who have used their personal qualities to gain success and reveals many principles for marketing oneself with a liberal arts degree.

Nadler, Burton. *Liberal Arts Power!* Princeton, N.J.: Peterson's Guides, 1985.

A book focusing on résumé development for liberal arts graduates. In an impressive array of examples, the author does a strong job of showing how résumés can intertwine coursework, out-of-class experiences, and career goals to make effective selling tools.

O'Brien, Mark. *High Tech Jobs for Non-Tech Grads.* Englewood Cliffs, N.J.: Prentice-Hall, 1986.

This book describes the language of "high tech," the specific jobs a nontechnical graduate can expect to compete for, and how to get a good start in this complex of industries. The author tells liberal arts graduates how to take fullest advantage of their backgrounds. "How to pick the winning from the losing high-tech company" is an especially helpful chapter.

Salzman, Marian, and Marx-Better, Nancy. *Wanted: Liberal Arts Graduates.* New York: Doubleday, 1987.

Interesting and detailed profiles of over 100 nationally prominent corporations and other organizations that hire liberal arts graduates on a regular basis. Featured companies include banks, advertising agencies, retailers, investment banking groups, stockbrokerage houses, manufacturers, and arts organizations. The book also includes a useful listing of hundreds of companies that actively recruit liberal arts graduates.

Index

357

definition, 73–74
exercises for stimulating, 79–81
Credibility, and referrals, 126–27
Crystal, John C., 120, 353
Curiosity, 101–102, 122
Cynicism, overcoming, 261–62

The Damn Good Résumé Guide (Parker), 207
Deadlines, coping with, as transferable skill, 215–16
DeBono, Edward, 76, 80
Decision making, 8, 13, 82–91
intuitive, 86–87
pleasure of, 91
sequence, 91
Defensiveness, as personal problem, 179
Degree programs, 280
Detail person, 60
Detective skills, 7, 8–9, 16-17. *See also specific skill*
applying, 106–107, 301–302
chart of, 7
definition, 105
need for, 106
Directory of American Scholars, 146
Directory of Professional and Trade Organizations, 144
Disadvantages, taking advantage of, 274–75
DISCOVER software, 84
Discretionary income, 53
Displays, as evidence of work you have done, 217
Dreamers, creativity of, 77
Dreams
pursuing, 252–53
values reflected in, 37–38
Dull, methodical person, 60

Earning incentives, 48, 51
Earning potential, and degree of risk, 52
Education. *See also* Liberal education
general, jobs available with, 319
requirements for, assessing, 287
vs. vocational training, 318–21
Education and Jobs: The Great Training Robbery (Berg), 319
Egan, Gerard, 160, 353
The Elements of Style (Strunk and White), 354
Emmons, Michael L., 353
Emotional issues, overcoming, 264–66

Employer(s)
dependence on least reliable data, 108
in job-search process, 107–108
prospective, locating, 113–15
specific, researching, 145–46
time pressure on, 108
Employer directories, 14, 109, 113–14
limitations of, 115–16
list of, 113–14
Employment agencies, 109
Employment agency interviewer, 221
Employment interview. *See* Interview
Encouragement, lack of, as excuse for not looking for job, 22
Encyclopedia of Associations, 116–17
Enthusiasm, demonstrating, in interview, 238–39
Entrepreneurship, 214
acquiring experience from, 214
Exaggerations, deliberate, 81
Excuses for not undertaking career search, 19–22
Experience, 209–18
acquiring, 9, 11, 111–12, 212–15
career-related, 320
combining, to your advantage, 294
identifying your, 209–12
importance of, 210
informal, 213–14
job requirements for, assessing, 287
kinds of, 212–15
lack of, overcoming, 12
mixed, and career progress, 290–95
physical evidence of, 217
presenting your, 217
as reality test, 98–99
relationship to future aspiration, 81
and values clarification, 42–44
Experts
career-choice, 17–18
relying on, 93

Fate, belief in, as excuse for not looking for job, 20–21
Fatigue, in job search, overcoming, 281–82
Fear, as excuse for not looking for job, 20
Fear of success, 268
Figler, Howard E., 351, 352, 353, 355
Financial counselor, private, career development of, 292–93
Finding Facts Fast (Todd), 353
Fine, Sidney, 62